Behind the Ballads

A Tribute to the People, Places, and Music of
Songbirds and Snakes

Thomas W. Paradis

Copyright © 2024 by **Thomas W. Paradis**

All rights reserved. No part of this publication may be reproduced, distributed, or transmitted in any form or by any means, without prior written permission.

Thomas W. Paradis has no responsibility for the persistence or accuracy of URLs for external or third-party Internet Websites referred to in this publication and does not guarantee that any content on such Websites is, or will remain, accurate or appropriate.

Published by Thomas W. Paradis
Indianapolis, IN. USA

Includes bibliographic citations and references.
Book Layout © 2017 BookDesignTemplates.com
Typeset in Alegreya

Cover designed and produced by Anna Burrous.
Cover photo: by Yoel J. Gonzalez, free use under Unsplash license.
Back cover photos: free use under Creative Commons license.
Guitar: by Alan Levine.
Olympic Stadium Berlin: by Paul VanDerWerf.

Behind the Ballads—1st ed.
ISBN 978-1-7334838-4-1 (paperback)
ISBN 978-1-7334838-5-8 (ebook)

Contents

Author's Note on Styles i
Foreword iii
Introduction 1
    From Collins' Mind to Period Piece 1

PART 1: The Music 9

1. The Backstory of District 12 11
    Just Where is District 12? 11
    Populating the Mountains 13
    Why So Many Ballads? 15

2. The Producers: Back in Business 19
    Collins' Latest Surprise 19
    Two Films or One? 21
    Nashville's Dave Cobb 23
    The Brilliance of James Newton Howard 27

3. Producing the Music 31
    The Savannah Recordings 31
    Being Lucy Gray, Live on Set 34
    Is *Ballad* a Musical? 38

4. The Covey: From Ballads to Bluegrass 45
    Covey Names and Meanings 45
    Covey Instrumentation: A Nod to Bill Monroe 48
    The Carter Family and "Keep on the Sunny Side" 53

5. The Ballads of Lucy Gray 57
"Nothing You Can Take from Me" 58
"The Ballad of Lucy Gray Baird" 60
"The Old Therebefore" 63
"The Hanging Tree" 65
"Pure as the Driven Snow" 69
"Lucy Gray" 74
What Happened to Lucy Gray? 77
A Successor to O Brother, Where Art Thou? 80

PART 2: The Places 83

6. Filming District 12 85
To Europe with Love 85
District 12 Peacekeeper Barracks 87
Filming District 12 at Landscape Park 89

7. Ghosts of the Third Reich 95
Enjoy the Show! The Arena Goes Indoors 95
The Troubled History of Centennial Hall 98
Olympic Park 102
Command Center for the 10th Games 104

8. Rebuilding the Capitol 107
The Snow Family Home 108
The Capitol Zoo's Monkey House 110
Peacekeeper Recruitment Center 111
The Mentor-Tribute Interviews 112
The City Circle and Statue 114
Capitol Train Station 120
Dr. Gaul's Lab and War Department 122
The Academy Lecture Hall 124

The Academy Exterior..125
Heavensbee Hall...126

PART 3: The People 131
9. Wardrobe and Makeup for a Postwar Panem............... 133

Differing Looks for the Capitol and Districts 134
Those Red Academy Uniforms... 140

10. The Performer: Lucy Gray Baird 143

A Forgotten Victor..143
The Backstory of Lucy Gray Baird...144
Comparing Lucy Gray with Katniss..148
Lucy Gray, Rousseau, and Frankenstein 150
A Rousseau-Plutarch Connection 153
A Prequel Love Story?..154
Portraying Lucy Gray in *Ballad*...157
Prepping for *Ballad*.. 160
Creating the Look of Lucy Gray... 161

11. Coriolanus: Snow Lands on Top 167

Coriolanus and Thomas Hobbes.. 168
The Meaning of *Coriolanus*... 171
A Childhood Nickname... 173
The Family Surname 174
Tom Blyth: Becoming Coriolanus..174
A Shirt with Tesserae 177
A Sympathetic Character? 178
Coriolanus Versus Anakin.. 181
Coriolanus in the Novel 184
A Façade of Friendship 188
Those Repelling Mockingjays.. 190
Cousin Tigris: An Alternative Voice..192

Snow's Nemesis: Dean Casca Highbottom 197
Close-Ups of Coriolanus (and Friends) 200

12. Sejanus Plinth: Up on a Pedestal 203

Sejanus in Rome 205
Sejanus and John Locke 206
Portraying Sejanus Plinth 208

13. Dr. Volumnia Gaul 211

Liar, Liar, Pants on 214
Volumnia Gaul and Shakespeare 215
Portraying Dr. Gaul 215
Gaul's Wardrobe and Makeup 218
Who Bombed the Arena? 220

14. Lucretius "Lucky" Flickerman 225

The Naming of an Amoral Character 226
Portraying Lucky 228

15. Of Mentors and Tributes 233

Casting for Inclusivity 234
The 10th Games: Film Versus Books 236
The Curiosities of Clemensia Dovecote 238
Arachne Crane: After the Crime 241
A Defiant Reaper 241
A Merciful End for Wovey 243
The Rise of Coral 244
Future Books or Movies? 248

APPENDIX 251
Twenty Callbacks and Easter Eggs in *Ballad* 253
Works Cited 263

Author's Note on Styles

To improve the flow of the narrative, all references to the film, *The Hunger Games: The Ballad of Songbirds and Snakes*, are shortened to *Ballad*.

Titles of books and films are in *italics* (e.g. *Mockingjay*, or *Mockingjay – Part 1*). Quotations are used for song titles (e.g. "Keep on the Sunny Side").

The following abbreviations are used to cite specific references to the four Hunger Games novels throughout the narrative:

> THG—*The Hunger Games*
> CF—*Catching Fire*
> MJ—*Mockingjay*
> BSS—*The Ballad of Songbirds and Snakes*

All other citations in the narrative include the author's last name of the referenced work, or the first word(s) of the title if no author is available. The names of authors mentioned directly within the narrative include no additional citations unless they have authored multiple works.

Foreword

Following his insightful book on Appalachian geography and music in *The Hunger Games*, Thomas Paradis is fascinating readers once again. He returns to Panem, this time to the prequel book and film: *The Ballad of Songbirds and Snakes*.

Suzanne Collins' unexpected offering returned readers to the haunting terror and call to social action that made up the trilogy. The latter provoked outrage about child soldiers and the governments that create them, exploitative entertainment and prurient spycraft, world hunger and poverty, and exploitation of the unfortunate. All was set in a dystopia that, alongside its touches of Roman culture, clearly evoked first-world America. Paradis touched on these much-analyzed themes while also exploring through the lens of his own specialties—the Appalachian culture and specifically its folk music. As Katniss sang haunting ballads and evoked the independent coal-miner culture, battling exploitation from those in power, Paradis delved into many recognizably cultural touchstones.

The Ballad of Songbirds and Snakes builds on the philosophy from the original trilogy—which shares Orwell's theme that revolutions change nothing, and power always corrupts in a cycle of endless wars. The new novel unveils the origin of the Games themselves, together with their motivation. Set against them, protagonists Coriolanus, Lucy Gray, and Sejanus voice opposing historic philosophies, evoking Thomas Hobbes, Jean-Jacques Rousseau, and John Locke. Those who teach classes on dystopia in general and *Hunger Games* in particular, as Paradis does, can find many recognizable allusions to the wider genre and world history.

This prequel leans even closer to Paradis' specialized knowledge, thanks to the sheer number of songs. In his previous book, he describes the impact of banjo and guitar, barn dances and blues, along with the history of country music. Popular folksongs, from "Clementine" to "Strange Fruit" clearly impacted Collins' lyrics. Further, the film gave it all new life, with evocative instrument, melody, and performance choices. All have deeper meanings that an expert reading can reveal for fans, from references to Wordsworth's classic 1799 ballad "Lucy Gray" to bluegrass guitar player Molly Tuttle's modern renditions.

Further, Paradis once more explores the setting—both District Twelve in its unfenced but still Appalachian early days—and the Capitol, now with a deliberately postwar aesthetic filmed in the former East Berlin. A close examination of all the locations, together with production and design interviews, reveals a great deal about the hidden meanings waiting to be unraveled. Likewise, a deep dive into costuming and looks for the characters, along with their casting and other choices, considers the symbolism and methods for making these characters come alive. A list of callbacks and Easter eggs in the Appendix makes a fun addition for fans.

Now let's dive in together, and explore the captivating tale Collins has created, with new insights and astounding revelations.

Valerie Estelle Frankel
Author of over 75 books on pop culture, including *Katniss the Cattail, The Many Faces of Katniss Everdeen,* and more recently, *Songbirds, Snakes and Sacrifice.*

Introduction

From Collins' Mind to Period Piece

Nearly five years following the release of *Mockingjay - Part 2*, the world learned that Suzanne Collins was back in business. She had written a prequel to her original series, looking back 64 years to the 10th Games and the teenage life of one Coriolanus Snow. Amidst some measurable skepticism over her featured character, the long-awaited book, *The Ballad of Songbirds and Snakes* was finally released to a global readership on May 19, 2020, in the midst of a global pandemic. On that very day, Scholastic released strategic promotional materials including interviews with the author herself. The first hint of Collins' inspiration and purpose for writing the prequel came with her comments below:

> With this book, I wanted to explore the state of nature, who we are, and what we perceive is required for our survival. The reconstruction period ten years after the war, commonly referred to as the Dark Days—as the country of Panem struggles back to its feet—provides fertile ground for characters to grapple with these questions and thereby define their views of humanity. ("News Room")

In a lengthier interview with Scholastic's David Levithan, she provides additional insights into her more personal reasons for crafting the story:

INTRODUCTION

Here's how it works now. I have two worlds, the Underland (the world of *The Underland Chronicles* series) and Panem (the world of *The Hunger Games*). I use both of them to explore elements of just war theory. When I find a related topic that I want to examine, then I look for the place it best fits. The state of nature debate of the Enlightenment period naturally lent itself to a story centered on Coriolanus Snow.

Focusing on the 10th Hunger Games also gave me the opportunity to tell Lucy Gray's story. In the first chapter of The Hunger Games, I make reference to a fourth District 12 victor. Katniss doesn't seem to know anything about the person worth mentioning. While her story isn't well-known, Lucy Gray lives on in a significant way through her music, helping to bring down Snow in the trilogy. Imagine his reaction when Katniss starts singing "Deep in the Meadow" to Rue in the arena. Beyond that, Lucy Gray's legacy is that she introduced entertainment to the Hunger Games. ("Scholastic")

To better envision the reconstruction period of Panem and the Capitol following the Dark Days, Collins pulled from a variety of real-world historical events and periods. Continuing with her interview, she explains these inspirations as well:

I thought a lot about the period after the Civil War here in the United States and also the post–World War II era in Europe. People trying to rebuild, to live their daily lives in the midst of the rubble. The challenges of food shortages, damaged infrastructure, confusion over how to proceed in peacetime. The relief that the war has ended coupled with the bitterness toward the wartime enemy. The need to place blame. ("Scholastic")

For those who had not seen Collins' interviews before reading her novel, she provided further clues to her underlying messages within the book's epigraph. While easy—or tempting—to overlook in favor of diving into the 10th Games, the one-page epigraph offers five thought-provoking quotes to set the stage for her story. This single page therefore provides the key to Collins' entire rationale for writing her prequel. And probably more to the point for readers and viewers of *Ballad*, this material helps us unlock the varied worldviews of Coriolanus, Sejanus, and Lucy Gray.

The epigraph's first three quotes provide carefully chosen perspectives of well-known Enlightenment-era philosophers, namely Thomas Hobbes, John Locke, and Jean-Jacques Rousseau. These are followed by a William Wordsworth poem from his *Lyrical Ballads*, and a passage from Mary Shelley's *Frankenstein*. All of these great thinkers had much to say about how the world works and the role of human beings within that world. Their specially selected quotes by Collins further point to their thinking about the nature of human beings and whether we are inherently decent or evil, or somewhere in between. This is one of the fundamental questions that Collins hoped her readers would explore throughout the book.

What is not readily apparent is that the three main characters, Coriolanus Snow, Sejanus Plinth, and Lucy Gray Baird can be interpreted as *avatars*, or embodiments, representing the beliefs of Hobbes, Locke, and Rousseau respectively. This knowledge opens up a whole new layer of meaning that lurks beneath Collins' story of Snow's rise to power (or at least his acceptance to university). Indeed, we can imagine how the dialogue between the prequel's three main characters could have been easily replicated between these timeless philosophers as well. These intriguing parallels are discussed in more detail for each respective character in Part 3.

INTRODUCTION

To the credit of the producers of *Ballad*, Collins' character dialogue on human nature was not overlooked. Rather, it was quite sincerely embraced. For her part, executive producer Nina Jacobson spoke extensively with Collins to better comprehend the worldviews she aimed to highlight. Jacobson even compares Collins to her character, Lucy Gray Baird. "That's what I was excited about; the same way that Lucy Gray says, 'I don't sing when I'm told to, I sing when I have something to say.' That's Suzanne," Jacobson says, adding, "She doesn't, like, crank out a book to crank out a book" ("Nina").

In this way, Jacobson gained an enthusiastic appreciation for Collins' big ideas and the bigger messages behind her story. She thus provides her own perspective on what Collins had in mind:

> She wanted to explore very different ideas in this one... which is much more about, are we fundamentally good, or are we bad? And if you believe that we are bad and that we will inherently destroy each other, you long for a more authoritarian government, someone to keep us in check. Your government should keep people in place so that they won't destroy you. If you're a person who sees the good and believes that people are fundamentally good, you want a government that protects their rights, their individuality, their liberties. And different characters are pulling Snow in different directions over the course of the story. And it felt very timely, democracy around the world is challenged right now; people are going to the polls and deciding what they want. And to explore how personal those choices are and how political the personal can become was a real opportunity for us, especially in seeing how a young Coriolanus Snow emerges from this boy into the man we know. ("Nina")

Director Francis Lawrence appreciated the story's philosophical underpinnings as well. He explains,

> Yeah, what's great about Suzanne is that she always starts her stories from theme. I think it's what's always separated her stuff out from the rest of the YA fair, is that she starts with theme and real ideas and builds stories around them. And the first series was about the consequence of war. This one, what she started to see and what she told me, was that around 2016 she started to see this real polarization, not only just in America, but really in the world. This idea that everybody in their thinking is so far apart from one another, that she wanted to write a story about the state of nature debate... This idea of, are we as humans innately savage and brutal, or are we innately good and deserving of freedoms and rights and independence? And that's what this is all about. And so, that's the thing that I think she got interested in and was inspired to go back into the world of Panem, and then take a character like Snow, and you can see how he fits into that world of being pulled toward the good by characters like Lucy Gray and Tigris and Sejanus, and pulled toward the more Hobbesian view of humans [as] savaged, by people like Viola [Davis] playing Dr. Gaul. (Stedman)

In their gallant attempt to bring such esoteric thinking to the big screen, Jacobson subscribed to what she calls a simple formula. That is, "adapt an actual book for what it is, then recruit a team well versed enough in the material to produce a full-blown *Hunger Games* period piece" ("New"). Given Collins' own comparisons between the war-torn Capitol and the reconstruction of Europe following World War II, the production team naturally turned to the historical

INTRODUCTION

experiences of Germany and Poland. And they looked more specifically at the postwar years of the 1950s.

To craft a full-blown period piece, producers hired German production designer Uli Hanisch (*Babylon Berlin*, *Cloud Atlas*) to ground the Capitol in the actual landscapes of his home country. During their research phase for on-site filming locations, Hanisch worked with the production team to determine the most appropriate sites. Many of them ultimately ended up in Berlin and, more specifically, the former East Berlin as it existed prior to the fall of communism in November 1989. The intriguing histories and backstories of these filming locations are detailed more in Part 2.

Still recalling his work on the *Mockingjay* movies, Francis Lawrence was no stranger to Berlin. A small part of those films had been set there, and thus Lawrence already had certain places in mind for *Ballad*. Now working with Hanisch, they both "discovered that Berlin had the perfect things" to emphasize the history of authoritarianism in Europe and Germany's own postwar reconstruction efforts. Lawrence explains,

> The story is a period piece [in relation] to the other films. It's not long after the wars that created everything about [the society in] these books and movies. We knew the Capitol was in a reconstruction phase, so we looked at the reconstruction era Berlin from the mid-1940s after World War II to the early 1950s. How long did it take to rebuild the classic buildings and to start to erect new buildings? What was the look and feel of that? The technology in the story is still somewhat rudimentary. We also looked at that era for car design, hair, makeup, and wardrobe. (Zelmer)

Overall, *Ballad* and its intentional filming locations point a spotlight on the imagery and lessons of fascist, socialist, and Soviet-era Europe. For Hanisch, this all comes down to the film's fundamental message. He reflects, "For me, as a German, I take the whole question of 'what if' more seriously," he explains. For Hanisch, his work on the prequel film took a personal turn, as his own parents had been born into the Third Reich. He adds, "When my mother was four years old, when she went to a bakery, she had to say: Heil Hitler... For me, it's a very real thing... the whole question of how would I have behaved, if I was born in that time, is a very present one... so I think it influenced me quite strongly." He adds that, while one might be "sitting very comfortably in the cinema watching the movie, there are moments where you get an idea of how it really could happen" (Rasker).

Before diving more thoroughly into the people and places that made this postwar period piece a reality, let us turn first to the world of Lucy Gray Baird and the Appalachian culture that underpins her own intriguing character. More specifically, let us turn to the musical and historical backstories behind the ballads.

PART 1: The Music

• CHAPTER 1 •

The Backstory of District 12

Just Where is District 12?

It is widely known that Suzanne Collins placed her coal-infused District 12 somewhere within the Appalachian Mountains. Beyond this geographical tidbit, however, she provides little direct information as to the whereabouts of Katniss' hometown. And the fact that this ancient mountain range extends through 420 counties in 13 states only adds to the confusion. The extent of this ongoing mystery is expressed quite creatively through numerous online and published maps of Panem. Their imagined borders of District 12 are wide-ranging, from the Great Lakes to the East Coast (post-global warming). And now, we see yet one more cartographic version in *Ballad*, referenced by Lucky Flickerman within his equally questionable weather report during the 10th Games.

Fortunately, Collins drops countless clues throughout her saga that collectively place District 12 somewhere in the central Appalachians—that is, roughly south of Maryland and north of

THE BACKSTORY OF DISTRICT 12

Georgia. This can be reduced even further with maps of coal deposits and historical mining activities. Combined with Collins' litany of cultural, musical, and environmental clues, current observers place Katniss' home somewhere within the realm of southern West Virginia, northeastern Kentucky, or extreme western Virginia (Paradis).

In one sense, District 12 is not really a "district" at all, but an isolated coal mining town of some 8,000 people, as Katniss tells us (*THG* 17). Even the Capitol would be hard-pressed to build a fence around such an expansive, multi-state region as imagined maps of Panem tend to indicate. As we well know, it was difficult enough to keep that pesky fence maintained around Katniss' hometown.

While many fans might attribute the district's inhumane living conditions to a fictional dystopian nightmare, Collins comes much closer to reality than one might prefer to believe. As Tina Hanlon notes, Collins "really nailed it with regard to the first half of the 20th century in the coal towns" (Hanlon). Even the coal dust described by Katniss, and the black lung disease referenced by Lucy Gray, were daily realities for these Appalachian company towns. And the strict, oppressive hand of the Capitol simply replaces similar real-world conditions imposed by dispassionate mining corporations. As Elizabeth Hardy explains, "Historical miners often suffered the same punishments as the District 12 rebels: lack of work, food shortages, physical punishment and humiliation in the guise of justice" (Poe).

Some better news is that all Hunger Games films highlight many of the Appalachian cultural and environmental qualities that Collins had in mind. Sure, maybe not the filming locations—the range of which now expands from an authentic North Carolina mill town and suburban Atlanta to rural Poland and industrial Germany. Still, film producers have credibly maintained a consistent focus on central Appalachian culture and history regardless of where the filming takes place.

Most recently with *Ballad*, director Francis Lawrence and his team intentionally sought to ground the story of District 12 in central Appalachia. Lawrence explains how the film's costume designer, Trish Summerville, "wanted to design something that felt authentic to the location of District 12, to the idea that [Lucy Gray is] part of this traveling troupe of musicians and performers; there's a slight can-can element to it, also this kind-of West Virginia—the hollows of West Virginia sort-of feel to it" ("Scene").

In an unrelated news release, Jessica Wang explains how the songs of Lucy Gray and the Covey were based on Appalachian-style country music of the early 20th century to correspond with District 12's location, "believed to be around West Virginia" (Wang, "Rachel"). Thus, while one might understandably have preferred a more authentic filming location, producers of *Ballad* still kept their eye on the Appalachian ball, so to speak. The ways in which they accomplished this are detailed further within the chapters below.

Populating the Mountains

Considering the real Appalachians, it is important to recognize District 12 as the product of numerous centuries of cultural mixing. This is even more true during Katniss' time, perhaps several hundred years beyond the present day. Even today the central mountains constitute one of America's most ethnically diverse regions. Aside from the Indigenous peoples already settled here, this area saw continuous waves of European immigrants streaming into the mountains during the 18th and 19th centuries. The vast majority of them were of Anglo-Celtic heritage, having arrived from Scotland, Ireland, and England. In turn, many of them were Scots-Irish immigrants (sometimes erroneously called "Scotch-Irish") whose ancestors had first migrated to the Ulster Province of Ireland from northern England or the lowlands of Scotland.

THE BACKSTORY OF DISTRICT 12

Only adding to this mixed European and Indigenous population was a continuous stream of largely involuntary newcomers from the African continent. Those of African descent appeared as early as the first European expeditions into the mountains, including those of early Spanish explorers. Such expeditions and later generations of settlers brought their African slaves as well, thereby starting a continuous trend of forced African migration into the mountains. In time, communities of slaves and free blacks added their own unique cultural and musical imprints to the region.

The central mountains therefore played host to a vast colonial stew—if not a true melting pot—of English, Scots-Irish, Indigenous, and African peoples representing three different continents. Later waves of Eastern Europeans and Italians came to the mountains as well, often desperate for work in the mines or other extractive industries.

This brings us to the local population of District 12 as Collins envisioned. Notably, the community consists of an ethnically and racially diverse population, with its "merchant class" inhabiting a small Philadelphia-style town with its central public square. Its more mixed-race population is relegated to the Seam on the edge of town, thereby separating the district's population along both socio-economic and racial lines.

As cultural geographers have observed, this region's human landscapes and place names largely reflect a Pennsylvania—and more distantly an Anglo-Celtic—heritage. Knowing all of this, one is less surprised to see a multiracial Katniss and her counterparts dancing to various Scots-Irish jigs and reels while holed up further north in District 13. Theirs is a microcosm of true cultural difference expressed in one place.

The majority of Scots-Irish newcomers arrived through the port of Philadelphia and first settled amidst the Appalachian Ridge-and-Valley Province west of there. They really had little choice, as all the good farmland around Philadelphia was already occupied by earlier

German immigrants. Ensuing generations of Scots-Irish families moved down those north-south oriented valleys to the central and southern mountains. Naturally, they brought their own familiar cultural traditions and lifeways with them—including their music, farming approaches, and town settlement plans.

In one interview, Collins provides a hint of this cultural diversity, saying that there has "been a lot of ethnic mixing" (Valby). Katniss tells us that she, Gale, and many of her Seam counterparts have "straight, black hair, olive skin, and gray eyes." These descriptors indicate their own racial ambiguity. This is in stark contrast to the generally Caucasian and better-off merchant class as represented by the likes of Peeta, Madge, and even Katniss' mother. And Collins remains consistent within her prequel, imbuing Arlo Chance's girlfriend, Lil with the same racial identity as Katniss. Thus, Lil is described similarly, with "olive skin and long black hair" (*BSS* 350). It is in this subtle way that Collins directly codes Lil as a resident of the mixed-race Seam.

Why So Many Ballads?

Without the geographical backstory above, the connections between Scots-Irish folk music and District 12 may remain something of a mystery. Just how did so many English and Celtic ballads survive in the hometown region of Katniss Everdeen? Starting with the basics, a *ballad* is a song that tells a narrative story with various characters involved. Three distinct forms of ballads are generally recognized, all of which make appearances within the prequel and its ensuing film adaptation.

The first is the *folk ballad*, which tends to be the oldest of the three types, many of them harkening back to the British Isles themselves. Their original sources are often lost to the passage of time (Paradis). Just one example is "Barbry Allen," for whom the Covey character, Barb Azure is likely named.

THE BACKSTORY OF DISTRICT 12

Appalachian variations of folk ballads tended to focus on the more serious topics of love, heartbreak, or death, though more humorous ones could be found as well. Further, it was often left to the women of a household to sing these ballads as they went about their daily routines, usually unaccompanied by musical instruments. This makes Lucy Gray's *a cappella* rendition of the Wordsworth poem all-the-more fitting.

Beyond the surviving folk traditions of Old-world Britain, a second form is the *literary ballad*. As the name implies, these are usually first written as poems or artistic creations. The William Wordsworth poem adapted for the *a cappella* tune "Lucy Gray" represents such a literary ballad. All the original songs penned by Collins likewise serve as excellent examples, not the least being "Pure as the Driven Snow" and "The Ballad of Lucy Gray Baird."

A third form was the *broadside ballad*, which became popular on both sides of the Atlantic up through the 19th century. In the age before cell phones and related electronic communications, local news, poems, and songs were often printed on single sheets of paper called "broadsides" and distributed through local communities. Perhaps strangely, many Appalachian ballads featured stories of homicide—often focused on young women murdered by their lovers. Popular examples included "The Banks of the Ohio" and "Tom Dooley." It follows that they were also called *murder ballads*, often culminating in the hanging of a guilty perpetrator. This may seem all too familiar to Hunger Games fans, given the saga's most prominent murder ballad of all, "The Hanging Tree." More on that later.

Elizabeth Hardy explains that the entire prequel—and its ensuing film—include themes that are "pure ballad stock" from the central mountains. The book's very title is no accident, of course, and for good reason. All those roses that Snow throws around are not just his; rather, they are the subject of countless historical ballads, often invoking themes of love or death. In fact, roses appear within two ballads for whom Covey characters are derived—namely, "Barbry Allen" and "Tam Lin."

Likewise, the literal snow that falls from the sky is a popular symbol in ballads. Hardy adds, "Coriolanus keeps telling himself that 'Snow lands on top.' It lands in a lot of ballads, too." The prequel's tale of murder and the ensuing attempts to erase the crime are common fodder for the ballads of Appalachia. This often involves the disposal of incriminating evidence—such as a body or guns—within a river or lake. Coriolanus thus falls right into line with a time-honored mountain tradition. And given Coriolanus' eventual fate and Lucy Gray's disappearance, Hardy makes her main point: "So we know, this will not be a happy story. Ballads rarely are" (Hardy, "The Ballad").

It is refreshing that *Ballad* producers treated the balladry and musical heritage of the mountains so seriously. They largely remained true to Collins' own intent, relying heavily on, among other influences, British and Anglo-Celtic source regions. Many immigrants from these places brought their own artistic and musical backgrounds with them. Such cultural traits were passed down to later generations of Appalachian families. This largely occurred—and still does—by aural tradition, with younger family members often emulating their elders through careful listening and practice. Printed sheet music was rarely used, and few amateur musicians knew how to read music anyway.

Katniss was no different, as her own knowledge and singing skills were passed down aurally from her father. Now armed with more clues from the prequel, Katniss' father likely gained his own musical talents—including "The Hanging Tree," of course—from his own parents. One of them was likely a member of the Covey. Though Appalachian ballads were certainly modified over time, memories of countless tunes from the "Old Country" survived well into the 20th century. These mountain communities had been largely bypassed by rapid industrialization and urban growth, which tended to hasten the loss of such traditions to modernizing influences.

This further explains Katniss' own musical inclinations. Unfortunately, she admits to having avoided anything musical in her life since her father's death. Still, he managed to pass down a wealth of musical knowledge to his oldest daughter. For instance, the mountain air or lullaby "Deep in the Meadow," along with the so-called "Valley Song," are examples of the oral traditions that clearly influenced the likes of District 12 centuries later. Although not included in the film, Lucy Gray's mournful "Down in the Valley" is largely based on the early country tune of the same title, one which Katniss learns years later. This is the infamous "Valley Song," to which Peeta refers while recovering in the cave.

Aside from a few such songs, Appalachian music traditions are mostly relegated to the background in the original books and films. However, remnants of Anglo-Celtic folk traditions do make a rare appearance during Finnick and Annie's wedding. Katniss and her peers enjoy some precious downtime to teach their District 13 counterparts a form of Appalachian clog or contra dancing, all to the sound of Scots-Irish fiddle tunes. Of course, it was District 12's lone surviving fiddler who provided accompaniment for the festivities. It is likely they learned much of their folk singing and dancing from more joyful times when the Covey and live audiences filled the Hob for their own barn dances!

• CHAPTER 2 •

The Producers: Back in Business

Collins' Latest Surprise

News of a new "prequel" book came as much of a surprise to director Francis Lawrence as with Collins' readership. Lawrence shares, "We had thought it was over in 2015 and then Suzanne surprised us with another book. She called me and Nina [Jacobson] in 2019 and said, 'Hey, I've got another one, can't wait for you guys to read it'" (Davids). Lawrence's own shock was genuine, as he had heard nothing word-of-mouth or through the proverbial grapevine that a new book was in the works. Collins had not yet even called Lionsgate to announce her latest contribution to the saga. Lawrence adds that, following the previous films, Collins "had no interest in really writing [a prequel]. It didn't seem like she was going to write anything else." He received the first call while working in South Korea on a commercial project (Jones). Jacobson and Lawrence read the manuscript soon thereafter and effectively said, "Ok, wow. Let's try to figure this out" (Stedman).

THE PRODUCERS

Collins reportedly first reached out to executive producer Nina Jacobson to announce her nearly completed book. At first, Collins revealed little more than two general facts—that her new story was a prequel set well before the original series, and that it would incorporate "a big musical element," as Lawrence recalls (Lynch). This latter aspect "sort-of surprised" him as well, given the minimalist role of local music within the original series. It turns out that Collins is not only well acquainted with the central Appalachians but is also an avid amateur historian and music history buff. She worked as a country music DJ during her college years and became well versed in the genre's early roots in mountain folk songs, balladry, and string bands.

During a lengthy conversation, Collins filled in Lawrence on her own passion for Appalachian music, especially focused on the 1920s and 1930s. She enlightened him on how these regional traditions were largely derived from earlier British and Scots-Irish folk songs, ballads, and poems. The birth of the country music industry occurred during this period as well, with the first recording companies and radio shows distributing this material to a national audience (Paradis). Collins coached Lawrence on these matters from their earliest conversations. She further directed him to digest Ken Burns' 16-hour documentary on the history of country music. As he recalls, "this was during the pandemic, so I had time" (Lynch).

The team responsible for the past three films was now confronted with an unexpected challenge. They would need to effectively blend two separate cultural worlds into a prequel film. The first would necessitate the invention of a proto-fascist Panem that existed some 64 years prior to Katniss' time. The second world would need to provide a veritable clinic in successive Appalachian music styles. If this were not enough to tackle, they would need to accomplish all of this within a single movie. This is because the idea of splitting the prequel into two separate films was ruled out from the beginning.

Two Films or One?

As the longest of the five Hunger Games films—2:37 including credits—viewers have considered whether *Ballad* should have been split into two separate movies. This would reduce the appearance of rushing through existing scenes and allow for a deeper, more nuanced storyline—and would, of course, allow for more Lucy Gray and the Covey. Even a short series would not be out of the question. Director Francis Lawrence has since addressed this issue through numerous interviews, and always with the same consistent response: no, not a chance. Responding to the idea of splitting the film, Lawrence says, "It was brought up, like, 'You could do it because it's a long book,' and I said, 'No way.' So, I said, 'No, you know what, I would rather do a long movie, and have it be one, full satisfying piece" (Dominick, "I Genuinely").

In a separate interview Lawrence explained that his decision was based largely on having split *Mockingjay* into Parts 1 and 2. Once supportive of the idea, he now deeply regrets having done so. He continues,

> The only person that ever said we could probably split [*Ballad*], and it was only because it's the longest of the books, was Suzanne at one point before I even knew what the story was. She just said, 'It's the longest of the books. It could probably be two movies. I don't want to tell you the story yet, so I don't want to talk about where it'd be split.' And even without reading it, I was like, 'Nope, I'm not doing that again. We got so much backlash.' You know what? I'd rather make a long movie. The truth is, splitting *Mockingjay*, gave audiences four hours of *Mockingjay*. Here we have two-and-a-half hours of *Ballad of Songbirds and Snakes*. I still think it's a more fulfilling experience to just get the whole movie in one go. (Stedman)

Lawrence looked back to his experience with splitting *Mockingjay*. "I totally regret it," he begins, adding, "I totally do. I'm not sure everybody does, but I definitely do." In contrast, he had initially defended the split, having been surprised by the extent of pushback producers received for doing so. He explains, "because we truly did think that there were two distinct stories to tell with their own dramatic questions" (Davids).

Still, he claims that splitting up *Mockingjay* had not been his decision. "That idea happened before I was even asked to do them," he says. According to Angel Shaw, splitting franchise films was standard practice up through 2015. One reason for splitting *Mockingjay* was to continue the Hunger Games' trend of remaining relatively true to the books. However, as Shaw explains, "this decision put the film's director in hot water since it was perceived as an effort to drag out the franchise's financial success. Unfortunately, finishing things off this way meant a lingering bad taste in fans' mouths regarding the Hunger Games" (Shaw).

Lawrence's own perspective had admittedly shifted with time. "What I realized in retrospect—and after hearing all the reactions and feeling the kind of wrath of fans, critics, and people at the split—is that I realized it was frustrating. And I can understand that" (Haring). He adds, had *Mockingjay* been done "in a nice, chunky, big, satisfying full movie, I think [it] just would've been a better experience for everybody" (Stedman). The difference between feature films and television is that viewers of a TV series need only wait for a week or less to enjoy a season finale, Lawrence explains further. "But making people wait a year, I think, came across as disingenuous, even though it wasn't." This is why, for *Ballad*, he says, "I would never let them split the book in two" (Haring).

Nashville's Dave Cobb

With the decision to create *Ballad* as one feature-length film, the reunited team received a welcome recommendation for producing the music. Lionsgate officials directed them to contact Nashville's Dave Cobb, who was still riding the coattails of success from his musical work for *A Star Is Born*, and *The Eyes of Tammy Faye*. He would soon sign on with *Elvis* (2022) as well. Already a fixture of Nashville's music scene, Cobb had proven his wherewithal to work on major Hollywood films without sacrificing his own genuine musical principles. A nine-time Grammy Award winner, Cobb's lengthy resume included the production of albums for the likes of Chris Stapleton, Brandi Carlile, Jason Isbell and Sturgill Simpson—that is, "country singers who value grit over studio polish" (Lynch).

The first step was to contact Cobb to determine his potential interest in the project. As Nina Jacobson recalls, "talking to him, he's an incredible historian of music and has such a passion that rivals Suzanne's for the origins of what we think of as American music." For his part, Lawrence came away from their first conversation equally impressed, saying, "It was his resume but also just the chat. He's such a great, smart guy and has such knowledge of the country music genre; he fit the family and is supremely talented" (Lynch). In a separate interview, Lawrence elaborated on their initial phase of collaboration:

> We had a great Zoom with him, and he's a really great guy... based in Nashville, really connected to a bunch of great musicians there too, so we just had lots of conversations, what the scenes were going to be like in the movie, and sort of tonally what I was looking for; Suzanne talked a lot about the sort of history references for the lyrics and the kinds of songs she was thinking about. And he ended up writing the melodies, the chords, the song

structures for these songs and brought together this great group of, I think primarily Nashville-based musicians to put these songs together. ("Cast")

Soon thereafter Cobb was brought on as executive music producer for the new film. While the lyrics for many of the prequel's songs were written by Suzanne Collins, it was Cobb who brought the songs to life with his own melodies and styling. In one special case, "Pure as the Driven Snow" was given the sweet melody used for "Streets of Laredo" and numerous other tunes that preceded it.

At first Cobb remained largely unfamiliar with the Hunger Games series. Not well versed in the dystopian universe of Panem, he had some catching up to do. Although Cobb sampled the earlier Hunger Games films for guidance, he gained more valuable insight from the prequel's author herself. About their extensive conversations, Cobb explains, "When she's telling you about each character in the series, she's got a backstory behind a backstory, behind a backstory" (Walsh). Earlier conversations between Cobb, Lawrence, and Collins found them "going down the rabbit hole" of traditional Appalachian music, as Cobb put it, adding that, "Francis knew his stuff, and that was an easy starting point. But Suzanne is a country music aficionado—she was a DJ in college—and is really well-versed. Suzanne knows everything about the Carter Family, Doc Watson, all of these turn-of-the-century records I adore also" (Amorosi).

After avidly consuming the books, he began to compose his own melodies to fit Collins' lyrics. They collaborated closely with one another and enjoyed sharing a sort-of musical shorthand between them. They especially enjoyed their mutual adoration for early country, folk, and bluegrass sounds. Favorite records were exchanged, allowing both to see eye to eye. Collins even had some time signatures in mind for various songs. Of this collaboration Cobb recalls, "Collins would talk about these characters so vividly you could see them... Suzanne has a universe beyond a universe beyond a universe, all with such depth. And she really pushed me to go for it. We made a great team. Plus, the lyrics were already in her books, so I had a master class in literature, and had the ability to go wherever I wanted with the music" (Amorosi).

Cobb was also in awe with Collins' impressive knowledge of the region, including its history, culture, and musical traditions. He explains, "Suzanne telling me the impetus for the story had me captivated. I'm a history buff, and everything in this film—everything she's written for Hunger Games—is derived from real history." The challenge for Cobb, however, was to make the songs "feel like turn-of-the-century, timeless classics. That's a very hard thing to do," he laughs (Lynch).

He was further faced with imagining how the music might sound centuries later in a dystopian District 12. Collins reportedly shared her own inspirations for Panem, including the English Civil War and early 20th-century mountain music (Walsh). Prior to production, Collins told him "every single detail and the feel and the sound and the inspiration for the songs." Cobb added that it was "going to be fun to take all this history of British Isles music and Southern music and mash it all together in this dystopian way, in the future. And gotta keep it raw and rugged and find a sound that isn't a sound that's been had before" ("Featurette").

With latitude to experiment, Cobb moved beyond the authentic genres of mountain music to consider more unconventional sources. "There's a lot of The Smiths in there," he admits, especially within the song, "Pure as the Driven Snow" (Amorosi). The song "could have been a Smiths melody, in a way," Cobb explains, adding that it "needed a little bit of a twist. I didn't want to make it completely period. There's very much an anchor in history, but there's also a little nod to a bit of the '80s music as well" (Wang, "Rachel"). To elaborate, he says, "I figure by the time we got to the future, [the characters] probably heard this stuff. It's definitely a melting pot" (Walsh).

In addition to pulling from early country music and—perhaps oddly—The Smiths, the songwriter-producer tapped into other favorite genres. These included the aforementioned folk music of the British Isles, the big-band era of the 1930s and 1940s, and "haunting vocalists" such as Jo Stafford (Wang, "Rachel"). The sound of Lucy Gray was also infused with elements of early Dolly Parton, Loretta Lynn, Patsy Cline, and most certainly Mother Maybelle of the Carter Family.

Cobb found himself digging back into his own personal roots to assist with this task. "My grandmother was a Pentecostal minister, so I grew up with hymnals my whole life," he explains, adding, "I'm very familiar with this sound growing up in the South and it was really fun to exercise that muscle of things I'd heard growing up, and put it into melodies" (Lynch). In another interview, Cobb adds that his grandfather was also a bluegrass musician, and his preacher grandmother "sang like Snow White." Altogether his rich musical family legacy only contributed to his own passions and career path (Walsh).

Everything Cobb produced went back and forth with the creative team, about which he says, "They were all such great cheerleaders... That gave me the confidence to keep digging... You're writing for this fictitious post-apocalyptic future, but you want to keep it honest. And honesty is the key factor in every film I do, whether it's [characters like] the larger-than-life Elvis or Lucy Gray Baird. I want everything I do to feel tangible" (Amorosi). Nina Jacobson witnessed the close collaboration unfold between Collins and Cobb, observing that they "have a shared love of the same music and the history of music." She adds that Collins attended a lot of the recordings virtually, and she continued her conversations with Cobb throughout the creative process.

For his part, Cobb found himself on a tight schedule; he was given less than a month to produce the songs and hand them over to the filmmakers. This expedited timeframe led to a quick turnaround with the recordings. He explains, "When you hear the soundtrack and the songs in the movie, they're very much first takes—first time we ever figured it out. I think the more you labor over something, the more it sounds intentional and cerebral, and I don't think there's much of a connection that way. Everything is very honest, raw, and first take, including Rachel's voice" (Walsh). In the end, Cobb's versions of the songs—including melodies, chords, and song structures—survived with only minimal modifications, as Lawrence confirms: "He wrote the full songs, and we barely did changes" (Lynch).

The Brilliance of James Newton Howard

If Rachel Zegler provides a fresh voice and style to *Ballad*, fans are treated once again with the familiar sounds of legendary composer James Newton Howard. Now a fixture within the Hunger Games franchise, Howard returned to score *Ballad* after doing the same for all four previous films. Perhaps in line with "Lucky" Flickerman who "needs no introduction," Howard's contributions to film and TV music are equally unrivaled. Since landing his first major role for scoring *Pretty Woman* in 1990, his lengthy resume includes seven nominations for the Academy Award and two nominations in the Best Song category. Just a few of his many recognizable projects include the scores for *The Fugitive, My Best Friend's Wedding, Defiance, News of the World, Maleficent, The Sixth Sense, Fantastic Beasts,* and *The Dark Night* with Hans Zimmer. His work on *Ballad* was also preceded by numerous creative projects in collaboration with director Francis Lawrence, including the features *I am Legend, Water for Elephants,* and *Red Sparrow*, starring Jennifer Lawrence. His list of accomplishments continues indefinitely. And his latest installment for the fifth Hunger Games film does not disappoint.

Howard's lengthy score for *Ballad* provides a full hour of music; its 40 cues are the most numerous yet of the five films. The score was recorded at the AIR Studios in London during May and June 2023. In keeping with Dave Cobb's efforts to honor the authentic musical history of the Appalachians, Howard decided to rely on an entirely orchestral, symphonic score. This was in contrast to his more electronic-infused compositions for the previous films (LeBlanc). His latest score incorporates some familiar themes from the preceding films, while it also adds fresh and original compositions to support *Ballad's* rather unique storyline. To do this he employed Baroque-era instrumentation including the viola de gamba and cello d'amore to infuse the score with more of a rural, folk feel.

This approach not only reflected the prequel's historical themes but also provided a "stylistic extension" of Lucy Gray's new songs (LeBlanc). In quite dramatic fashion, the symphonic score intersects with Lucy Gray's "The Old Therebefore" while she attempts to survive Dr. Gaul's reptile onslaught. In more eloquent words, Ivan Korrs writes, "The orchestral thunder of James Newton Howard's score marries well with Lucy Gray's songs, in which executive music producer Dave Cobb crafts rousing tunes around Collins' lyrics, adding fire to the heroine's rebel spirit" (Korrs).

In one interview, Howard explains more about his approach to the prequel. He begins, "I think the musical opportunities were huge; I think originally we had a mandate to keep the score in the spirit and in the feelings of all the Hunger Games movies that came before." And the producers originally expected him to reuse much of the thematic material from earlier films. To this he explains, "But what I discovered soon was that this is an entirely new set of characters, there's a different sensibility to this movie than the others, it's tougher; I just found it very easy to write to this movie, but in a very distinctive way; it defied my expectations for sure.

When I first saw it, I thought, 'Oh, there's not much action music in this movie,' and then once I started working it was just monster action piece after piece. That's always kind of amazing to me" ("Cast").

One theme Howard did not include was "Rue's Fairwell." He adds, "We tried using it a couple of times, and we all kind of agreed that that wasn't going to happen." Likewise, Howard and his team "tried to stay away from Katniss' theme because she's obviously not in the movie." One exception is a well-placed cue when Lucy Gray mentions the katniss plant to Coriolanus at the lake. Viewers are immediately treated with her theme from the opening of *Catching Fire*, as she attempts to hunt in the woods. Howard later admits, "there's a resonant Hunger Games bit of the score which I think people will enjoy because I think they're touchstones" ("Cast"). One such "bit" includes another throwback to *Catching Fire*, when the arena crumbles and Katniss is pulled to safety. Among other thematic elements, Howard includes a minor-chord, almost insidious variation of the hopeful "Searching for Peeta" cue from *The Hunger Games*. In these ways the highly original score for *Ballad* still provides a variety of subtle and obvious callbacks to the earlier films.

One surprising newcomer to Howard's symphonic score is world-renowned Chinese pianist, Yuja Wang. Her newfound status as featured artist in *Ballad* has generated a buzz in its own right. Not only are her musical talents integrated throughout the tracks, but she also contributes three solo piano suites highlighting emotional themes from the previous films. One solo is infused into *Ballad*'s end credits, and all three are included within the 40-track album. Her themes can immediately elicit a sharp pang of nostalgia, reminding us of the earlier films' more emotional moments. Her tracks specifically include "Friendship," "Rue's Fairwell," and "Victor." If these poignant variations do not tug at our heartstrings from the ghosts of Hunger Games past, it is difficult to say what will.

THE PRODUCERS

Just how Yuja Wang came to be involved with the film is an intriguing story in its own right. Rather than actively seeking her out, the opposite happened. Howard elaborates, "At one point her people reached out to me, and I heard that she actually wanted to work with me, which of course I didn't believe at all; I had to verify that with a number of sources… Once I knew she was on board, I started writing different kinds of piano parts. I think what it did was give us a really interesting… expression of the score which we wouldn't have had before." He further explains how, for some of the film's more tense moments, "we used piano in a more elaborate way than I ever would have before. And I think it became a very important voice in the score" ("Cast").

• CHAPTER 3 •

Producing the Music

The Savannah Recordings

Eventually it came time for Cobb to test drive his tunes with actual musicians. For this purpose, he decided to think well outside the (music) box. A traditional recording studio was not suitable enough, he felt, to create the raw, authentic, dystopian sound he strived for. Instead, he and his team sought out just the perfect site to produce the future songs of Lucy Gray Baird. "The big thing for me was to get the ability to be completely unorthodox," explains Cobb, adding, "We had this crazy idea to come down to my hometown of Savannah, Georgia and rent an old mansion and record in that" (Lynch). To that end, Cobb converted the lower floor of a historic home into a makeshift studio for approximately two weeks.

In so doing he looked to 20th-century folk archivist Alan Lomax for some posthumous inspiration. Among numerous lifetime accomplishments, Lomax was known for his tireless field recordings of folk songs and ballads across Scotland and Ireland. It was not enough for Cobb to take advantage of the old mansion's acoustics.

PRODUCING THE MUSIC

As a serious nod to Lomax, he brought in vintage recording equipment and musical instruments from the 1940s era, which only added to the production's authenticity (Amorosi). Cobb explains with some understated giddiness, "We mic'd the walls... and obviously the wood sounds different because it's nearly petrified." He continues, "I wanted to have this real authenticity to match the recordings we were influenced by—and you can feel that super Southern dystopia" (Walsh).

This approach contrasted greatly with a clinical recording studio. Cobb claims, "With all the creaks in the walls, you can hear the history in the recordings... The old microphones we used looked like they'd been under a bed for 75 years. Molly Tuttle played a big part—she played the guitar of Lucy Gray, and I found this old '30s Gibson that she played on. It wasn't just a regular acoustic guitar—it has character" (Lynch). He envisioned having the songs "sound like they were on a porch in a rocking chair, singing and strumming like an Alan Lomax recording" (Amorosi).

In a four-minute "featurette" video, Cobb is seen with various assistants and musicians sprawled across the lower floor of the Savannah property. Microphone stands are placed in corners and along walls as he described. A litany of musicians, acoustic (string) instruments, and recording equipment have taken over the floor's period furnishings. In one scene they are in mid-performance of the background music for "Keep on the Sunny Side." While Cobb bangs on a Maude Ivory-type drum, four others are clapping and stomping on the staircase to simulate a joyful Hob audience. This was Cobb's unique approach to replicate the raw acoustics one might encounter at such a rural venue ("Featurette").

Of course, authentic reproduction can only go so far. The Covey actors, for instance, are not playing their own instruments while performing on the Hob's makeshift stage. Rather, professional musicians were brought in to reproduce and pre-record the Covey's instrumental sounds. They include none other than Molly Tuttle, one of the world's top guitar players and bluegrass musicians. The "California phenom" has become a recent fixture within the modern bluegrass genre in recent years. She plays Lucy Gray's guitar throughout the film's musical numbers, and she did not hold back her excitement about doing so. "It was crazy," she said during one interview. "Dave Cobb called me about a year and a half ago and was like, 'I want you to play guitar on the new Hunger Games movie.' I was super excited because I read all those books as a kid, and I'm a really big fan of the series" (Mower).

On an Instagram post Tuttle further claimed to be "nerding out the whole time" while she worked on the project, adding, "Fun fact: guitar I recorded with is the same one that you see [Rachel Zegler] play in the movie." She explains the guitar was inspired by the archtop Gibson model once played by Maybelle Carter of the famed Carter Family. In a separate interview, Francis Lawrence adds that "Maybelle [Carter] inspired the guitar Lucy Gray plays in the movie. Maybelle was small, and she had this giant guitar that looked too big for her. So that's what we sort of designed for Lucy Gray" (Dominick, "I Genuinely").

Cobb enlisted the talents of other professional musicians as well. Country musician Carmella Ramsey was hired to stand in for Clerk Carmine's fiddling parts. Cobb gushes about Ramsey, saying "she's amazing and [is] coming in to play the fiddle. She's played with Reba McIntyre, played on tons of incredible country records" ("Cast"). Of course, this means we do not hear the instrumental magic of actor Konstantin Taffet, who plays the Covey's young Clerk Carmine in the film. His exceptional violin playing has won awards and wide acclaim in Germany, making him a clear choice for the role.

To play the mandolin parts, Cobb brought in Dominic Leslie, another up-and-coming bluegrass phenom. He recently partnered with Molly Tuttle on her band's 2023 Grammy-winning album, *Crooked Tree*. For his part, Leslie has produced recently acclaimed albums with his own band, Hawktail, including *Formations* in

January 2020. He had been playing various acoustic instruments since age four, eventually settling on the mandolin and releasing his debut solo, "Signs of Courage," at age 15. Prior to that he was the youngest ever to win his state of Colorado's *Rockygrass* mandolin contest in 2004. Now based in Nashville, Leslie's reputation led to an invitation to replicate the Covey's own mandolin phenom, Tam Amber. With Leslie and all of Cobb's exceptional hires, there was no lack of talent in replicating the Covey's Mountain sounds.

Being Lucy Gray, Live on Set

One impressively authentic element—and a surprise for film producers and fans alike—was the powerful voice of Rachel Zegler. After she completed the *pre-record*, or the in-studio recordings of her songs, Zegler agreed with Lawrence that she should sing her musical numbers live on set to provide maximum impact. Singing live while filming is virtually unheard of within contemporary movie production. Of her numerous and multifaceted roles, Zegler was particularly proud of her ability to sing on set. In one interview, she discusses how her decision affected both her acting and singing, in that performing live "adds something audiences miss when it's gone. Singing in a film and singing live onstage are two different types of performances, sure, but you should be able to demonstrate both in your art when you're working in the world of both musicals and film. Singing live for every take five days a week is not easy. But it brings something alive to the world of a film" (Amorosi).

Zegler adds that Cobb's song compositions become like an additional character in the film. The songs provide more information about Lucy Gray than what the spoken dialogue alone can accomplish. She continues, "And there's a rawness to the music that truly fits in District 12—solace in the midst of the pain and suffering in a post-war society. Singing live added layers to a performance that canned vocals cannot" (Amorosi).

Dave Cobb recalls, "We knew that Rachel could deliver on that over-the-top vocal quality, so when she actually got to us, filming and singing in Germany and Poland, doing scratch vocals and pre-records, it was even better than I could imagine... No matter how high our expectations were of her, Rachel surpassed them. Nothing was impossible for her; she did everything in one or two takes." Along with Lawrence, he immediately knew that she could sing live on set after hearing her first vocals. Normally this is a demanding task for any actor to accomplish, given the triple duty of singing, reacting to the audience, and acting per the script. "Very few people can do what Rachel does," adds Cobb (Amorosi).

For her part, executive producer Nina Jacobson recalls her own astonishment with Zegler's live performances:

> Watching Rachel sing on set was, something that, I would get chills, or just sit there, sort-of stunned especially because she mostly chose to sing live. Which is really rare. Usually, you lay down a track of your actor, and then they lip-sync, maybe sing softly along, but they don't bring it every time because that would be exhausting. She brought it every time, and it would leave you stock still, sort of staring, unable to take your eyes off of her, unable to believe that this voice could come out of this tiny little person. ("Cast")

In a separate interview, Jacobson mentioned the added challenge with a lead actress who also sings on stage. Portraying that type of character in a film "still feels like a big leap," she says, adding, "It's certainly not something Katniss Everdeen would ever be caught dead doing. Having a character like Lucy Gray and getting to give her that stage and to see the incredible arrangements and Rachel's command over the songs and her range, her ability to blow the roof off." She concludes with added emphasis, "She sang live virtually every take, every time that you're seeing her sing in the movie. She's not singing playback" (Gomez).

Asked whether the team knew they would include Zegler's live vocals from the start, Francis Lawrence clarified that they still had Rachel complete the in-studio sessions for the album and other purposes. He then adds thoughtfully,

> But weirdly, the studio sessions were almost like a rehearsal. They were really Rachel's first time singing to the tracks that had been recorded with the musicians, and she was able to work with Dave Cobb, our producer-songwriter, to make sure we got the tone right for the genre of music that we were doing. And luckily, she's just so talented, and she slipped into it perfectly and immediately. And because singing is so easy for her, my goal was always to have her sing live. So we took the knowledge from the recording studio [to set], but you also can't recreate some of these scenes that we were doing, especially emotionally, by sitting in a dark recording studio with a couple of candles lit and a big microphone in your face. It's very different than singing an *a cappella* song in an arena while you're pushing yourself up a slab of concrete in fear, defiance and rage. So, we just wanted her to be more present, and it was great that she could do it. (Davids)

Any lingering doubt about whether Zegler should—or could—effectively sing live was likely put to rest the first day of filming. This is when she belted out "The Old Therebefore," surrounded by fake rubble and equally fake dead bodies inside Wroclaw, Poland's Centennial Hall. Lawrence vividly recalls his experience that day, saying, "That's the first song she sang in the filming of the movie... The sound of her solo voice in that big cement space was pretty incredible. It gave everybody chills. Some people were even tearing up" (Wang, "Rachel").

Some concern remained as to whether Zegler could sustain repeat performances, given the intensity of the scene. Lawrence explains, "Because it does get pretty big," he says in an understated way, "that was the only time where we couldn't do take after take... Usually singing for [Zegler] is super easy and she's happy to do it, but there was only so much she could do without blowing her voice. So, we had to be careful there" (Wang, "Rachel").

Not surprisingly, the difference between singing in a studio versus live on set did not escape Rachel Zegler herself. She explains there is "nothing like hearing one's voice in a space live, and as somebody who has been training vocally for ten years, it was really important to me as a viewer of movies and musical alike. When you're witnessing it, you can tell it adds emotion when someone is singing live in the room; emotion for other people who get to watch and listen, but also for someone who is singing" (Campione).

Aside from singing live, Zegler was required to shift her vocal style from the Broadway musical genre to that of a movie production. She had only recently finished working with director Stephen Spielberg on his Oscar-winning adaptation of *West Side Story*. Still, she passed this veritable skills test with flying colors. "We knew she could really sing because Zegler played Maria," writes Craig Havigurst for Nashville's WMOT Roots Radio, adding, "but any fears she'd bring Broadway mannerisms to this acoustic country material can be set aside." In his positive review of Zegler's songs within the soundtrack, Havigurst offers that the original song, "Pure as the Driven Snow," is a "fine plaintive and bittersweet song. But the showstopper... is 'Nothing You Can Take from Me,' a high-stepping minor-key song of self-possession that shows the savvy range and sweet tone of Zegler's voice." He further compares that song favorably to the acclaimed "Man of Constant Sorrow," the upbeat tune from *O Brother Where Art Thou?* two decades earlier. This is all high praise indeed from a specialist in old-time, Americana "roots" music.

In an email conversation with *Variety*, Zegler provides a more technical explanation for shifting from the voice of Maria to that of Lucy Gray on rather short notice. After mentioning her years of training, she explains, "It rests in how one approaches their consonants (or a consonant orchestra), the positioning of their larynx, their glottis, their epiglottis, even their tongue... Maria was approached with much more softness, with her volume rising with her confidence." In contrast, Zegler's voice for Lucy Gray was much more powerful, and frequent. As Maria, she had only sung with such a powerful voice in three of the musical's numbers. "The rest was very quiet, very pensive," she adds. For Lucy Gray's character, Zegler was given the green light to let loose with her own powerful voice. She further explains, "[Lucy Gray] even says, 'I don't sing when I'm told, I sing when I have something to say.' And working with Dave Cobb made that especially exciting, as he tends to work with musicians who have the same attitude toward their talents" (Amorosi).

Is *Ballad* a Musical?

Given Zegler's extensive singing role, some observers have considered whether *Ballad* is the franchise's first Broadway musical. Do we see a truly theatrical production here, or is it something else? A *musical* as a distinct form of theater can be defined as either a stage or film production that features popular songs, either to contribute to the storyline itself or to showcase the talents of a specific writer or performer. Other broad definitions distinguish a *musical film* as including various songs interwoven into the narrative, sometimes accompanied by dancing. A common theme is that the songs need to be linked into the storyline.

BEHIND THE BALLADS

According to Lee Hamilton of *Shore Scripts*, what distinguishes a musical from a drama, horror, or comedy is that the musical numbers "function, not as light relief from storyline, but like any other element, the dialogue or the scene, it must be active, advance plot or develop character." Some relatively recent productions considered excellent examples of TV/film musicals include *La La Land*, Spielberg's' *West Side Story* remake, *The Greatest Showman*, *Mamma Mia!*, *Bohemian Rhapsody*, and *A Star Is Born*. There are countless others, of course, though these provide an appropriate baseline from which to compare.

A case can certainly be made that *Ballad* fits at least partially into this general framework. The film features a string of songs, or numbers throughout the story. And—for the film, at least—they are integrated to showcase the incomparable voice and talents of Rachel Zegler. Although Suzanne Collins did not likely have Zegler in mind while writing her prequel, Zegler was on the producers' collective radar from the onset. Further, several of Zegler's more emotional songs help us understand Lucy Gray's character, inner thoughts, rebelliousness against oppression, and past relationships. This education comes to us most notably through "The Ballad of Lucy Gray," "Pure as the Driven Snow," and "Nothing You Can Take from Me." Her unaccompanied version of "Lucy Gray" likewise provides similar character development.

Additionally, author Valerie Estelle Frankel notes how several songs in the prequel book are repeated, or reprised, later within the story. This is standard practice for Broadway musicals, where earlier songs are revisited later with a twist, or to re-emphasize an earlier mood (Frankel, "Songbirds"). One prominent case in point involves "The Hanging Tree," which is reprised several times in various contexts within the book. While the film returns to the haunting song only once—as Coriolanus gives chase to Lucy Gray in the forest—it is indeed reprised as the closing song.

Another song that makes a grand return is "Nothing You Can Take from Me." Lucy Gray first performs this song unaccompanied and under duress during the reaping. This later becomes Lucy Gray's opening number at the Hob, backed up by the full complement of Covey musicians playing for a raucous crowd. Likewise, "Keep on the Sunny Side" is treated similarly, first sung in the book as a sing-along number by Maude Ivory. The song is reprised later in what Frankel calls an "ironic juxtaposition" (Frankel, "Songbirds"). That is, while the crowd is being entertained by this uplifting number, dramatic acts of violence and death are transpiring in the shed next door. In the film, we only hear the song within this particular scene, and mostly relegated to the muffled background. For viewers unfamiliar with the original book, it would likely be a stretch to recognize what was once considered a Carter Family staple.

Other writers for various media outlets have likewise compared *Ballad* to a musical. Writing about the film's largely unexpected music component, Katie Campione and Anthony D'Alessandro suggest that many viewers may expect little more than a story devoted to Coriolanus Snow. Others may assume that Lucy Gray Baird is just another Katniss from District 12. Such generalizations would be mistaken, however, "for at its core this sci-fi political action thriller has the underpinnings of a sublime romantic country western musical, and when you finally see it, you'll get what we mean." What sets this film apart from the earlier ones with Jennifer Lawrence, they continue, are the "raw and rugged, rural Scottish and Irish influenced ballads sung by Rachel Zegler's Lucy."

Even more emphatic is *Slate's* Nadira Goffe, whose article is headlined with the not-so-subtle title, "The New Hunger Games Movie Is a Musical, Thank God." In separating *Ballad* from its predecessors, Goffe claims, "The original movies were action dramas that featured rare musical performances, but the newest action drama is an actual movie musical." She then admits a key counterargument: "Ok, no one randomly bursts into song. But like such fellow movie musicals as *Once, Sing Street,* and *A Star is Born,* [*Ballad*] is best when spotlighting Lucy Gray Baird." In support of her claim, she continues, "While perhaps not every dystopian franchise would be a natural fit for staging a musical, The Hunger Games is, because, as Zegler suggested, the idea of performance has always been central to the series... Between her talents and Coriolanus' astute ideas about how to keep viewers invested, the orchestrators of the Games begin to understand, and weaponize, the idea of spectacle... What better way to make a movie about performance and spectacle than to make a musical?" Goffe's most insightful message comes near her conclusion: "In the end, if any Hunger Games fan doesn't appreciate the power of theatricality, they've missed one of the key lessons of the franchise—and it doesn't get more theatrical than a musical."

Despite such enthusiastic arguments, the case becomes more difficult to make when considering a musical's specific characteristics. One attribute not seen within *Ballad* is characters randomly breaking into song and dance as part of the storyline. To do so would immediately add the element of fantasy rather than reality. In his own introduction to the musical genre, Jason Hellerman notes that, within bona fide musicals, "characters break into song and choreographed dance routines, allowing their emotions, thoughts, and motivations to be expressed in a lyrical and often larger-than-life manner."

More vaguely, the definition of "musical genre" is largely in the eye of the beholder. Theorists have offered numerous perspectives on how a musical should be defined, let alone the musical genre. According to Lee Hamilton of *Shore Scripts*, "one film may constitute as a musical, or not," depending upon which theorist is talking. She adds that having "characters spontaneously burst into well-rehearsed song and dance routines cannot do anything but shout at us that this isn't real life, it's fantasy."

PRODUCING THE MUSIC

One should therefore ask seriously whether *Ballad* screams "fantasy" in this way, which arguably it does not. Though severely truncated for the film, Suzanne Collins' original storyline remains remarkably intact in its own right and is not dependent upon singing and dance routines. Rather, as Zegler's character clarifies, Lucy Gray only sings when she has something to say, not when she's told to do so. Her songs are built into the plot simply because she happens to be a performer, around whom much of the storyline revolves.

Perhaps the most useful comparison is to size up *Ballad* with the genre's most common characteristics. For this purpose, Hellerman provides a useful list of such *tropes*, or aspects that audiences have come to expect from every musical. Of the top fifteen tropes he discusses, *Ballad* appears to only include three. These include a *love ballad* (which could be interpreted as "Pure as the Driven Snow"), a *reprise* (Lucy Gray's repeated version of "The Hanging Tree"), and a *showstopper* (possibly "Nothing You Can Take from Me"). Aside from Lucy Gray's full complement of songs throughout the film, it is these tropes that are cited most often by those who interpret *Ballad* as a musical.

That said, Hellerman's other twelve tropes are nowhere to be seen or heard. Briefly for purposes here, these include (1) an *opening number* (2) an *"I want" song*, in which a character expresses their desires and goals (3) a *villain's song*; Coriolanus does not sing, nor does he want to do so (4) *dance numbers* with elaborate routines (5) an *11 O'clock number*—a powerful song near the end to signify a character's realization or transformation. Coriolanus does neither, aside from quietly "breaking bad" (6) characters *breaking into song*; Lucy Gray does this only as part of the narrative, when she is expected to sing and perform (7) a *big finale* (8) *fantasy sequences* (9) *group numbers* with ensembles of characters performing lively singing and dance routines (10) *tap dancing* (11) *parallel songs*—two characters singing separate songs opposite one another, and finally

(12) *breaking the fourth wall*, in which characters might directly address the audience or acknowledge they are in a musical. While musicals within the genre are not required to include all these tropes, it is commonly expected to see many of them.

With only three tropes clearly making an appearance within *Ballad*, it becomes all the more difficult to label it a musical. Does it trend in that direction? Certainly. And it was admittedly a surprise—if not an outright shock—for readers and audiences to experience such a musical focus within its otherwise dystopian story. As indicated earlier, even the film's producers expressed their own initial befuddlement. That said, should *Ballad* be considered a full-blown musical? Probably not.

If anyone enjoys at least partial authority on this debate, it might be Francis Lawrence. Not only did Rachel Zegler leave her "Broadway mannerisms" out of the film as noted earlier. But Lawrence offers his own perspective. After indicating how her powerful voice gave everybody chills inside the arena, he adds, "It was a big [moment] because the musical element of this movie is one of the biggest differences from the other movies." Despite this fact, Lawrence confirms, "it's not a musical, so it was finding the right balance of that" (Wang, "Rachel"). Lawrence and his team were therefore not aiming for that particular genre. Beyond this, viewers and interpreters can make their own conclusions. At the end of the day, this is all part of the fun.

• CHAPTER 4 •

The Covey: From Ballads to Bluegrass

Prequel readers must have been shocked upon moving into the book's third part. Unlike the original series books, the last third of the story occurs after the Games, back in District 12. And not only do we witness raucous concerts at the Hob, but the future president of Panem is actually in attendance—as one of Panem's "newest, if not shiniest, Peacekeepers" (*BSS* 320). This is only for starters. The prequel takes us back to central Appalachia to offer up more of District 12's music and culture than at any time previously. Let's take a deeper dive into the musical roots and inspirations behind Lucy Gray's "pretty birds," the Covey.

Covey Names and Meanings

Along with Coriolanus, readers are introduced to the full complement of Covey members during the first Hob concert. The cinematic version omits Maude Ivory Baird's detailed introductions, replacing them instead with the upbeat "District 12 Stomp." Still, we finally meet Lucy Gray's younger cousin, Maude Ivory as she jumps on stage to introduce the group. In *Ballad* Maude Ivory is played by actress Vaughan Reilly, a New York native and singer descended from several generations of circus performers. She is likely known best for her co-starring role opposite Natasha Lyonne in *Russian Doll* for her small-screen debut. She also provides voices for a variety of Russian-accented characters, podcasts, narration, and commercials. She now makes her big-screen debut in *Ballad*.

Within the novel, the first to be introduced on stage by Maude Ivory is Tam Amber, playing the mandolin and described as a "tall, rawboned young man in a feathered hat" (*BSS* 361). He is all business, ignoring the crowd's applause and walking straight to Maude Ivory's side. Actor Eike Onyambu, who is Kenyan by birth, portrays Tam Amber in *Ballad*. Prior to graduating from the Music and Arts University of Vienna in 2022, Onyambu was already acting for radio programs and voiceovers as a child. He further plays the violin, viola, and saxophone, skills that made him a shoo-in for the Covey.

The Covey's fiddle player, Clerk Carmine Clade is announced next in the book. He is around age 12 in the story and is Billy Taupe Clade's younger brother. Lucy Gray nicknames him "CC" and praises him at the lake for finding some katniss plants, although they are not yet in season for eating. In *Ballad* Clerk Carmine is played by the acclaimed German violinist, Konstantin Taffet. He has placed first in a number of his home country's violin competitions and has been a member of several orchestras in Potsdam since 2015. Given that the fiddle and violin are technically the same instrument employed for widely varying musical styles, his role in *Ballad* made excellent sense for his feature film debut.

Next to be introduced on stage is Lucy Gray's other cousin, Barb Azure Baird, on upright string bass. Older than Clerk Carmine and Tam Amber, Barb had "started seeing a gal down the road" and was probably "glad to have the place to themselves for a day," as the Covey and Coriolanus ventured off to the lake (*BSS* 430). She is one of the prequel's three characters confirmed as part of the LGBTQ community, in addition to Pluribus Bell and Cyrus ("Barb"). In *Ballad* she is portrayed by Honor Gillies, who was making her professional acting debut with the role.

Then Maude Ivory says excitedly, "And now, fresh from her engagement in the Capitol, the one and only Lucy Gray Baird!" (*BSS* 361). At this point the film closely mimics the book as Maude Ivory welcomes Lucy Gray to the stage. Our star performer then teases the crowd before launching into her first number.

It should come as little surprise that the term *covey* refers to a flock of birds, thereby explaining the name of Lucy Gray's traveling family. Collins does not stop with that metaphor, however, as each of her Covey characters is purposely intertwined with Appalachia's musical heritage. The book's Maude Ivory tells us that the first names of Covey members derive from historical ballads, while their second names are based on colors. For her part, *ivory* is the color of piano keys. This naming convention fits Billy Taupe as well. *Taupe* does not describe a single color, however, but is more a vast range of blended colors from dark tan to brownish gray. This quite fittingly represents his own troubled and complicated personal history.

Lucy Gray is special, of course, taking her name directly from William Wordsworth's poem of the same name (see "Lucy Gray" in Chapter 5) (*BSS* 436). Beyond these tidbits, Collins leaves it up to her readers to uncover the rest. And there is plenty more.

One principal source of Appalachian folk ballads was Francis James Child, who compiled an impressive collection of 305 ballads primarily from England and Scotland. He managed to include a few American variations as well. Many of them date to the 17th and 18th centuries and are sometimes even older. His eight-volume series was published simply as *English and Scottish Ballads* in 1860. A later version was published as a five-volume set in the United States, thereby introducing these Old-world folk tales to Americans after 1882.

With time the so-called "Child Ballads" found their way into the folk customs of Appalachian communities and were passed down to future generations. These later Americans added their own tales and folk songs to the vast mountain repertoire, many now derived from more local experiences and stories. Ballad topics expanded to include the theme of extractive industries such as logging, ranching, and mining, not to mention woeful tales of environmental desecration, family tragedy, and of course, murder. The experiences of Black communities were likewise mixed into the full complement of mountain balladry, which in their case often featured their own first-hand experiences with grief or celebration. They often relied on real-life events as inspiration for their own tales (Paradis).

Enter Suzanne Collins and her own dystopian tale from central Appalachia. Already famous for her themed character naming system, she now adds the Child Ballads and related tunes as additional sources of inspiration. One of the first authors to unlock this connection was Valerie Estelle Frankel, who first wrote about the Covey character names within her follow-up book, *Songbirds, Snakes, and Sacrifice*. Based on some background research, Frankel learned that Barb Azure owes her first name to the ballad, "Barbry Allen," while Maude Ivory derives from "Maude Clair." The Child Ballads kick in directly through the names of Tam Amber and Clerk Carmine. Frankel posits that the Covey's "finest picker alive," Tam Amber owes his first name to "Tam Lin," in Child Ballad number 39. Likewise, fiddler Clerk Carmine seems to reference "Clerk Colvill" in Child Ballad number 42. In this way Collins has creatively married the Covey band's characters with Appalachia's folk ballad traditions and history.

Covey Instrumentation: A Nod to Bill Monroe

The instrumentation of the Covey band is no accident, either. As I uncovered within my earlier book, the Covey of the novel can clearly be interpreted as a traditional Appalachian bluegrass band. True to her cunning ways, Collins never reveals outright the origins or meaning of the Covey's carefully chosen instrumentation. Still, she provides a litany of clues as to their performance style and its connections with Appalachian—and more generally Southern—music history. Compared to the early country music genre of the 1920s and 1930s, bluegrass evolved within the region largely after 1940 and World War II. It is likely no mistake that Collins included the precise instrumentation of what is considered America's first bluegrass band, *Bill Monroe and the Blue Grass Boys*.

In their case, "Blue Grass" referred to the nickname of Kentucky as the Blue Grass State, and the home of Bill Monroe. Bluegrass music as a genre would not be identified as such until a full decade later. Eventually dubbed the "Father of bluegrass music," Bill Monroe and his string band introduced this up-tempo genre at Nashville's Grand Ole Opry in 1939, much to the audience's shock and delight. They first performed a rousing rendition of "Mule Skinner Blues" by hillbilly music star, Jimmie Rodgers. At the time, country music was still referred to as *hillbilly music*, a term which survived until the more acceptable "country" descriptor became standard in the 1940s. Regardless, many scholars have identified this specific concert as the night Bill Monroe ushered in the bluegrass era (Paradis).

Most curiously, Bill Monroe's original group included himself on mandolin and three other musicians who played the fiddle, string bass, and guitar. If this mix of all-acoustical instruments sounds familiar, it is. The Covey band replicates this instrumentation precisely, just as the Blue Grass Boys performed between 1939 and 1942. In that year Monroe rounded out their band with their first banjo player, making history as they did so. Ever since, the banjo has been considered a necessary instrument for traditional bluegrass bands, ideally including five acoustic instruments. Given that Collins' prequel serves as a veritable tour of Appalachian music history, it is no stretch to imagine she based her Covey on the inaugural version of Bill Monroe's outfit. This further explains the conundrum as to why the Covey band does not include a banjo. Neither did Bill Monroe, until 1942 (Paradis).

Supporting this argument is a litany of clues indicating the Covey's principal performance style. Despite what we see and hear in the film, the Covey is not conceptualized as a country band. Certainly, bluegrass is often interpreted as a "cousin" or sub-genre within the larger country music umbrella. Still, it comes with its own distinct instrumental and vocal styling, along with a unique, team-based performance approach on stage. As the outgrowth and expansion of earlier Appalachian string bands, later bluegrass ensembles typically included between four and seven musicians playing combinations of the five standard acoustic instruments mentioned above. Additional instrumentation was occasionally added, especially the "dobro" (resonator guitar), and less commonly the mouth harp (harmonica), and accordion. Given that many of the Covey's relatives had been killed during or after the war, it is entirely possible that additional family musicians had once been a part of their traveling group as well.

We further know that Billy Taupe played the accordion and clearly wanted back into the band. In the book he carries around his boxy, wheezing instrument almost everywhere, indicating his strong personal identity with the Covey. It is clear that the Covey had included him prior to the 10th Games, until he was unceremoniously booted from the group after some poor decision making. Given that the accordion was never a standard instrument for a bluegrass ensemble, it is perhaps fitting that both the instrument and the character who played it were considered superfluous, or supplemental (Paradis).

What distinguishes the Covey of the book versus that of the film is their performance style. If one did not know better, we could very well be watching two different musical groups from several decades apart. The Covey of *Ballad* best represents an early country or mountain string band. Country music is defined in part by its reliance on one lead singer and a series of backup musicians. This approach was an outgrowth of the earlier mountain string bands that began first with a fiddle-banjo combination and later added the mandolin and string bass. During the 1920s and 1930s the mandolin had not yet been elevated as a lead instrument, but instead was relegated to the background. Its purpose was little more than to help maintain the rhythm and beat through its characteristic "chop" chords (Paradis). That is, until mandolin prodigy Bill Monroe transformed the Italian-bred instrument—along with himself—into a lead performer.

True to the country music genre, Lucy Gray sings and carries the melody throughout each of her numbers. Dave Cobb seemed content with such a style, as his primary aim was to replicate the mountains' early country music of the 1920s and 1930s (Wang, "Rachel"). Unlike in the book, there is no vocal harmony or swapping of lead instruments, nor is there an effort to showcase different musicians as bluegrass outfits would do. At no time in the film do we see multiple Covey members gathered around the single mic to sing two- or three-part harmonies for their selections. Yet, this is how the book describes them.

We further do not get the sense of teamwork or sharing the spotlight—another trait of the bluegrass style. Even in numbers with a lead singer, bluegrass performances often include multiple instrumentalists taking turn to be featured at the mic, while the lead singer drops to the background. As Collins' narrator thus describes, "the Covey had a wide and varied repertoire, and played straight instrumental numbers as well. At times, some of the members would exit, disappearing behind the blanket to leave the stage to a pair or a solo performer" (*BSS* 364).

This is how we learn that Tam Amber proves to be "something of a standout" on his tear-drop shaped mandolin, which represents an A-style mandolin in real life. Likewise, sometimes Lucy Gray "relinquished the mic, allowing Clerk Carmine to step up and do some fancy finger work on his fiddle" (*BSS* 363). In the world of bluegrass, such featured improvisations are referred to as *breaks* and *breakdowns*. This even explains why Lucy Gray can occasionally leave the stage to take her own break, most notably when she is dealing with the tomfoolery occurring in the shed next door. Either way, there is little of the bluegrass performance style to speak of within the film.

Perhaps most intriguing is that *Ballad* producers introduced dancing to the Hob—not the least being the *country waltz* (see "Pure as the Driven Snow" in Chapter 5). As Mayne Smith describes the standard bluegrass experience, "The band's business is clearly to play music," while the audience sits and listens more or less attentively. In true form, the Hob audiences of the book are there primarily to listen and enjoy passively—not to dance. And many of them are Peacekeepers, though they seem to constitute a minority within the film.

And just as the Covey demonstrates within the book, bluegrass musicians are there first and foremost to display their *virtuosity*, or their respective technical and artistic skills as musicians. And unlike rural dance bands, bluegrass ensembles tend to exhibit a wide range of musical styles and singing, including harmonized duets, upbeat tempos and rhythms, creative song arrangements, and clear, high-pitched, falsetto singing—the latter of which intriguingly seems to define Katniss' late father in the original series.

It follows that, while Collins has clearly given us a standard bluegrass ensemble within her book, the film's producers have somehow perceived the Covey as a mountain dance band. The latter represents more of the early country music era of the 1920s and 1930s—that is, pre-bluegrass. These were the decades when mountain folk singers and string bands were discovered and elevated to a national stage. Beyond her references to bluegrass,

Collins highlights one such early country group within her prequel, none other than the Carter Family of Maces Spring, Virginia.

The Carter Family and "Keep on the Sunny Side"

What is certainly the prequel's most up-tempo and cheerful number, "Keep on the Sunny Side" is one that Collins did not write herself. Though performed twice within the book, the song is heard only once in *Ballad*, while the teenage drama is transpiring next door to the Hob. During this sequence, Coriolanus is attempting to manage Sejanus and the rebels while the Covey is performing what Frankel calls an "ironic juxtaposition"—that is, a happy song heard over the top of two cold-blooded murders (Frankel, "Songbirds"). The song is further ironic given its general message of encouragement to remain optimistic and hopeful in the face of life's challenges.

In the book as in the film, a spritely Maude Ivory is featured as lead singer on this one, serving as a snappy, crowd-pleasing sing-along. Collins modified only one verse to render it more secular. Rather than having faith in "our Savior," we are entrusted to the more inclusive "tomorrow" instead. Invoking a Christian figure in the original song made sense at the time, having been originally penned in 1899 by Ada Blenkhorn and J. Howard Entwisle as a gospel hymn. The tune's main theme was apparently inspired by Blenkhorn's disabled nephew who preferred to have his wheelchair pushed down the sunny side of the street.

The tune is often described as a veritable theme song for the famed Carter Family singing group, originally consisting of Alvin Pleasant Carter (known as A.P.), his wife Sara Carter, and his sister-in-law, Maybelle Carter. With their home base in Maces Spring, Virginia, theirs was a genuine Appalachian family dedicated to collecting and performing traditional ballads and other folk songs from the mountains. They first built their budding reputation locally, mostly through performing for weddings, house parties and church events, much in a similar vein to how the Covey perform in District 12. The Carters eventually recorded some 300 *sides* or numbers, making it one of the more significant repertoires of mountain music at the time (Ledgin).

For his part, A.P. was an avid collector of rural mountain music passed down aurally from one generation to the next. His growing collection of ballads and folk tunes included fragments of Old-world, British ballads, Victorian "parlor songs," African American material, gospel music, and 19th-century pop tunes (Malone). He and his family further developed a fondness for the blues, with clear African American origins. They regularly performed such songs, including "Worried Man Blues" and "Bear Creek Blues," showcasing the multicultural origins of mountain music. This somewhat rare affinity for such ethnically diverse source material is in part attributed to a Black musician named Leslie Riddles. He often accompanied A.P. on his "song-hunting expeditions" through the mountains. His influence only contributed to the Carter Family's vast and diverse "reservoir" of Appalachian folk music.

Also contributing to the Carters' budding musical fame was Maybelle's unique style of guitar playing. Hers was a technique which came to be immortalized as the "Carter scratch." Basically, this involved her striking one string as the lead note with her thumb while brushing the other strings with her index finger. Since then, guitar players everywhere have sought to imitate her trademark technique.

It is perhaps not surprising that historians have traced Maybelle's own guitar style back to Leslie Riddles. Her technique closely resembles that of Black banjo playing (Conway). While religious music like gospel songs and spirituals comprised about 40 percent of the Carter's full repertoire, half of those songs find their origins with Black musicians. Two examples included "Little Moses" and "When the World's on Fire," taken either directly from Black artists themselves or from their previous recordings (Ledgin).

BEHIND THE BALLADS

The Carters were propelled almost instantly to the national stage in July 1927. This is when producer Ralph Peer brought his recording crew to Bristol, Tennessee to capture the sounds of various mountain musicians and groups. While Peer had originally intended to record the songs of Ernest Stoneman, he also advertised in local newspapers to attract other musicians to his temporary studio. His efforts proved fruitful, in more ways than one. He ultimately recorded nineteen differing music groups and performers during his Bristol sessions, thereby "preserving" a total of 76 recordings.

One of those performing groups was none other than the Carter Family, having responded to Peer's call for musicians. Together with the "Singing Brakeman," Jimmie Rodgers, the Carter Family members were credited with becoming America's first hillbilly (i.e. country) music stars, due primarily to Ralph Peer's Bristol recordings and distribution (Paradis). Some of the earliest standards performed by the Carters included "Wildwood Flower" and "Keep on the Sunny Side" (1928), joined later with "Wabash Cannonball" and "Will the Circle Be Unbroken" in 1932. It is likely that Suzanne Collins chose to revive "Keep on the Sunny Side" in her prequel to highlight the beginnings of the country music era, along with the Carter Family's role in that history. The song became a national hit soon after its first recording in 1928.

For decades thereafter, both the Carters and country music star Johnny Cash featured the song in their albums and performances, sometimes appearing together on stage. Of course, after a lengthy partnership and romance, Johnny Cash eventually married June Carter, the daughter of Maybelle and Ezra Carter, in 1968. If it was indeed Collins' intention to honor this remarkable Appalachian family, she could do much worse than include "Keep on the Sunny Side" as a standard sing-along by the Covey.

Despite the challenge of comprehending the song's words within *Ballad*, the snappy Carter Family staple can be heard in its full glory on the movie soundtrack of songs or on YouTube. Ten-year-old musician Josie Hope Hall provides the delightfully lively singing voice for Maude Ivory in the film and on the soundtrack. Though actress Vaughan Reilly plays Maude Ivory, it is Josie Hope who sings lead on the number. According to their web site, she and her two older sisters comprise the Bennett Hall Band, named in honor of their older brother who passed away in 2010. Playing all around the middle Tennessee region and beyond, Josie Hope is a regular, real-life Maude Ivory, competent as she is on the drums, ukelele, tambourine, and in "killer solo and sibling harmony." It is to everyone's benefit that *Ballad* producers discovered her talents for this upbeat role.

• CHAPTER 5 •

The Ballads of Lucy Gray

Out of the eleven full-length songs woven throughout the prequel, seven are performed by the film's star—technically eight if we count Parts 1 and 2 of "Lucy Gray" separately on the soundtrack. Additional tunes are performed by the Covey without Rachel Zegler at the helm. On the flip side, several songs from the book did not make the film's final cut, namely "I'll Sell You for a Song," the humorous ballad, "Clementine," and—perhaps more surprisingly—"Down in the Valley," the country tune that Lucy Gray sings from the Capitol Zoo. Fans know this better as the "Valley Song," mentioned in the first book by Peeta during the famous cave scene.

Whether in the book or film, we learn much about the life of Lucy Gray Baird through her ballads. This is emphasized through one of her more important lines of the film, when she declares to Coriolanus, "I don't sing when I'm told, I sing when I have something to say." It follows that each ballad provides unique insights into Lucy Gray's life experiences, coded messages, or inner thoughts at the precise times she wishes to convey them. In this spirit, then, let's explore the life of Lucy Gray Baird as we consider each of her ballads in turn below.

"Nothing You Can Take from Me"

This is Lucy Gray's first song in the prequel, highlighting the dramatic moment she is introduced to Panem. After stuffing a snake down Mayfair's dress, she continues onto the Justice Building's steps, only to be swatted down by Mayfair's father, Mayor Lipp. Wearing her signature ruffled skirt, she collects herself as members of the Covey sing the first lines of the song from the audience. Now encouraged by her musical family, she pushes herself to her feet, grabs the mic, and lets loose (*BSS* 27). In the book Lucy Gray manages to finish the song and even acknowledges the crowd as a Peacekeeper carries her back to the middle of the stage.

The song is truncated in the film, ending with her screaming its most insolent line to the Capitol. This is perhaps a rare instance when the film is more realistic than the book's counterpart. Having the Peacekeepers and all of District 12 patiently waiting out Lucy Gray's full number is somehow hard to swallow.

Regardless, unbeknownst to Lucy Gray this is the first time Coriolanus and his fellow mentors hear her sing. For her part, Lucy Gray is employing the tune as a song of defiance against the Capitol—and perhaps against the Mayor and his daughter as well. This is not unlike the style of American protest songs around the turbulent 1960s. Written first as a literary ballad by Suzanne Collins, its melody was provided by producer-songwriter Dave Cobb. He explains, "I gave it a sad melody, while its lyrics are filled with joy and strength, and real empowerment from Rachel, based on history and the reinvention of it" (Amorosi).

At the conclusion of her impromptu song during the reaping, Zegler's Lucy Gray performs a prolonged, sarcastic bow with her arms fully extended. Fans immediately questioned whether this was an intentional callback to Katniss' own bows to the Gamemakers after demonstrating her chosen skill in *The Hunger Games* and later in *Catching Fire*. Hanging an effigy of Seneca Crane in the latter film was one of Katniss' earliest instances of rebellion. Francis Lawrence admits that Lucy Gray's similar bow was no coincidence. Rather, he says, "It was something that I made up on the day and had Rachel do because we're constantly looking for, in the making of this, little sort of Easter eggs that would excite the fans... I thought, 'Wow, this is really cool. If she does this then, you know, Katniss could have heard generations later about this kind of rebellious, irreverent act of this woman that was a singer and did this sort of bow curtsy at the reaping" (Piña).

Much later in *Ballad*, the song from the reaping is reprised triumphantly as the Covey's opening number at the Hob. Although the foot-stomping tune is cut short, reviewer Craig Havighurst considers it a showstopper, comparing it to "Man of Constant Sorrow" from the acclaimed film, *O Brother Where Art Thou?*. This is the first time Coriolanus sees Lucy Gray perform at the Hob, while finally confirming that she is, in fact, still alive.

Somewhat disappointingly, the song is soon interrupted by an inebriated Billy Taupe (Dakota Shapiro). In the book, the Covey rattle through a number of tunes prior to the Billy Taupe intrusion, though the lack of time for such escapades in the film is understandable. Further, the book's version of the Hob concert has the Covey performing "That Thing I Love With," one of Collins' several original songs not included in the cinematic adaptation. It is during this lengthy concert that readers—and Coriolanus—are introduced to the Covey one by one, along with their traditional bluegrass performance style (see Chapter 4).

Later in the book's concert, Collins does include "Nothing You Can Take from Me," though only one verse of the song is provided. The concert concludes, and Maude Ivory makes her standard rounds to collect contributions as payment *in kind*, if not in cash. This is when Coriolanus places the rest of Ma Plinth's popcorn balls into the basket, after which Maude Ivory indicates to Lucy Gray who did so. Their eyes finally connect, acknowledging one another, at which point Lucy Gray takes the stage one more time. As an unplanned encore, Coriolanus actually tears up as she sings "Down in the Valley,"—that is, the Valley Song—for the second time.

In *Ballad*, of course, this first concert is seriously trimmed, featuring only the so-called "District 12 Stomp" and "Nothing You Can Take from Me." At which point, Billy Taupe arrives prematurely, and the requisite fighting begins.

"The Ballad of Lucy Gray Baird"

After the arena bombing, Coriolanus is recovering in bed watching Lucky Flickerman's tribute interviews. And finally, the film's Lucy Gray has "something to say," through her own personalized ballad. Much to Coriolanus' dismay, she sings the story of her own troubled life and her relationship with Billy Taupe Clade from back in District 12. The song further confirms Grandma'am's snobbish if wise observation about Lucy Gray in the book, claiming, "She's district. And trust me, that one hasn't been a girl in a long time" (*BSS* 77). Her telling line appears in *Ballad* as well.

More so in the book, Coriolanus is clearly disturbed by the ballad and indicates this to Lucy Gray later. Steeped in his own self-centered thinking, he finally considers the girl had already experienced much in life prior to meeting him on the Capitol's station platform. Still, he remains personally hurt and profoundly jealous. While he does inquire about her song when they meet again in the film, his thoughts and emotions are largely downplayed.

As the film's Lucy Gray prepares to sing her ballad at the interviews, she has magically received a guitar—although just how this occurs remains unclear. Perhaps the producers felt it was enough for her to ask Coriolanus to find one beforehand. In the book we learn that the guitar was on loan from Coriolanus' long-time family friend and neighbor, Pluribus Bell, whose nightclub, pet cat, and various backstories augment readers' understanding of the storyline. One backstory provides readers—and Coriolanus—with further insights into the early friendship between Coriolanus' father and Casca Highbottom. Regardless, Pluribus' character and role did not survive the film's screenwriters.

Pluribus Bell or no, Lucy Gray's main point for singing the ballad is heard within its last two lines, about "being the bet you lost in the reaping." This is code to inform Maude Ivory and the Covey what really transpired during the reaping ceremony. The "bet" refers to Billy Taupe's brazen decision to become romantically involved with both the mayor's daughter, Mayfair, and Lucy Gray at the same time. It is strongly implied in both book and film that Mayfair implored her father to send Lucy Gray as tribute to the 10th Games. This even becomes obvious to Sejanus within the book while he watches the reaping with his peers. He is convinced the drawing was rigged, suggesting, "Her name wasn't on that slip" (BSS 27).

Afterwards Coriolanus and Lucy Gray discuss the song's meaning, and she explains why she sang it. Their dialogue within the book is more protracted, of course, as the now disgruntled Coriolanus prods her about the song. After some thought, she explains directly, "I left some loose ends back in District Twelve. Me being tribute... Well, there's bad luck and then there's bad business. That was bad business. And someone who owed me plenty had a hand in it. The song, it was payback of a kind. Most people won't know that, but the Covey will get the message, loud and clear." He then asks how they would understand her meaning after hearing it only once, to which she responds, "One hearing's all my cousin Maude Ivory needs. That child never forgets anything with a tune" (BSS 173).

This latter line serves as a key if subtle Easter egg connecting with the original trilogy. In *Mockingjay*, the similarity with which

Katniss describes her own childhood is uncanny. While reflecting back on when her father taught her and Prim "The Hanging Tree," she claims that "back then I could memorize almost anything set to music after a round or two" (*MJ* 124). This and other clues have pointed to a possible, and likely, family connection between Katniss and Maude Ivory (Paradis).

The film's melodic version of the ballad comes with its own story. While Collins wrote the lyrics herself, she mentions in her Acknowledgements that the song is "meant to be sung to a variation of a traditional ballad tune that has long accompanied tales of the unfortunate ends of rakes, bards, soldiers, cowboys, and the like." It turns out that the particular melody she had in mind is the one heard in the famous country-western tune, "Streets of Laredo." Also known as "The Dying Cowboy," this was an American cowboy ballad in which a dying ranger tells his own story. Laredo refers to the ranching town of Laredo, Texas.

The lyrics appear to be derived from an 18th century Irish folk song called "The Unfortunate Rake." In this historical context a *rake* can be defined as a man predisposed to immoral and otherwise troubling conduct. With time the song evolved with a completely different time signature and melody into the New Orleans standard, "St. James Infirmary Blues." For its part, the melody of "Streets of Laredo" has become a folk music favorite and performed with many variations over the years.

One well-known recording was by the Grammy-winning country singer, Marty Robbins (1925-1982). It is likely not a coincidence that the song appears on his "All-Time Greatest Hits" album together with another familiar ballad, "The Hanging Tree." This "other" hanging tree ballad served as the title song for a popular Gary Cooper cowboy film in 1959. This one involves what is likely a happier tale than its Hunger Games counterpart. It relates the story of a man who enjoys a reunion with his own true love after barely escaping the noose himself. Given Collins' personal history as a country music aficionado, it is unlikely that this album and its collection of storied songs completely escaped her attention.

"The Old Therebefore"

If the defiant "Nothing You Can Take from Me" is the prequel's showstopper, "The Old Therebefore" serves as the story's powerful and heart-stopping climax. One writer declares, "No other moment in [the film] made us feel like we should be holding our breath like this one" (Gawaran). This is basically Lucy Gray's "goodbye" to the world, as she considers what she has accomplished in life and prepares herself for the "sweet old hereafter." The book's Coriolanus considers the "old therebefore" to be "a funny line," as likely do many of Collins' readers. We catch a glimpse of his thinking, however, which helps us define the term. He contemplates, "That must mean the present. Here. Now. While she was still alive" (*BSS* 303). Dictionaries variously define *therebefore* as "before that time" or "beforehand." It further could be interpreted as a twisted play on words, in direct opposition to "hereafter."

With the title so defined, this number is treated similarly within both the book and film. It is gallantly performed by a nervous Lucy Gray Baird while Dr. Gaul's mutated rainbow snakes slowly engulf her body. She is under the impression that it is her singing that calms the weaving reptiles, thereby preventing an outright attack. She and Panem's viewership are unaware that the snakes are actually subdued by her scent. This scent was strategically provided by one Coriolanus Snow, having made yet another impulsive decision to place his handkerchief inside the snake terrarium. Lucy Gray had previously wiped her face with it, which—as Coriolanus had shockingly learned earlier—should adequately familiarize the snakes with Lucy Gray. Of course, the handkerchief in question was embroidered with his late father's initials, for Crassus Xanthos

Snow. This evidence was later used by Dean Highbottom to implicate him in the transgression.

As Lucy Gray patiently awaits rescue in both book and film, the film's storyline diverges markedly in its own unique direction. From here we witness almost two parallel realities. The cinematic experience shows Coriolanus and other mentors pleading with Dr. Gaul to free Lucy Gray and to declare her the victor. Despite the efforts of the entire student body chanting "Let her out," it is Coriolanus' poignant reminder to Dr. Gaul that nobody will watch the Games if there is no victor. This also likely serves as a callback to the dramatic scene in *The Hunger Games* when Peeta declares that the Capitol always has to have a victor. After this the pair wisely calls the Gamemaker's bluff by pretending to commit suicide. In this way, the power of the spectacle in entertainment becomes apparent to Dr. Gaul just as it would to the Gamemakers of Katniss' time.

Collins' book takes an entirely different tack. As the story's climax concludes, the snakes begin to relax their grip—something not apparent in the film. Lucky Flickerman then gathers his wits and publicly recognizes Dr. Gaul and demands she take a bow. Heavensbee Hall erupts into a standing ovation, a far cry from the film's risky protest chant. Having humbly acknowledged the applause, Gaul then quickly redirects everyone's focus on the now deceased mentor, Gaius Breen—not Felix Ravenstill. Lucky complies quickly and darts around the hall looking for spontaneous thoughts from Gaius' classmates.

Meanwhile—quite unlike the film—Lucy Gray continues to "hum to her pets" and—for the non-readers among us—*four other tributes still remain alive in the arena* (BSS 306). The reptiles did not usher in the end of the Games after all. Rather, Teslee disappears behind a barricade while Mizzen, Treech, and Reaper hold their lofty positions. A thunderstorm and ensuing downpour engulf the outdoor stadium as night falls. Lucy Gray disappears from view, and by the next morning "dead snakes litter the arena." The narrative explains away this outcome with, "Some genetically engineered creatures didn't do well outside the lab" (*BSS* 309). Coriolanus and a recovering Clemensia(!) retake their places, and the Games continue apace.

In an interview for the *Into the Arena* Podcast, actress Mackenzie Lansing, who plays District 4's Coral, explains that director Francis Lawrence and his colleagues preferred to wrap up the Games more definitively and cleanly with Dr. Gaul's reptile terrarium, rather than prolong the already lengthy film with specific story arcs for each tribute ("Episode").

Not only does *Ballad* wrap up the Games with "The Old Therebefore," but Dr. Gaul's story arc is altered dramatically as well. Her character in the book does not seek to eliminate all remaining tributes along with Lucy Gray. This is because she is not vengeful against a rebel group that supposedly blew up her arena. Unlike what transpires in *Ballad*, the true culprit of that apparent act of terror remains quite the mystery. This is discussed more thoroughly in Chapter 13.

"The Hanging Tree"

In Collins' third book, *Mockingjay*, Katniss recollects how her father had taught her and Prim "The Hanging Tree." The scene is definitely worth a rare chuckle. The sisters had practically known it as a household song and were singing it while crafting necklaces from scraps of old rope. That is, until their mother walked in and hit the roof. As Katniss recalls, "Suddenly, my mother snatched the rope necklaces away and was yelling at my father" (*MJ* 124). With Prim wailing, Katniss ran to the meadow to hide. Later her father reassured her that all was fine, "only we'd better not sing that song anymore." Katniss adds that her mother just wanted her to forget the song. "So, of course, every word was immediately, irrevocably branded into my brain," Katniss says.

Of course, this explains her ability to sing the disturbing tune aloud for her camera crew. The rest is history. Katniss' song is built into Plutarch's propos, and "The Hanging Tree" is deployed as a veritable call to revolution. At least two questions emerged from the scene with Katniss' parents. Just how had her father learned the song himself, and why did her mother become so upset?

Prior to Collins' prequel, "The Hanging Tree" was interpreted in various ways without yet knowing that Lucy Gray had written the song. Its lyrics were often compared with a *protest song* of the Civil Rights Movement. Many such politically inspired tunes—along with their singers—sought to raise awareness of various rampant injustices at the time. Most prominent among them were race-related killings and segregation up through the 1960s. So-called protest songs were further employed to raise attention to environmental destruction and inhumane working conditions imposed by coal mining companies and other extractive industries. As discussed in Chapter 1, Collins' own song of rebellion can likewise be considered a *murder ballad*, representing one common form of broadside that circulated through the Appalachians.

In his own interpretation of "The Hanging Tree," self-proclaimed "Hogwarts Professor" John Granger claimed we "can't talk about a 'hanging tree' song if you're in my generation and not think immediately of 'Strange Fruit'" (Granger). As with many literary ballads, the metaphorical song, "Strange Fruit" was first written as a poem, in this case by Abel Meeropol (pseudonym Lewis Allan). Meeropol was a teacher, poet and songwriter who also composed more uplifting songs during the early twentieth century. The poem tells the "tale of a lynching told via the rich description of a lifeless body hanging from a flowering tree" (O'Dell). During the late 1930s Meeropol approached the then-popular blues and jazz singer, Billie Holiday (1915-1959), who was at first reluctant to sing or record it. She was especially wary of its overtly political and shocking content. However, she eventually came around and made it a staple of her evening shows. Soon after the "inflammatory" song was recorded and released in 1939, "Strange Fruit" leaped to number 16 on the charts and became Holiday's best-selling record to that point in her career (O'Dell).

As Cary O'Dell writes for the Library of Congress, "So-called 'protest songs' were nothing new, but to have the story of a brutal lynching laid out so blatantly, yet so poetically, at this time in US history was unusual indeed." Given Collins' extensive knowledge of music history, it is difficult to imagine she was not somehow inspired by "Strange Fruit" as she penned her own ballad. What are the odds she happened to overlook one of the First Ladies of the Blues, as Holiday is considered—someone who performed perhaps the most influential protest song of the twentieth century?

At the risk of reading too much into Collins' possible clues, there is nonetheless a suspiciously high number of instances of the word, "strange" within both "The Hanging Tree" and now the dialogue within the prequel. While discussing the song with Lucy Gray, Coriolanus simply declares, "It's a strange song" (*BSS* 491). The word further shows up repetitively within the chorus: *Strange things did happen here, No stranger would it be*. Might this be a subtle nod to Holiday?

Regardless of Collins' own inspiration, Rachel Zegler's rendition of "The Hanging Tree" takes a considerable step to approximate Holiday's own raw, drawn-out style. For instance, both songs utilize deliberate vocal styles and similar chord progressions. According to J'na Jefferson, Holiday's version of the song, despite being accompanied by jazz piano, "is incredibly macabre, resulting in a sonic dichotomy just as bone-chilling as its lyrics." Likewise, Zegler adopts a more melancholic, eerie, and haunting style for her rendition of the folk ballad than we hear sung by Katniss (Jennifer Lawrence) in *Mockingjay, Part 1*. In place of a jazz piano, Zegler is accompanied only by a simple guitar rhythm. This is in stark contrast to the steadier rhythm and symphonic accompaniment of

Katniss' version, composed by James Newton Howard and the folk-pop group, the *Lumineers* (Paradis).

And Collins' tune is not the only song about a hanging tree. Another "Hanging Tree" tune appeared as the title song to a popular western film of the same name, starring Gary Cooper in 1959. Based on a 1957 booklet by Dorothy Johnson, "The Hanging Tree" western is set within Montana's post-Civil War gold rush. The film's title song, performed by Marty Robbins, is considered a western ballad that tells the tale of a man who reunites with his own true love after narrowly escaping being hung himself. The song was performed widely and was nominated for best song at the 32nd Annual Academy Awards.

Incidentally, Marty Robbins' "All-Time Greatest Hits" album (1991) includes not only "The Hanging Tree," but the "Streets of Laredo" as well. As discussed earlier, this latter tune adopts the same popular melody as "The Ballad of Lucy Gray Baird." Two references to Collins' songs therefore appear on the same album. More to the point, Granger suggests that if one had grafted the country-western version of "The Hanging Tree" with the powerful lyrics of "Strange Fruit," we would likely approach the style and intent of Collins' own creation.

Little did anyone know that Collins was setting up her readers to finally learn the backstory of "The Hanging Tree." In the prequel we learn that Lucy Gray had actually penned the song, thereby adding yet another layer to its meaning. It was likely jaw-dropping to discover that the lyrics were inspired by an actual event in District 12. Lucy Gray sings specifically about the fate of Arlo Chance, who had apparently "murdered three" down in the mines. Just before he is dropped from the gallows, he notices "a young woman with olive skin and long black hair" shrieking through the crowd, to whom he responds, "Run! Run, Lil!" (*BSS* 352). This is also when Coriolanus gains a painful lesson about mockingjays, which horrifically pick up Arlo's cry in the trees above.

Prior to our witnessing the event ourselves, Collins deftly foreshadows this upcoming scene when Lucy Gray quips to Coriolanus, "The show's not over until the mockingjay sings." Upon asking if a mockingjay sings in her show, she replies curtly, "Not my show, sweetheart. Yours. The Capitol's anyway" (BSS 352). While witnessing the hanging of Arlo Chance and the ensuing mockingjay performance, Coriolanus thinks back to his conversation with Lucy Gray prior to the tribute interviews. He now understands better what she had meant. Alas, this otherwise significant dialogue is not included in Ballad.

Additional dialogue in the book likely foretells the future of "The Hanging Tree" song in District 12. Given that the commander told her not to sing the "dark" song again following his birthday celebration, Lucy Gray promises that "he'd never hear it from my lips again." This is when Coriolanus responds, "It's a strange song." She then offers what is probably one of the book's more telling clues for the future, saying "Well, Maude Ivory likes it. She says it has real authority" (BSS 491).

Numerous interpretations of this exchange have rippled through the fandom and media alike. One version incorrectly presumes that "The Hanging Tree" has been banned outright from District 12, when it is only the Hob concerts that have ultimately been banned. Further, if we take Collins' dialogue at face value, only Lucy Gray has been told not to sing the song, to which she readily complies. This does not mean the song cannot be sung privately and passed down to future generations. It is possible—if not probable—that Maude Ivory will do just that when she eventually teaches it to Katniss' future father.

"Pure as the Driven Snow"

Lucy Gray writes and sings this country waltz for Coriolanus at the height of their amorous feelings for one another. While the song lyrics in *Ballad* remain true to the book, the setting and context are widely divergent. Notably, in *Ballad* Lucy Gray becomes visibly puzzled midway through the number. Her new love in the audience suddenly gets up, looks around, and leaves with barely an acknowledgement to Lucy Gray. In the film's storyline, Coriolanus is distracted with the disappearance of Sejanus, which ultimately leads him to the rebel meeting. It is difficult not to sympathize with Lucy Gray, as the remainder of her heartfelt song goes unnoticed by its intended recipient. She still manages to finish the song, after which she rushes off stage and unwittingly stumbles into the ensuing drama next door.

In stark contrast, the book's version of the tune appears much later, well after the murders at the shed. Sejanus has already been hung at this point, and Coriolanus has recently been interviewed and exonerated by Commander Hoff—for the time being. It is in this context that the Covey band has been hired to perform for the commander's birthday at the Peacekeepers' base. The gymnasium was decorated with banners and flags for the special event. As the narrator comments, "Whiskey flowed freely, and many impromptu toasts were made over the mic brought out for this purpose." Coriolanus remains unaware of the impending concert until soldiers start setting up chairs. An officer then confirms for him, "We hired that band from the Hob. The commander gets a kick out of them" (*BSS* 477).

With this news, Coriolanus springs into action, returning to the barracks to retrieve the replacement guitar strings Lucy Gray needs. He then stands in the back of the audience to watch the show. It is important to note that Coriolanus remains in a highly distraught and confused state of mind here, still unsure of his eventual fate. He might still be found guilty of shooting Mayfair, he contemplates, and even feels gratitude that Lucy Gray could go on surviving for the both of them. At this point he views himself as the one in trouble, not her.

BEHIND THE BALLADS

After the Covey band sings "Happy Birthday" to Commander Hoff, Lucy Gray appears once again in her signature rainbow dress. Believing she wore the dress for him, the narrator tells us, "An overwhelming flush of love ran through him at her reminder that he was not alone in this tragedy. They were back in the arena, fighting for survival…" (*BSS* 478). Just before she starts to sing, she pats the pocket of her dress, just as she had done during the Games as a signal. She then begins "an unfamiliar song," as every nerve tingles within his body. It is in this context of plot development that "Pure as the Driven Snow" is performed.

Rather than having an apathetic Coriolanus leave halfway through the number, the book's Coriolanus remains entranced for the full song while he carefully interprets its meanings. First his eyes fill with tears, knowing "they would hang him, but she would be there, knowing he was still a genuinely good person." Any remaining doubt the song was written for him evaporates when she sings, "I've got three and twenty," meaning the number of reasons she trusts him. He knows immediately this refers to the other 23 tributes in the Games. In the end she mentions trust, the "thing she valued most." The whole scene smacks of a profound emotional exchange between the two of them (*BSS* 40-481).

Not only does the film largely downplay this touching romantic connection, but the meaning of certain lyrics is lost as well. Here we watch Rachel Zegler replicate the song word-for-word, to the producers' credit. Hers is yet another stunning performance and a musical highlight of the film. The catch is that she is singing about her previous experiences with Coriolanus, many of which *Ballad* simply leaves out. Her lyrical mentions of "rough as a briar," or turning "goat's milk to butter," or "ice blocks to water" are likely all lost on viewers. Each one serves as a subtle reference to a time she cherished with Coriolanus. Much of this occurs during their visits to the lake and to the Covey's home in the Seam. Another reference from the third verse involves "cake with the cream," which does make a brief appearance when the pair is first stuck in the monkey house. For these reasons, the original lyrics of the song do not entirely align with the screenplay. Perhaps the silver lining is that Lucy Gray (i.e. Zegler) is allowed to perform it in the first place.

While the song's romantic lyrics and title are, well, sweetly naive, Lucy Gray eventually comes to this realization in due time. One of the more intriguing questions that arises is whether—or perhaps the extent to which—Coriolanus and Lucy Gray are truly in love. This is discussed more thoroughly in Chapter 11 with respect to Coriolanus' character. To the credit of *Ballad* producers and actors alike, they wisely keep the true nature of their relationship purposely vague. This is seemingly what Collins intended from the outset. While some form of a romantic relationship certainly develops, one is hard-pressed to determine conclusively whether their mutual affections are genuine and everlasting.

More likely, theirs is primarily a relationship of circumstance, whereby each of them is manipulating the other for self-serving motives. Whether their respective motives are justified in some way remains open for discussion. As we gather from the chilling and desperate sequence in the woods, however, neither seems intent on sticking with the other through "thick and thin." Lucy Gray devolves into another burden for Coriolanus to overcome on his way back to a coveted career. And, for her part, Lucy Gray decides quickly and wisely to not "stand by her man" to preserve whatever affections she felt for him. Whether the pair was somehow genuinely in love at one point or not, this is clearly no Katniss and Peeta reboot.

Readers will likely note another curiosity about those Hob concerts in *Ballad*. Unlike the comparatively passive attendees of the novel, now there is dancing! Collins' prequel makes no formal mention of dancing at the Hob, likely due to the group's primarily bluegrass-inspired style of performance. The crowds might cheer and get rowdy, but they do not dance. This is more in keeping with a traditional bluegrass concert. At such venues, audiences typically sit and appreciate the music in a less participatory fashion (more on this in Chapter 4).

In this case the addition of dancing at the Hob provides an instructive lesson on the genre of country music. "Pure as the Driven Snow" is performed as a *country waltz*, typically defined by its fast-paced tempo and three beats per bar, or measure. It replicates its European predecessor, the *Viennese waltz*, which is historically the first ballroom dance performed in the "closed hold," or "waltz" position. This is compared to today's standard, slow waltz—often referred to simply as a *waltz*—which is typically performed at only 90 beats, or 30 bars per minute. This form of music therefore originated not within the country music genre, but amongst the traditions of ballroom dance centuries earlier in Europe. The faster Viennese waltz was actually the original form of the two. What is most popularly known as the *waltz* today came later, known originally as the English or slow waltz.

Here in America the faster Viennese waltz style was adapted over time by various country music songwriters and artists. True to form, both "Pure as the Driven Snow" and "The Ballad of Lucy Gray Baird" exemplify this unique amalgam of country music and ballroom dance. Even "The Old Therebefore" loosely adopts the Viennese waltz form, though Rachel Zegler performs a more dramatic and halting version with varying tempos.

In this way we can say that traditional ballroom dance has been infused into the film, in addition to the Appalachian traditions of folk singing and balladry. Country dancing can be traced back to other forms of ballroom dance as well, including the Foxtrot and the Swing. The Two Step, for instance, is considered the "country cousin" to the Foxtrot within the ballroom world. It is the country waltz that makes its debut within the Hunger Games franchise, however.

Aside from *Ballad*, fans may recognize one other instance when ballroom dance makes an appearance. This was during the dance between Katniss and Plutarch Heavensbee at the presidential mansion during the victory tour. They and their counterparts danced to the deliberate "Waltz in A (Op. 39, No 15)." This traditional waltz tempo is in stark contrast to the energetic, faster-paced Viennese waltz we encounter twice in *Ballad*.

Whether the fast Viennese or slow waltz, both are considered rotary dances, whereby the couples move (hopefully) in a single flow to avoid collisions. This further explains the disciplined dancing at the Covey's Hob concerts. District 12 has indeed learned to ballroom dance! We are thereby treated with watching couples in the closed-hold position, rotating in a loose circle in front of the stage. Rachel Zegler provides a rare, behind-the-scenes view of this dancing from the stage perspective on YouTube. Her video shows the couples easing their way around a loose circle. Meanwhile, Zegler is singing "Pure as the Driven Snow" while Tom Blyth is being filmed further back on set ("Rachel").

"Lucy Gray"

Readers and viewers alike are understandably puzzled about the reason for leaving Lucy Gray's fate open-ended. For more clarity on this issue, one need only look to the historical poem for which she is named. Specifically, Collins created her musical character to mirror the subject of English poet William Wordsworth's own "Lucy Gray" (1799). This became one of Wordsworth's best-known poems and was published more widely in his *Lyrical Ballads* (1800). This publication included his own work along with that of his close friend, Samuel Taylor Coleridge. Together, their collection of ballads helped focus English literature more on the rural folk culture of the British Isles. This was in direct opposition at the time to standard classical modes derived from Greek and Latin poetry (Miller). A champion of the working class, Wordsworth condemned what he considered the artificial "gaudiness and inane phraseology" of his time. He favored more readable and realistic language to which the general population could better relate. Perhaps this is why Collins adopted such a popular Wordsworth poem for her own story, to champion the cause of Panem's struggling working class (Miller).

Wordsworth's "Lucy Gray" was based on a true story he had heard from his sister about a little girl in Yorkshire, England. After becoming lost in a snowstorm, her parents traced her footsteps to the middle of a canal lock where they mysteriously disappeared. Sadly, the girl's body was recovered from the canal. The story inspired Wordsworth to write "Lucy Gray," though his own character simply disappears without a trace (Paradis). It was this poem that inspired Collins' own Lucy Gray Baird.

Collins does alter the original poem in minor ways. The book's Maude Ivory says vaguely, "We mixed it up a little" to better match the story of the Covey's own Lucy Gray (*BSS* 424). Still, a comparison between Wordsworth's original poem and that of Collins indicates only minimal modifications. She mostly replaced older English words that modern-day readers may not easily recognize. Beyond that, the fundamental meaning and storyline of the poem remain virtually unchanged.

And Wordsworth's poem is by no means short. The film only includes four of the poem's sixteen total *stanzas*, or *verses* when sung as a song. Fortunately, Collins' own "Lucy Gray" is published in its entirety within the prequel. Likewise, all verses may be heard on the film's soundtrack of songs, split into "Parts 1 and 2." As in the film, Rachel Zegler sings both parts *a cappella*—without instrumental accompaniment. This style was characteristic of Appalachian folk traditions, in which women often sang ballads around the home unaccompanied. These women were, as described by Debby McClatchy, "fulfilling roles as keepers of the families' cultural heritages and rising above dreary monotonous work through fantasies of escape and revenge."

THE BALLADS OF LUCY GRAY

While certainly entranced by Zegler's voice, audiences may be hard-pressed to audibly comprehend the shortened version in *Ballad*. For this purpose, viewers will need to refer to the book or soundtrack for a more thorough accounting of Lucy Gray's backstory. Coriolanus may not have been alone in his confusion about the tune.

On that note, in *Ballad* Coriolanus asks Lucy Gray while relaxing in the meadow whether the poem's character ultimately survives. Her response is unhelpful, as she suffices to say, "It's a mystery, like me." This scene does appear to set up one of Dean Highbottom's most dramatic lines back in the Capitol, saying emphatically that "mysteries have a way of driving people mad." The particular mystery of Lucy Gray's whereabouts is likely to haunt Coriolanus for the rest of his life. This is emphasized dramatically with the return of actor Donald Sutherland's haunting voice just prior to the credits, reminding us, "It's the things we love most that destroy us." At which point, we are treated to Olivia Rodrigo's powerful song, "Can't Catch Me Now." Its lyrics only confirm that Lucy Gray will haunt Coriolanus' every move until the day he dies. It is satisfying to contemplate President Snow's own internal horror with the emergence of Katniss Everdeen six decades later—along with many of Lucy Gray's favorite tunes, and those relentless mockingjays to boot!

Some might be surprised to learn—or recall—that it is not Lucy Gray who sings Wordsworth's poem in the book, but Maude Ivory instead. She does so during the second Hob concert, the night before the Covey members drag Coriolanus and Sejanus out to the lake for the first time. Coriolanus attends this second performance, albeit admittedly plied with too much white liquor—a regional moniker for moonshine. He gallantly tries to focus on Maude Ivory and the song despite his inebriation. Before beginning, she provides an introduction for the audience (and readers), telling everyone, "I promised a friend I'd sing him something special tonight, so this is it." This is when she explains, "Every one of us Covey owes our name to a ballad, and this one belongs to this pretty lady right here!" Leaving nothing to chance, Collins additionally has Maude Ivory explain that the ballad is "a really old one by some man named Wordsworth" (*BSS* 423).

Coriolanus does his best to pay close attention so that he might "say something nice about it" the next day out at the lake (*BSS* 424). Throughout the ballad, readers gain insight into Coriolanus' attempts to make sense of the story. This provides for a rather humorous string of thoughts. He ultimately ends up despising the song, concluding, "Oh, a ghost story. Ugh. Boo. So ridiculous" (*BSS* 427). He then considers a litany of practical questions that do not seem to make sense in the story. This is because the literary value and meanings are lost on him; he admits to not having been a stellar student in rhetoric class. And the book's narrator adds, "the white liquor wasn't helping," which is worth a chuckle. In any case, one must turn to the book for a more complete understanding of how Coriolanus tries to grasp Wordsworth and the fate of Lucy Gray.

What Happened to Lucy Gray?

This remains the fundamental question of the prequel and film alike. While some presume that Lucy Gray perishes at the other end of Coriolanus' rifle, others believe she survives to outlast the story. Both the book and film versions are equally ambiguous by design. Aside from Coriolanus detecting "a faint cry" after he attempts to shoot her through the trees, there is no direct evidence of injury or death. Rather, he cannot see her clearly through the brush. When he finally arrives at the spot she may have been, she is nowhere to be seen. The intended meaning of her cry, therefore, is left intentionally vague. This mystery parallels Wordsworth's poem precisely. He does not indicate within his "Lucy Gray" whether the little girl perishes.

Technically she disappears, leaving her whereabouts open to interpretation.

A related puzzlement involves the filmmakers' decision to remove the concluding lines of "Lucy Gray." Granted, the second to last verse serves the purpose well enough, thereby perpetuating endless discussion over her fate. The film's last verse is as follows:

> *Yet some maintain that to this day*
> *She is a living child;*
> *That you may see sweet Lucy Gray*
> *Upon the lonesome wild.*

Nonetheless, it is arguably the poem's last stanza that provides an uncanny parallel to the final chase scene:

> *O'er rough and smooth she trips along,*
> *And never looks behind;*
> *And sings a solitary song*
> *That whistles in the wind.*

The first two lines can be interpreted as Lucy Gray running away from Coriolanus through the woods, perhaps never looking back. She then sings her "solitary song"—a reprise of "The Hanging Tree," which then "whistles in the wind." The whistling consists of the mockingjays picking up the tune and appropriately terrorizing Coriolanus until he is driven suitably mad. In this way Collins deftly crafted her climactic sequence to virtually replicate Wordsworth's own Lucy Gray. As Lucky Flickerman might say, "Take . . . a . . . bow!" (*BSS* 305).

For his part, director Francis Lawrence says, "We tried to make everything add up as much as possible, even if there's some mystery left." He even offers an opinion about Lucy Gray, saying, "I think she's alive for sure. I think she vanished into the woods and made a life for herself" (Wang, "Mysterious"). In an interview for the *Into the Arena* podcast, actress Mackenzie Lansing (Coral), believes similarly. After admitting the question is open to interpretation, she logically posits, "I think she's alive… She's so smart, I can't imagine she went out to get katniss and just got shot, like 'Oh dang it.' In my head she had a plan and figured something out" ("Episode 76").

This fits a more nuanced read of possible foreshadowing within the book. Earlier Lucy Gray had told Coriolanus that she and the Covey know the way to the lake because it's their "second home" (*BSS* 430). It follows that she likely knows the woods around the lake like the back of her hand and could easily outwit a bumbling Coriolanus when she had to do so. It's her home turf; she has the advantage.

As to whether Lucy Gray makes a new life in the woods, this is more uncertain, if not completely unlikely. She tells Coriolanus earlier that she is not so keen about living in the wild—Katniss Everdeen she is not. She says, "It's not just how hard it will be. It's too lonely. I might've made it for a few days, but then I'd have come home to the Covey" (*BSS* 491). While this is admittedly prior to the murders near the Hob and the mayor's ensuing vendetta, this reality likely remains true. Her fundamental interest is to protect her Covey family. This presumably motivates her to eventually return to, well, face the music in District 12. At some point she needs to deal with the mayor and tie up loose ends. She is clearly smart enough to do so if she chooses this route. Does she return permanently to continue performing with the Covey? Perhaps not, given that Katniss knows nothing about her within the original series—save for her music.

One additional theory supports the notion that Lucy Gray survives. That is, could Coriolanus have been experiencing hallucinations—knowingly or otherwise—from the snakebite? After having evaded him for so long, not to mention with endless forest around her, why would she have crossed his path at such a close range? And why would she magically begin singing a reprise of "The

Hanging Tree"—and *after* she had apparently been shot, nonetheless?

In support of the hallucination theory, observers have considered the color of her dress, which is clearly tinged with orange as she briefly crosses Coriolanus' path. Some contend that the dress is different than the one she wore earlier to the cabin. Upon closer inspection, however, her dress does appear to be the same in both instances, displaying a white background with a repetitive orange print pattern. Although its coloring looks muted inside the cabin, this is due to the low lighting conditions. Different dress or not, the theory is an intriguing one that likely deserves further exploration. Until Collins decides to reveal the ultimate fate of Lucy Gray Baird, this mystery is likely to persist indefinitely—a mystery that may indeed find a way to drive us all mad.

A Successor to *O Brother, Where Art Thou?*

For enthusiasts angling for more of Lucy Gray's folk tunes and ballads—not to mention Rachel Zegler's incomparable voice—one need only begin with the film's expansive soundtrack of songs. Importantly, the soundtrack includes all eight of Rachel Zegler's numbers, along with the foot-stomping "Keep on the Sunny Side" and the Covey's "District 12 Stomp." These are supplemented with seven additional tracks which, as described by Ivan Korrs, highlight the "prowess and excellence of the bluegrass, folk, and country artists" making waves within these genres right now. Noting that the country and roots music genres are enjoying something of a revival, *Saving Country Music* celebrates that "the makers of the new Hunger Games movie are taking notice. Under the guidance of producer Dave Cobb, they've taken some of the most preeminent up-and-comers in the movement and placed them on the soundtrack..." ("Soundtrack"). Their writer was further impressed that Suzanne Collins directed Francis Lawrence to binge watch the 16-hour

Country Music documentary (2019) by Ken Burns to better prepare for his directing role.

The culminating result is a soundtrack that features some of folk music's most acclaimed and upcoming young artists. After the pop-star Olivia Rodrigo leads off the album with her original "Can't Catch Me Now," new and original material is interspersed among Rachel Zegler's numbers. These include selections from Flatland Cavalry, Sierra Ferrell, Molly Tuttle, Bella White, Billy Strings, and Charles Wesley Godwin. In addition to bluegrass music sensations Billy Strings and Molly Tuttle, the latest mandolin virtuoso, Dominic Leslie, accompanies Tuttle on the recorded tracks for Rachel Zegler. It follows that "the power of this soundtrack to expose its participants to a wider audience makes it one to watch, especially if many watch the movie, and seek out the music from it" ("Soundtrack").

Those who call the Appalachians home have likewise noted the album's focus on so-called *roots music*. Also referred to loosely as *Americana*, roots music includes an ambiguous blend of old-time folk music, ballads, early country, rhythm and blues, and bluegrass styles. As Rachel Leishman wrote soon after the film's release, one surprising element consisted of the "influences that inspired Zegler, which included Loretta Lynn, Dolly Parton, and the Carter Family." She continues, "As someone who went to school in the Appalachian Mountains, we often sang songs native to the region. One of those songs I performed at school made an appearance in the film's soundtrack." She was referring to the Carter Family's rendition of "Bury Me Beneath the Willow," performed by Molly Tuttle.

Whether this album ultimately matches the influence of its predecessor, *O Brother, Where Art Thou?* (2000) remains to be seen. The satirical comedy-drama film starring George Clooney is set in rural Mississippi in 1937 and follows three escaped convicts searching for treasure. More to the point, the acclaimed soundtrack features 1930s period folk music harkening back to an array of styles reflecting the Old South, including a combination of gospel, delta blues, country, swing, and—some say—bluegrass. The soundtrack ultimately won a Grammy Award for Album of the Year in 2002 and launched one of America's more recent folk music revivals.

This is why numerous reviewers have been quick to compare its music with that of *Ballad*. Either way, as Craig Havighurst writes, "a lot of folks will likely have their first exposure to old-time roots music through the film." He was further pleased to see that the "special guests" on the album "stand on their own as great additions for 2023 roots music." That reviewers like Havighurst are positively recognizing *Ballad's* musical qualities is high praise indeed. It appears Suzanne Collins can "take a bow" herself for bringing central Appalachia's folk music traditions into the global spotlight.

PART 2: The Places

CHAPTER 6

Filming District 12

To Europe with Love

Of all the intriguing decisions associated with the production of *Ballad*, perhaps few surprised more than its European filming locations. Eyebrows were certainly raised upon learning that District 12 had somehow shifted to Germany and Poland. Those who looked forward to film crews returning to the actual Appalachians were understandably puzzled if not outright disappointed. Nonetheless, director Francis Lawrence remained enamored with the wealth of potential filming sites in and around Berlin. He even had specific locations in mind when his team began working with the prequel's production designer, Uli Hanisch, based in Berlin himself.

Together with Lawrence, Hanisch imagined how Panem and the Capitol might look only ten years following the so-called "Dark Days" of the first war. In so doing, Hanisch believed that the experience of Panem likely paralleled that of Berlin's own reconstruction in the aftermath of World War II. He explains, "Six decades ago, in our history, we were at the end of the 1950s, and the beginning of the

1960s… Berlin at that time is comparable to the film's Capitol: You have a capital city 15 years after a devastating war, and everything is different. I found that very inspiring in designing the Capitol of Panem" (Allen). With the main intent to produce *Ballad* as a postwar period piece, perhaps it is forgivable that District 12 took a back seat to all that Berlin and nearby cities had to offer.

Lawrence readily agreed to root the story within a significant period of European—and world—history. His personal aim was to ensure that the scenes of rebuilding the war-torn Capitol and the gritty District 12 still felt grounded in historical reality. To that end their team relied upon meaningful historical sites and urban locations in Germany and Poland. Lawrence explains in his director's lingo, "I didn't want to be in giant screen and blue screen environments and to be doing everything digitally… It's not as immersive for the actors or the crew and I wanted to root everything in reality." During his research phase with Hanisch, Lawrence adds, "we discovered that Berlin had the perfect things" (Zelmer).

Staying grounded in reality also meant minimizing the use of stage sets. Only two sets were specially constructed for *Ballad*—namely the Snow family apartment and the monkey house at the zoo. More about both of these sets is discussed in Chapter 8.

Filming in both countries required seventeen weeks, beginning with Centennial Hall in Wroclaw, Poland where the 10th Games were filmed. Production then turned to *Zalew* (Reservoir) *Grzedy* and a nearby meadow in the Polish countryside to film the Covey's day at the lake and the story's climactic forest sequence. Crews then turned to Germany, specifically Duisburg-Meiderich at a former steel mill complex now called *Landscahaftspark*. The District 12 industrial scenes, the public square, the hanging tree, and the Hob were all filmed here. This facility is described more thoroughly below.

The Rhenish Industrial Railway Museum in Cologne provided an appropriate setting for the Capitol train station, as it may have appeared not long after the Dark Days. Brandenburg's Nauen

Transmitter Station was where Coriolanus received his Peacekeeper training at the base in District 12, and it is where he meets Commander Hoff during a rather nerve-wracking encounter. The production wrapped up its European tour with numerous filming sites in Berlin, and particularly within the former East Berlin (Allen). All of these locations are discussed in more detail in the chapters below. For now, the remainder of this chapter focuses on District 12 filming locations—whether they could realistically be found within the Appalachian Mountains or not.

District 12 Peacekeeper Barracks

Located in the Havelland district of Brandenburg, Germany, the Nauen Transmitter Station was chosen as the filming location for the District 12 Peacekeeper Barracks. It is here where Coriolanus receives his Peacekeeper training after first arriving from the Capitol. One can catch a first glimpse of the main Transmitter Station building in the background behind the entrance gate as the truck drives in with the new recruits. Later we see the interior of the building's main hall and its impressive array of windows backlighting Commander Hoff's desk. This is where Hoff meets a visibly nervous Coriolanus. Some of the facility's historical radio equipment is presumably featured when Coriolanus contacts Tigris over Panem's own antiquated network.

The historical building and its surrounding campus are honored as the world's oldest continuously operating radio transmitting installation. Germany's first high power radio transmitter was constructed here in 1906 during the early days of radio technology. Early financing for the site came from Germany's Post Office, the leaders of which desired a strategic link with Germany's colonies overseas, such as Togoland in Africa. The facility further served as a hub for handling telegram traffic to the Americas. After the station was upgraded during the 1920s with shortwave transmitters, it became the country's most advanced facility for long-range communications. The main transmitter building featured in the film played a large role in these upgrades, designed as an Art Deco-styled, cathedral-like building in 1920 by Hermann Muthesius. It is thus appropriately referred to as the Muthesius Building. Art Deco was becoming a popular version of early modernism in both Europe and America at the time, with its vertical orientation, geometric shapes, and lack of historical references.

During World War I the station served as Germany's main connection to the outside world after its submarine communication cables were disabled. The facility continued to serve as an important radiotelegraphy station through World War II, after which it was all disassembled by the Soviet occupiers. No record exists of the whereabouts of the transmitters, though the Soviets blew up their supportive masts on the property. The Muthesius Building was also slated for destruction and was for some time used as a potato storehouse. Eventually the communist German Democratic Republic (GDR, East Germany) restored the site once again to its original purpose. After doing so, the site served as the Eastern Bloc's second most powerful radio station behind that of Moscow. It therefore became an important source of propaganda to the West and to other Eastern Bloc countries. For these reasons the facility's history was well suited to its cinematic role in *Ballad*, representing an outpost for an emerging authoritarian regime.

After reunification in 1991 the facility has continued its relevance through its use by Deutsche Telekom, Germany's state telecommunication service. Contemporary photos of the site online reveal almost space-age like communication towers and equipment installed around the campus.

BEHIND THE BALLADS

Filming District 12 at Landscape Park

Based on what we see in *Ballad*, the industrial might of District 12 appears to be impressively over the top. One might ask, just how much massive infrastructure is necessary to move coal from the ground to awaiting railway hopper cars? Perhaps never before has an Appalachian coal town seen such gargantuan manufacturing complexes. No matter, in this, the third version of District 12 to appear within the franchise, the producers discovered one of the most creative filming locations yet. The bulk of District 12 filming took place at an abandoned steel mill complex that was permanently shuttered in 1985, leaving a seriously polluted landscape in its wake.

Today the site is far from abandoned, as it has entered the next chapter of its own unique history. The former steel works have since been converted into a public park, providing an irresistible opportunity for filming. The expansive site is known as *Landschaftspark*, or the *Landscape Park, Duisburg North*. Not one's ordinary park for strolling, the site's 180 hectares (445 acres) makes use of the abandoned Duisburg-Meiderich steelworks. Instead of being demolished as some might have preferred, the entire collection of old factory buildings, blast furnaces, gasometer, and associated infrastructure have been creatively preserved as an industrial heritage site. Without a doubt, this industrial playground would become a District 12 like no other.

As promoted on the park's German web site, the mill's preserved infrastructure provides numerous opportunities for recreation, education, and even ecological nature walks, of all things. The site of the gasometer, used within the former smelting works, was flooded to create Europe's largest indoor diving pool. A lookout tower has been crafted out of the defunct blast furnace to provide impressive panoramic views of the park below and beyond. Climbing enthusiasts can challenge themselves on a high ropes course within the old casthouse, or inside the former ore deposit bunker. The park remains open at night as well, allowing visitors to enjoy the unique lighting installations by Jonathan Park. If one prefers walking and cycling amidst more natural environs, the perimeter of the park includes numerous nature trails for exploration. Guided tours provide more educational opportunities. Visitors can learn about the mill's former operations, the workers who labored there, and their living conditions throughout that era ("Landscape").

The steel mill comes with its own intriguing backstory even after its closure in 1985. Around 1991 a competition between five international planning teams was held to design a park out of the derelict site. The winning plan belonged to Peter Latz and his team, which proposed significant preservation of the existing industrial facilities (Diedrich). He recognized the educational value of the site and intended to help people understand the industrial past rather than outright reject it. The plan's main notion was that a grandfather who once worked there could explain the machinery and his own job to his grandchildren. Once given the green light, Latz remediated the polluted soils and contained the most toxic material inside existing bunkers. Likewise, a former sewage canal was converted into an approach to expedite the site's cleanup efforts.

Latz and his team further repurposed numerous existing plant facilities as recreational uses more befitting a public park experience. These included the aforementioned gardens created out of concrete bunkers, scuba diving pools from old gas tanks, and old concrete walls turned into a climbing gym. Perhaps most unexpectedly, the wider parkland itself has become recognized as a local hotspot for biodiversity within the western Ruhr Region. The park is especially recognized for its high ecological value, contributing to the preservation of many rare and endangered plant species. These diverse plant communities in turn provide unique habitats for all kinds of wildlife. In one sense, the industrial past has become an approach to celebrate and promote natural processes on the site once again.

One prominent design element particularly drew the attention of *Ballad* filming crews, namely the park's new public square. One of the steel mill's central places was redesigned as a comfortable space for public gatherings and community events and performances. Now known as Piazza Metallica, the landscape architects adapted 49 aging steel plates for the piazza's flooring. They had once lined the foundry pits and were now envisioned as a highlight of the square's new design. They are not meant to last permanently, however, as it is expected they will slowly decay through natural weathering processes. The idea is that the flooring plates represent natural processes occurring on the site overall, with a variety of plants growing up between them.

Not surprisingly, Piazza Metallica proved to be the perfect location for District 12's public square. Most prominently, the reaping ceremony was filmed here, requiring some 3,000 extras for this and related District 12 scenes. The piazza itself is featured prominently in the film, as the ragged community of District 12 assembles for the unprecedented events of the 10th reaping ceremony. Viewers can see the hulking industrial infrastructure towering around the square, making this otherwise rural district appear immense. The expansive steel plates on the ground are visible as well, including the wide gaps between them. This is most prominent as Mayfair falls onto the plates attempting to dislodge that pesky snake.

From a symbolic perspective the reinvention of the steel mill could parallel the future rebirth of District 12 in Katniss' time. As she and Peeta return to their hometown after the war, they are far from alone despite what some readers had interpreted at the conclusion of *Mockingjay*. Instead, she describes nothing less than the gradual rebirth of her hometown, literally and figuratively, up from the ashes (*MJ* 388). The mines have been permanently closed, and the ashes from the firebombing are being recycled back as nutrients for agricultural fields. Likewise, a new factory is being built to produce medicines, symbolizing the blending of regional healing remedies with more modern medical practices now available outside the Capitol. Just as District 12 witnessed its own post-industrial revival, so too did the creative visionaries of Landscape Park. An industrial relic had been creatively converted into a celebrated public park and recreational facility. For this reason, the filming of District 12 at Landschaftspark was more than fitting.

That said, for those looking for a more accurate, literal interpretation of District 12 within *Ballad*, some may find this hyper-scaled version just too fantastical. From a creative standpoint this is the franchise's third unique version of an imagined public square. Curiously, none of them come particularly close to Collins' original vision. Though easy to overlook within her narratives, she had modeled the center of District 12 as a quintessential small town and public square, the likes of which many Americans would recognize. In her original series and reinforced within the prequel, Katniss and Coriolanus separately describe a typical grid plan of streets, modest homes, and local businesses at the center of town, all focused on an open public square. Katniss especially notes that the "square is surrounded by shops" (*THG* 16). Even 64 years earlier, the prequel's Smiley notices the town square, "with its smattering of small shops and tradespeople" (*BSS* 335).

Likewise, the now-famous bakery of Peeta's family is not located on an isolated property as seen in the first film. Rather, it is simply one of the numerous small businesses that front the square. This is consistent with the bakery in the prequel, where Coriolanus and Sejanus likely encounter an ancestor of Peeta's grumpy mother.

One block beyond the business district and public square we find the more lavish homes of the merchant class, including an even more elaborate mayor's house. As the prequel's narrator informs us, the home "might count for a mansion in District 12 but would be unremarkable in the Capitol" (*BSS* 372). This urban pattern mirrors that of countless smaller towns and cities, where businesses still clustered along main street or around the public square up through the 1960s. America's downtowns then experienced an era of economic decline as suburbs and shopping centers shifted to the edge of town. Additionally, many of the community's elite residents, politicians, and businessmen once lived in the more distinguished, Victorian-era homes within walking distance of downtown. On a smaller scale, this is what we find in Collins' own downtown of District 12.

This is in stark contrast to the various layouts we see within the cinematic versions. For the first franchise film the crews made use of a private collection of warehouses in Shelby, North Carolina. The scene certainly provided a reasonable portrayal of a possible District 12 public square. Rather than modest, wood-framed storefronts enclosing the square, however, the open space is bounded on two sides by metal sheds or warehouses. A conventional railroad siding and coal hopper cars comprise the background, while the Justice Building occupies the front. Then, in *Catching Fire* we see a square surrounded by 19th century brick manufacturing buildings. This was filmed at the Goat Farm Arts Center on the west side of Atlanta, Georgia. Now in *Ballad*, the District 12 industrial complex is upscaled yet again, essentially supersized within the impressive grounds of Landscape Park.

Missing from this latest installment was the outpost of Capitol authority, the Justice Building. As the prequel clarifies, some version of this edifice already exists in Lucy Gray's time. When Mayor Lipp resists the Peacekeepers on stage during the reaping, the narrator says, "they hauled him back into the Justice Building" (*BSS* 26). In reality the layout of Landscape Park did not allow for a Justice Building, nor was one added through CGI (computer-generated imagery). From the perspective of cinematic production, this is all well and good. It remains intriguing, however, that each of the franchise's versions of District 12 has become progressively more elaborate—ever further from Collins' original small-town feel.

FILMING DISTRICT 12

Beyond Piazza Metallica, other District 12 scenes were filmed within the park as well. The Hob and its makeshift dance hall were filmed within walking distance of the piazza, as were the street scenes packed with Peacekeepers and residents. Francis Lawrence gushed about the entire park during one interview, saying,

> We had an opportunity because it's so many years before the other films, so we could do something different. It made me wish we'd had access to these places when we were doing the original movies. We found a place called Landscape Park in Duisburg, Germany, which is so immersive and massive and grimy and industrial. It is actually all about coal and steel, which is what District 12 is. Everything we shot there was geographically connected. The Hob was in one of the big industrial structures. When you see the guys walking down the road to go there, they're truly walking into [where] The Hob is. (Zelmer)

Aside from the Hob and public square, the park further hosted the artificial prop for the infamous hanging tree. In those dramatic scenes one can easily see the old mill's massive platform crane looming nearby. The physical prop for the tree includes only its bottom half and branches. As various fan photos reveal online, the top of the artificial trunk was wrapped with a blue screen. This enabled the completion of the tree's top half through the use of CGI. For this and the litany of reasons above, Landscape Park became a veritable candy store for District 12 filming opportunities. It is easy to understand why Francis Lawrence and his team quickly became enamored with the place.

• CHAPTER 7 •

Ghosts of the Third Reich

Enjoy the Show! **The Arena Goes Indoors**

R eaders of the prequel were understandably surprised upon seeing the 10th Games on screen. The circular, covered arena contrasts markedly with the book's expansive, open-air stadium. And common to such large-scale sporting venues are the so-called *luxury boxes*, or luxury suites, isolating the wealthier spectators from the outdoor elements. Likewise, we learn in the prequel that members of the privileged Snow family had once enjoyed their own luxury suite, thereby insulating them from the Capitol's lower social classes.

This leads to an amusing sequence during the book's mentor-tribute tour of the arena. For the first time Coriolanus navigates the stadium entrance designated for commoners. As the narrator relates, the soldiers lead them "deep within to the far side of the lobby. A bank of full-height turnstiles, each with three curved metal arms, [stand] covered in a thick layer of dust" (*BSS* 135). The turnstiles require a token for admittance, the same used for the Capitol trolley fares. Of course, this is where readers are introduced to the rather ironic, if cheery voice imploring patrons to "Enjoy the show!" This happy directive is heard at each rotation of the turnstile and is vaguely reminiscent of Monty Python humor. As *Ballad* viewers can attest, the turnstile voice was one element that producers wholeheartedly embraced for the feature film.

As the mentor-tribute tour proceeds in the book, Peacekeepers are posted at the turnstiles to pump tokens into the slots, still somehow necessary after all these years. The group's chaperone, Professor Sickle, even questions the absurdity of this, asking, "Can't you override the ticket barrier?" To which a Peacekeeper replies, "We could if we had the key, but no one seems to know where it is." As Coriolanus navigates a turnstile, he quickly thinks to push backwards and realizes that no exit is possible. This scene foreshadows later events when Coriolanus does indeed need to escape quickly with Sejanus. This is also how Sejanus badly injures his knee in the film, still recovering later as the new Peacekeepers rumble off to District 12.

In the book, Coriolanus does not recognize this particular entrance, as more privileged families had entered in a separate location "demarcated by a velvet rope" (*BSS* 135). When testing the turnstiles, he guesses that the "patrons of the cheap seats" had to leave the building elsewhere. As a way to highlight the Capitol's own social inequities, Coriolanus surmises that this entrance must be for the "poor people." He then quickly corrects himself to describe them as "plebeian." Within our own history, this term refers to the commoners of ancient Rome, yet another Collins reference to the Classical Era. The narrator then tells us, "Certainly, their [luxury] box could not be accessed with a trolley token. Unlike much of the arena, it had a roof, a retractable glass window, and air conditioning that had made the hottest day comfortable." As children, he and Tigris could nap on the plush seats while an Avox catered to their every need. In this way, we learn that the Capitol's brutal punishment for dissenters was already in existence prior to the first rebellion, only raising more questions. It does provide one indication of the Capitol's oppression that rebel districts were fighting against in the first war.

In producing *Ballad*, German production designer Uli Hanisch and his team deviated widely from the book's open-air stadium. Instead, they chose a closed-in facility which purposely added a "prison-like" quality to the set (Rasker). In one respect this is even more consistent with Collins' original intent than her open-air stadium suggested. One of her fundamental goals of the story was to take us back to how the Games began. She thereby constructs her own intriguing history of this evolution, from a time without pre-game festivities, tribute parades, splashy interviews, interactive arena landscapes, tribute sponsorships, on-screen betting, and related high-tech wizardry. During the 10th Games, there was no spectacle, as the Realty TV-type infrastructure and entertainment approach had yet to be developed.

The 10th Games therefore reveal a compact, unadorned, rudimentary facility which forces all of us to (finally) confront the raw violence without the showy spectacle glossing it over. After all, one of the story's fundamental points involved how young Coriolanus—together with an unwitting Lucy Gray Baird—contributed many of these new ideas to only prolong the future of the Games.

In addition to the book's narrative, Collins revealed her own vision for the 10th Games in an interview with Scholastic's David Levithan. She explains,

> Even as the victor in the war, the Capitol wouldn't have had the time or resources for anything elaborate. They had to rebuild their city and the industries in the districts, so the arena really is an old sports arena. They just threw in

the kids and the weapons and turned on the cameras. The 10th Hunger Games is where it all blows wide open, both figuratively and literally. ("Scholastic")

In light of Collins' original intent, Francis Lawrence describes the type of facility his team sought out for their own bare-bones arena:

> For the 10th annual Hunger Games, because we're seeing the early, early days of the arena and the Games themselves, we needed something that felt almost Colosseum-like, almost like a place you would find in Rome. And my production designer and I searched—Uli Hanisch, the production designer—searched around the world and found a fantastic arena called Centennial Hall in Warclow (Wroclaw) Poland. And luckily, we were able to secure it for about six weeks. It was the very beginning of our schedule, we got to shoot there right away and bring our Games in. ("Scene")

It is important to note that we only see the interior of Centennial Hall—and its computer-enhanced bomb-scape—within the film's version of the 10th Games. All exterior shots make use of Berlin's *Olympiastadion* (Olympic Stadium), discussed in more detail below.

The Troubled History of Centennial Hall

For its part, Centennial Hall was designated as a UNESCO World Heritage Site in 2006, recognized in part for its groundbreaking architecture and engineering ("Centennial"). Beyond that, the storied facility has played significant roles in European history and cultural symbolism. It was first built as a monument to commemorate the 100th anniversary of the four-day Battle of

Leipzig in 1813, also referred to as the Battle of the Nations. This is when French Emperor Napoleon Bonaparte and his occupying armies were soundly defeated by the unsuspecting coalition of Austria, Germany, Russia, and Sweden.

Aside from its commemorative purpose, the German architect and urban planner Max Berg designed the facility as a multi-purpose recreational building. This was when Wroclaw was a part of the German Empire. That era came to a tragic climax as the city witnessed rampant persecution of its Polish and Jewish residents prior to and during World War II. These populations were deported to forced labor camps and to the infamous Nazi concentration camps. Adolf Hitler himself "regularly ranted at the Centennial Hall" through his own rallies in support of the Nazi party (Tonkin). Remarkably, the bulk of Centennial Hall survived the war nearly unscathed, with the exception of the colonnade roof above the main entrance.

When the city later became part of the Republic of Poland in 1945, the facility was renamed *Hala Ludowa* (People's Hall) by the communist government installed by the Soviets. During this communist period the hall played host to various "Soviet-inspired propaganda stunts" (Tonkin). Given the cautionary tale of Suzanne Collins' Hunger Games saga, Centennial Hall's period of authoritarian history provides an appropriately symbolic backdrop for the heart of the Capitol's oppression against the districts.

Upon its completion in 1913, the facility was considered the largest reinforced concrete dome in the world. Its structural engineering was groundbreaking for the time, as its innovative construction approach was highly experimental. Its central, circular area is designed in the form of a symmetrical quatrefoil, similar to a four-leaf clover. The original seating capacity of 6,000 people was increased to 10,000 following extensive renovations in 2011.

The structure was built with such high standards that it can withstand a load-bearing weight six times greater than the original design required. During its construction, however, workers on the project were not so sure about its structural integrity; many were still unfamiliar with concrete projects of this scale. They consequently feared the entire structure might collapse when the wooden supports were removed. Max Berg needed to prove his design by pulling out some of the supportive planks himself, with the assistance of a volunteer (Wilmering).

To this day the hall provides an outstanding example of early modernism, which became the architectural mainstay of the twentieth century. Proponents of modernism emphasize a building's function over its exterior ornamentation, typically avoiding the use of historical designs. The hall was also pioneering for its time as a multifunctional facility, built to accommodate theater performances, exhibitions, and sporting events as it still does ("Centennial").

And now Centennial Hall's impressive resume includes the latest installment of the Hunger Games saga. Francis Lawrence discusses how the filming crew transformed the storied hall for the purpose of the 10th Games:

> And they let us do a lot. We had to add a bunch of rubble, a bunch of dust, a bunch of dirt. We also did some digital augmentation to the walls. There's a big sequence early on with explosions that damages the structure. This is the first time in any of the stories, in any of the Games where, because of explosions, the landscape of the Games has changed. And so, when you see the rubble, that's all because of these explosions that have now blown holes into the floor or given access down to tunnels or access into air vents. That's [created] a big pile of rubble in the center, which you can tell is probably the beginning for the idea of the cornucopia that's set in the center of the Games after this. ("Scene")

BEHIND THE BALLADS

With its substantial digital augmentations for the 10th Games, the facility now needed actors. Notably, the tributes and their violent movements needed to be carefully choreographed well in advance. In an elaborate, behind-the-scenes description, Francis Lawrence discusses the preparation, well before filming begins:

> For a sequence like this, we spent a long time choreographing it. I worked with my stunt coordinator, Scott Attia, very, very closely, and what we'll typically do is take the sort-of beats that are important for the story, and we'll kind of map that all out, and then we draw diagrams of what we think the arena's going to look like and where we want tributes to be. We also have sort-of another list; we're supposed to know which tributes are actually supposed to die in the sequence. And then we send Scott off with a bunch of stunt people to start to choreograph. And one of the last things I wanted to do was to have shots link up and last for long periods of time. And usually very focused on Lucy Gray. So, he would choreograph some of the fighting and the battles and what everybody is doing because you have close to 24 tributes in this arena all vying for weapons and fighting with one another. He'll choreograph all of that, and we'll start to design the camera moves around that. Once we lock in on all the story beats and what the fighting is all like, and who's dying, and where they end up, and get the story right, we then bring the actors in. We train them in the sequence, almost like learning a dance. And then we bring our camera operator in and our cinematographer in, and we start to choreograph the camera moves. And this is all done on a stage, not even on set yet. Not even with big cameras, but even just with iPhones and things like that. So, we have everything perfectly planned out so that on the day when

we're there, and everybody's in costume and hair and makeup, and we've got all the rubble around and the set pieces, we can move really efficiently through the sequence. ("Scene")

Beyond their own staged fighting, the fact that Centennial Hall played host to Hitler's rallies during World War II was not lost on the actors. Tom Blyth took this troubling historical connection to heart. He says of the facility, "There was this tangible feeling of terror in there. I think that energy lives in spaces sometimes, so to be there to [tell] this story about the rise of a tyrant was something I felt came into the performance" (Bythrow).

Olympic Park

For the exterior of *Ballad's* arena, filming crews turned to Berlin and its Olympic Park from the 1930s. The Park's centerpiece is the *Olympiastadion*, or Olympic Stadium, constructed by the Nazis for the 1936 Summer Olympics. The imposing structure serves as a backdrop in the film for the Capitol's arena, including scenes underneath its exterior colonnade. From here we see the mentor-tribute pairs being ushered in for the initial tour of the arena. In more dramatic fashion, the tributes are marched in at gunpoint to begin the Games.

It is easy to see why Uli Hanisch and his team chose this grand exemplar of fascist architecture to frame the 10th Games. Hanisch recalls, "The first thing we did was research the aesthetics and architecture of restrictive systems [like] the Soviet Union, fascist Germany, Italy and Spain" (Rasker). The stadium and its surrounding grounds are replete with difficult memories of the Nazi era and the ensuing atrocities of World War II. Earlier in 1931, Berlin was selected to host the 11th Summer Olympics, at which point the government decided to restore the existing 1916 stadium. With the

Nazis coming to power in 1933, however, the new government decided to build an entirely new stadium and complex for the upcoming 1936 Games. It was none other than Prince Imperial and Chancellor Adolf Hitler who initiated the project, with architect Werner March in charge of design and construction. When completed in 1936 the open-air Olympiastadion could hold 110,000 spectators.

Reminiscent of President Snow's own lofty perch for the tribute parades, the stadium came complete with a special stand for Adolf Hitler and his associates from which to preside over the events. Of course, the 1936 Olympics were officially inaugurated at the opening ceremony by Hitler himself. In perhaps another parallel with Collins' prequel, this was the first Olympics to be televised, with 25 viewing places scattered around Berlin and Potsdam for the occasion.

On a lighter note, Olympics fans still point to these 1936 Games where African American track and field athlete Jesse Owens won four gold medals. This was all during Hitler's Games where the Nazis looked to demonstrate the superiority of the Aryan race. *Oops.* To this day, one of the streets outside the stadium is named Jesse Owens Allee in honor of his achievements there (Rasker).

The Olympic Stadium's imposing architecture provides an equally profound connection between the Hitlerian Third Reich (1933-1945) and the Hunger Games. Featured prominently in the film, the massiveness of the stadium's exterior columns reflects Hitler's own obsession with the Roman Empire. He ended up being more of a modernist, however, which meant he had no use for historical revival styles, nor for elaborate ornamentation. His own simplified version of ancient Roman architecture has been dubbed by historians as "starved neo-Classicism." The stripped-down style was widely adopted by the Nazis for public and government buildings. As Kevin Martin adds, "Its designs became, in essence, tributes to the power of the state that created such out-of-scale monuments to the ego of the Führer himself." The monumental exterior colonnades of the stadium exemplify the Third Reich's minimalist classical architecture.

Command Center for the 10th Games

Practically next door to the Olympic Stadium is a smaller, circular building known as the *Kuppelsaal*, or Dome Hall. The facility was first used as the fencing arena during the 1936 Games. Today it is primarily deployed for gymnastics events and training. More recently for *Ballad*, the space proved more than suitable for the command center of the 10th Games. This is the viewing auditorium from where Academy students, mentors, and Lucky Flickerman all watch the proceedings on television. Francis Lawrence describes their approach to the command center's set design and how it played into the film's overall thematic period:

> A bunch of the tech, which is a big conversation that we had with Suzanne Collins and amongst ourselves was that everything, again, needed to be much more rudimentary. And because we were looking at sort-of reconstruction-era Berlin as a reference point for the city, of the capital of Panem in general, we decided to look at the 40s, the 50s, for technology, also for some of the aesthetics. This informs the hair and makeup and styling, some of the screens and all of that, and you can really see that 40s, 50s influence throughout the movie, almost like a retro-future kind of a feel. What we have here [in the viewing auditorium], we actually had the stage built, the screens, the control room, we had some interactive iPads that you can see are on the screens [mentors sitting down front with them], on the mentors' desks... Those were actually iPads that were programmed live. ("Director")

Snapshots of all the tributes had been taken at various points throughout the shooting. Their images were then projected onto the 24 smaller screens that flanked the massive, central television. As each tribute is killed, a rudimentary buzzer sounds to announce the death, at which point the tribute's image is removed and replaced by the standard logo of Panem. This basic approach to announcing the deaths of tributes would of course evolve by Katniss' time, involving cannon blasts and digital face shots projected above the arena.

Lawrence further notes—quite proudly—that the footage of the Games watched by the mentors consisted of the actual fight scenes filmed earlier at Centennial Hall. "Because we shot the Games ahead of time," he explains, "we could pump footage of the Games through the TV for our actors to watch. So, [for instance], when we were watching the tributes walk in, they could literally see these shots as if shot by TV cameras in the arena itself." The result is that viewers of *Ballad* are watching the mentors, who in turn are watching their tributes fight in the Games as if it was being filmed live on television ("Director").

• CHAPTER 8 •

Rebuilding the Capitol

In the Capitol of the original films, producers embedded design elements from the austere, minimalist architecture and public spaces of the communist Soviet Union. They had also studied Adolf Hitler's original vision for the future city of *Germania*. This Renaissance-inspired city plan was drawn up by Hitler's architect, Albert Speer, to be imposed on Berlin had his Nazis won World War II (Rasker). A creative amalgam of these various design modes contributed to the urban plan of the original trilogy's Capitol.

Our cinematic placemakers have now returned to conjure another version of the Capitol more than six decades earlier. At its core, *Ballad* is a period piece, specifically telling the story of a fascist state's postwar reconstruction. To this end, Berlin-based production designer Uli Hanisch recalls, "We had the idea to compare the fictional history of Panem with our real history. If you count back 60-something years... then you have Berlin in the 60s, in a very comparable situation" (Rasker).

This aligns well with Suzanne Collins' own inspirations for her dystopian nation, both within her original series and the prequel. It is no mistake that she gave Katniss a birthday of May 8. On that day in 1945, the Allies formally accepted the unconditional surrender of Nazi Germany to officially end World War II in Europe. This is often abbreviated as V-E Day, or Victory in Europe Day. Collins' own references to the war carry over in a big way to her prequel, and now to its follow-up film as well.

Fortunately, *Ballad* production and design teams did not skimp on the placemaking. Rather, they relied heavily on a strategic variety of local sites to ground the film in real geography and history. It is considered rare for a major franchise to still film on location, rather than rely heavily on digital makeovers and CGI (computer-generated imagery). As Elizabeth Fazzare describes of this earlier rendition of the Capitol, its "filming locations, visual references, and buildings conjure subliminal connotations about its brutality, and its fate."

Although Panem is a fictional setting itself, Hanisch offers that, "we can use a combination of real historical architectural elements—fascist architecture from Germany's Third Reich, from Italy and Mussolini, from the Soviet Union, and the newer East German GDR state—as the base for our thinking" (Fazzare). In one sense, the film takes viewers on a historical tour of the former Berlin and East Germany. This represents a virtual "Who's Who" list of 20th century restrictive governing systems. Having already explored some of the film's references to the Third Reich above, this chapter continues along that vein to consider *all places Capitol*.

The Snow Family Home

As one of the production's only two set builds, the Snow family apartment was dreamt up to represent different stages of disrepair. The set was assembled at Germany's Babelsberg Studio, and production designer Uli Hanisch based Coryo's home largely on Collins' descriptions from the book. The derelict condition of the apartment provides visual evidence of how the Snow family continues to struggle after the war (Allen).

Lawrence recalls, "We shot in it a few times, so we had a pristine version for the end of the movie and more dilapidated versions" (Zelmer). This subtle distinction may reflect the good fortune of Coriolanus finally winning the Plinth Prize at the film's conclusion. When Tigris says her now-famous last line, "I think that you look just like your father, Coriolanus," their home is in pristine condition once again with fresh, modernist wallpaper or paint, working lights and chandeliers, and no sign of disrepair. One might wonder just how they received the prize money to renovate so quickly. Regardless, we do indeed see the restored version of their home near the film's conclusion.

Whether derelict or not, the apartment in the film curiously resembles a confusing mishmash of décors and irregularly shaped rooms. The floor plan seems disjointed and even unpredictable, with oddly shaped rooms and passageways. This is no mistake, however, given the eclectic array of design ideas that fed into the set. Most metaphorically, the apartment was designed to resemble the shape of a snowflake, with a deliberately confused interior plan. Discerning viewers can further detect a variety of stylistic themes, from early 20th century Art Deco to Czech Cubism and unrelated furnishings and finishes (Fazzare). Thrown into the mix is some worn, inexpensive furniture to signify the family's reliance on second-hand products after the war.

What is not apparent is the apartment's location on the twelfth floor, with its penthouse or roof garden. Nor do we see the dysfunctional elevator or any family members laboring to climb the stairs. While such omissions admittedly make sense for the film, the book offers such nuances to accommodate additional family stories. Especially during the early chapters, Coriolanus is forced to navigate twelve flights to the *Corso* below, the grand avenue which is also omitted from the film. Still, producers do acknowledge this context.

Complete with his freshly renovated shirt, Coryo is shown racing down the building's lower flight of stairs into what is likely the inner courtyard of a Renaissance-era palace building. True to the book, he does not take the elevator.

Whether in the book or film, one is pressed to consider why their home's twelve floors, penthouse, and open-air rooftop provide such a remarkable resemblance to the Tribute Center of the original series. Why would the District 12 tributes be privileged—as Effie crows to Katniss and Peeta—to enjoy the penthouse suite? Could a future President Snow have assisted in the design of the Tribute Center facing the City Circle? While the Snow's family home and Tribute Center do not represent the same building or location, they certainly do share the same layout and scale. It is not unreasonable to believe that we are seeing the influence of Snow's lingering nostalgia for his past dalliances with one Lucy Gray Baird and her current home of District 12. He did, after all, first introduce himself to Lucy Gray at the train station with a rose in his hand. Perhaps Grandma'am's former rooftop garden is still offering up its symbolic roses to his first love.

The Capitol Zoo's Monkey House

The other set constructed for the film consisted of a specially designed animal enclosure. In the book this is more specifically the old monkey house at the abandoned Capitol Zoo. The set for this scene was assembled and filmed at *Britzer Garten*, a public park in Berlin. Francis Lawrence adds, "We found this great roundabout that was part of a little road, and we took it over and fenced it all in and made a backing. It fully looked like an old animal enclosure. It felt so real. Most of, if not all, the cast thought it was actually part of a former zoo. They thought we had lucked out and found this old, abandoned zoo" (Zelmer).

Peacekeeper Recruitment Center

After Dean Highbottom "finally" hears the "sound of snow falling," Coriolanus is whisked off to the Capitol's Peacekeeper Recruitment Center for processing. He is subsequently transformed into what Suzanne Collins describes as "Panem's newest, if not shiniest, Peacekeeper" to close out Part 2 (*BSS* 320). The gargantuan structure filmed for this purpose is *Ullsteinhaus*, constructed for *Ullstein Verlag*, a printing and publishing company. It was built during the 1920s for the Ullstein family according to plans by Eugen Schmohl. At the time the structure was recognized as Germany's largest reinforced concrete frame building. Its construction approach mirrored that of Centennial Hall in Poland, used for filming the interior of the arena. In this case, the structure's façade was faced entirely with red clinker bricks, the design of which was heavily influenced by the popular expressionism of the 1920s. This is one of the few, if not only, brick structures featured within the film. The massive structure stood as Germany's tallest building for 30 years, until 1957. It is now preserved as the primary architectural landmark of Berlin's southern district, Tempelhof.

The Ullstein family was dispossessed through the process of *Aryanization* in 1934 under the Third Reich. At that time the company was renamed "Deutscher Verlag" and the building "Deutsches Haus." After the war the complex was restored and returned to the Ullstein family. The structure remains an excellent example of *adaptive reuse*, a popular approach of historic preservationists to adapt older, specialized buildings like this one to new, contemporary functions. This provides an economic incentive for not tearing them down to build something new. Today the facility serves as office space for numerous companies, along with various retail stores ("Ullsteinhaus").

As Coriolanus arrives outside for processing, viewers can see an oversized owl perched atop the corner entryway. This was a fortunate bonus for filming this particular entrance. The bronze sculpture has served as the trademark symbol of the Ullstein family and their business since the beginning. It further somehow survived the purges of the Third Reich.

The Mentor-Tribute Interviews

Considered the largest war memorial in Europe, the Monument to the Battle of the Nations (or Battle of Leipzig) in the city of Leipzig was used for several interior and exterior shots. Much like Centennial Hall in Poland, the structure was completed to commemorate the 100th anniversary of the decisive battle, which took place over several days in October 1813. This pivotal event marked the beginning of Napoleon's downfall, when a coalition of armies defeated the French Emperor's troops. The size of the memorial reflected the immensity of the battle itself, with more than 600,000 soldiers from across Europe clashing in one of the continent's bloodiest battles to date. An estimated 100,000 were killed. Nonetheless, the coalition was ultimately responsible for Napoleon's defeat, when he lost control of Germany once and for all. The event played a major role in establishing the future German state.

The monument was erected on the battlefield itself. Standing at nearly 300 feet (91 meters) tall, the massive concrete and granite structure was funded mostly through donations and the City of Leipzig. More than 500 steps help visitors reach a viewing platform at the top, from which one can scan the battleground and nearby city. The monument was sited where some of the bloodiest fighting occurred, including where Napoleon ordered his army to retreat. This area would become the scene of another historic battle during World War II, when the Nazis in Leipzig made their last stand against U.S. forces. Prior to that Hitler used the monument to stage rallies in support of the Nazi cause (Moon).

The monument's awe-inspiring interior includes two main floors, the second of which is largely open so as not to interrupt the vertical view from below. The more compact first floor is comprised of a circle-shaped crypt with sixteen larger-than-life statues of warriors standing guard. This space was designed as a symbolic tomb for all the battle's fallen soldiers. In the Hall of Fame on the second floor, four large corner sculptures symbolize the alleged virtues of the German people—namely bravery, faith, people's strength, and sacrifice. Leading upwards toward the massive central dome are arched, pillared windows with 96 sculptures reminding us of the suffering of war. Overall, the interior space provides a unique venue for various concerts due to the unusual acoustics.

Two scenes in *Ballad* are filmed here. The second floor is where the mentors are instructed by Dean Highbottom (Peter Dinklage) to interview their tributes, albeit with little success. This is amidst the Hall of Fame and its four gargantuan sculptures. All mentor-tribute pairs are spaced around the periphery because the center is open to view the first floor below. The solid stone barrier is visible behind tributes such as Dill, Reaper, and Lamina.

Later, Coriolanus arrives back here after the Games, hoping to reunite with Lucy Gray. To his chagrin, he only finds Dean Highbottom accusing him of cheating. This takes place at the center of the symbolic crypt on the first floor. Encircling Coriolanus are the sixteen warrior statues standing guard, almost as if to condemn his actions, just as Dean Highbottom is about to do. In both scenes, viewers gain at least a sense of the acoustics here, mostly through Dinklage's low, booming voice echoing throughout the structure.

The monument's colossal exterior is featured within the film as well, essentially cut and pasted into the background as seen from the Academy steps. Its digitally altered form is clearly visible behind Coriolanus and Tigris as they climb the Academy staircase to watch the Games. The monument's artificial body of water—essentially a reflecting pool—is visible as well. This is known as the Lake of Tears, intended to remind visitors of the horrendous death toll on both sides of the fighting. As it is part of the memorial, no one is allowed to bathe or swim here ("Monument"). To either side of the monument, CGI was deployed to show the Capitol's high-rise buildings in various states of reconstruction. Given that one of Collins' fundamental goals is to educate young people about the atrocities of war, one could do little better than including this solemn memorial prominently within the film.

The City Circle and Statue

What is likely the most stunning urban scene in *Ballad*, the Capitol's expansive City Circle is portrayed quite differently than earlier films. This version, meant to represent the Capitol's earlier decades, consists of a massive European traffic circle complete with a colossal statue at its center. Around the statue—which producers have amusingly dubbed the *Panema*—is a circular fountain with water shooting upwards. Beyond the circle are the city's high-rise buildings under reconstruction following the war. Taken together this scene reeks of the recovering totalitarian power of the state.

Although greatly enhanced with CGI, the underlying geography of the scene was filmed at one of Berlin's major traffic circles, called *Strausberger Platz*. The expansive boulevard leading into the circle is that of *Karl Marx Allee*, one of Berlin's primary thoroughfares from the city's post-war period. Prior to 1961, the boulevard had been named *Stalinallee*, in honor of the early Soviet leader, Joseph Stalin, and his occupying government. It follows that Strausberger Platz had been located behind the so-called *Iron Curtain* and was a part of communist East Germany until the Berlin Wall fell on November 9, 1989.

The extent to which this real location parallels that of the Capitol following its own war is uncanny. Together with its central axis and boulevard, Strausberger Platz was constructed during the post-war

1950s to showcase the emerging prestige of communist East Germany. The entire collection of apartments constructed along the boulevard and around the circle celebrated the uniform austerity of Soviet, Stalinist architecture. Today Strausberger Platz marks one terminus of Europe's longest contiguous historical monument along Karl Marx Allee. This corridor is further recognized as the westernmost extension of Soviet-style Classical architecture ("Strausberger").

Much like Panem's struggling Capitol, this part of East Berlin revealed a sea of rubble and destruction following the bombings of World War II. A huge demand for decent housing necessitated the construction of massive apartment blocks, and quickly. The Cold War had now descended upon Berlin, dividing the city into east and west. Wanting to prove its political strength, the Socialist United Party of Germany (SED) sought to demonstrate they could provide a better life for its residents than could western democracy and capitalism. With that goal in mind, the construction boom was on. The new apartment high rises appearing along Stalinallee and Strausberger Platz were admittedly luxurious by the standards of the day—true palaces for the working-class population ("The Former").

In this way, construction of East Berlin's first major "socialist prestige building project" began in 1952, with the thoroughfare of Stalinallee made exceptionally wide from one side to the other. The purpose was to provide enough space for future civilian and military parades ("The Former"). This might all sound familiar to prequel readers who recall the Capitol's own central boulevard, the *Corso*. It was within the Corso's elite housing blocks where the Snow family lived stylishly in their twelfth-floor penthouse. The Corso was so wide, says the narrator, that eight chariots could ride side by side. This was more common back when the Capitol had staged its own military parades (*BSS* 12). Just as the former Stalinallee served as East Berlin's principal thoroughfare, so too did the Capitol's Corso, leading to its own City Circle.

REBUILDING THE CAPITOL

The uniform appearance of the architecture was inspired by the socialist classicism of the Soviet Union. It is instructive to recall that East Germany after the war was occupied by the Soviets, and it was the Soviet Union that installed the German Democratic Republic (GDR) to govern this occupied zone. Thus, the GDR naturally looked no further than the 19th-century neoclassicism of Moscow, including that city's own residential apartments of the 1930s. For that reason, Stalinallee became a sort-of mini-Moscow that reflected socialist-inspired architectural trends. Eventually critics ridiculed this socialist architecture and derided it as "wedding-cake style." By the end of the 1950s the process of "De-Stalinization" had already begun. This involved the removal of Stalin's memorial and the renaming of his namesake boulevard to Karl-Marx-Allee in 1961.

It should be noted that despite how well Strausberger Platz and Karl-Marx-Allee double for the Capitol, this was apparently not Collins' original source of inspiration. Given her propensity to pull insights from ancient Rome, this case is no different. The actual *Via del Corso* served as Rome's main street since the Baroque era of the eighteenth century. The fashionable thoroughfare was the place to be for the city's primary social and cultural events, and the corridor remains one of the city's primary thoroughfares today (Paradis).

Likewise, the eight-chariot width of Collins' Corso is another direct reference to the Roman Empire. The Corso itself can be traced all the way back to the city's Classical era when the corridor was referred to as Via Lata. This essentially translated to "Broad Way." Historical records point to its construction during the second century BCE to connect the center of Rome with the Adriatic Sea (Paradis). Today Via del Corso follows the same path through the city, from Piazza Venezia at one end to Piazza del Popolo at the city's northern gate. Unlike Panem's Corso and Berlin's Karl-Marx-Allee, however, Rome's Corso was much narrower and remains so to this day—only two lanes wide, plus sidewalks.

Within the film we see little to nothing of the broad avenue the Snows call home. Nor do we see the trolleys (streetcars) plying the avenues as they are described within the book, transporting Coryo back and forth to school—if he could pay the fare (*BSS* 45). In *Ballad*, the Snows' street address is barely visible as Tigris skims an ominous tax statement or eviction notice. Producers have apparently changed the name of their avenue to the Road of Hope. Alas, all traces of the Corso are erased from the film.

At the heart of Collins' own design for the Capitol is a distinctive urban street plan beloved by former autocrats and monarchies across Europe. The city circle she relies upon for all her books comes straight out of Baroque-era urban planning in European cities. Known generally as the Grand Manner, this *Baroque* (pronounced "Bar-OKE") urban layout of the 18th and 19th centuries relied upon an extensive radial street system sometimes described as the "hub and spoke" pattern. At the core of this urban plan was a series of expansive city circles, with wide boulevards and esplanades radiating outwards like spokes on a wheel.

All major roads thus led to city circles, which strategically doubled as the power centers of government. This is because these hubs were reserved for state-owned palaces, government buildings, or monuments demonstrating the political hierarchy. Urban scholar Peter Kostof summed up this Baroque pattern as "a phenomenon of capital cities. It served the tastes and representational needs of absolutism."

Is it any wonder that Collins chose this urban pattern to represent her own authoritarian Capitol? Numerous European cities could easily provide the inspiration for her City Circle. Earlier, small-scale versions of this radial pattern appeared in Madrid, London, Amsterdam, and Copenhagen. Then Baroque planning was introduced to Rome in a big way during the late 1500s. In their efforts to remake Rome into a Renaissance ideal, an ambitious string of Popes imposed an expansive network of straight thoroughfares radiating out from central urban nodes. Their primary intent was to facilitate movement between the city's main churches for incoming religious pilgrims.

This hub-and-spoke pattern still defines much of Rome's urban layout to this day. Paris then adopted the Grand Manner in a serious way during the 1600s and continued developing its radial boulevards and circles until World War II. This impressive urban pattern of grand avenues and civic monuments (think the *Arc de Triomphe*) serves as a main attraction for visitors today.

This favored plan of Europe's autocrats diffused to other cities across Europe, including Berlin, and even to Russia's St. Petersburg. That city, dubbed the "Venice of the North" for its extensive network of canals, was designed by its founder, Russian Emperor (Tzar) Peter the Great in 1703. Its urban plan relied heavily on western street and architectural designs.

These ideals also spread the other direction across the Atlantic, where America's own founders took notice. It was none other than Washington, D.C. that became America's principal showcase of the Grand Manner, with wide boulevards converging on central nodes of power or public spaces. Think Pennsylvania Avenue, Capitol Hill, the White House, and the likes of DuPont Circle (Paradis).

At the time of its founding, the new United States and its emerging capital city were promoted as a revolutionary (pun intended) experiment in democratic government. In that spirit, the city's principal designer, Pierre Charles L'Enfant overlaid a more egalitarian, rectangular street grid over the top of his otherwise European Baroque avenues. The standard rectangular grid is considered more democratic because it provides equal access to all areas of the city. In stark contrast, the radial, hub-and-spoke plan accentuates social hierarchy and political status. More practically, this further explains the city's litany of bizarre intersections and oddly shaped properties to this day. The silver lining is that the nation's capital is considered by many as one of America's most charming, walkable, and livable cities—aside from the housing costs.

Although Collins has apparently not yet confirmed her direct source of inspiration for her City Circle, there is likely no better model for the Capitol than that of Washington, D.C. Aside from her story's countless references to the Classical period and Roman Empire, she has likewise invoked plenty of imagery from American history and democracy as well. For starters, her choice to include 13 districts reflects America's 13 original colonies, while reaping day is held on July 4.

The references to early America continue. Collins' first book begins with the 74th Games. Readers may have glossed over this apparently mundane decision, at least until they do the math and realize the actual revolution in *Mockingjay* would have occurred during the 76th Games. In one sense, they did. Prior to arriving in the Capitol with the Star Squad 451 (a reference to the novel, *Fahrenheit 451*), Finnick comments, "Let the Seventy-sixth Hunger Games begin!" (*MJ* 251). This is Collins' not-so-subtle nod to the "Spirit of '76," and America's own revolution and the ensuing Declaration of Independence. It is therefore not unreasonable to presume that Collins looked no further than Washington, D.C. to help model her own capital city of Panem (Paradis).

Returning to the City Circle seen in *Ballad*, this Baroque urban plan is carried over grandly from the original series. In the first book, Katniss describes the outdoor scene during the tribute interviews, observing, "the City Circle and the avenues that feed into it are completely packed with people. Standing room only" (*THG* 124). She is unwittingly recognizing the Capitol's radial street plan. We learn more about the City Circle in *Mockingjay* when Katniss returns as a disguised refugee. She arrives on foot this time to find the Circle's wide expanse lined with grand buildings and the president's mansion (*MJ* 345). This implies the circle center remains an unbuilt, open space.

In contrast to the unbuilt Circle of the original series, this space in *Ballad* has been adorned with a colossal CGI-added centerpiece. This is a creative, new addition to the Capitol's urban landscape. Production designer Uli Hanisch provides further insight to the Circle's central statue and fountain, conceived as a direct opposition to America's Statue of Liberty. There's "this big statue, which we call *Panema*," Hanisch begins. "It looks like Lady Liberty, but instead of having a torch and a text, welcoming everybody, it has two swords [crossed together] that says really clearly: [Go away]" (Rasker). Discerning viewers will further notice a simplified emblem of *Panema's* double swords emblazoned on various interior walls and fascist-style décor. For Panem, this emblem consequently served as the centralized image of state authority.

The film closes out dramatically as Coriolanus approaches the imposing *Panema* to contemplate his newfound future, with—as suggested by Dean Highbottom—"nothing standing in [his] way." He somehow ignores and dodges the CGI-added 1950s autos darting around the Circle, hinting at a bustling Capitol returning to life after the war. Behind the statue is the socialist Karl-Marx-Allee, flanked on both sides by the GDR's tiered, wedding-cake apartment blocks of the 1950s. Various digital modifications provide the appearance of a half-built, grungy cityscape topped with construction cranes (Fazzare). This scene could very easily be imagined as the reconstruction of East Berlin after it has been permanently closed off from the West. As the *Panema* statue might imply, *Welcome to the Capitol. Now go home.*

Capitol Train Station

The Rhenish Industrial Railway Museum in Cologne provided an appropriately gritty and industrial setting for the Capitol train station. Founded in 1987, the museum's primary mission is to preserve railroad equipment from the region, including the research and documentation of railroad history. The collection includes approximately 70 locomotives from different eras, likely including the early diesel engine that heads up the tribute train pulling into the station. As the train screeches to a stop, Coriolanus greets Lucy Gray for the first time inside the museum's historic locomotive maintenance facility. One can see the sunken bays below the tracks to make equipment repairs.

Various railway locomotives and train cars from the museum were used to emulate early 20th century train travel in *Ballad*. Of course, the railway equipment is distinctly European and, more specifically, of German heritage. This is why American viewers may find the aesthetics of these trains to be largely unfamiliar and somehow foreign. From an American perspective, this works well for portraying Panem's fictional railway system. For one thing, we see the distinctive *buffer and chain* coupling mechanisms visible on each railway car and locomotive. Two spring-loaded buffers stick out on either side of the couplers to soften the jolts from slowing down, stopping, and taking sharp curves. These and other features are not found on American railway equipment.

And unlike the high-speed, levitated trains we see in the earlier films, the Panem of the prequel still relies on conventional railroad travel. Then as now, numerous days were necessary to cross the continent by rail. This is well represented in the film through the creative deployment of mid-20th century German railroad equipment. Perhaps the closest approximation to an American steam locomotive is the smooth, streamlined engine we see pulling our shiny, new peacekeepers into District 12. Such metallic, sleek-looking exteriors were characteristic of the 1930s and 1940s to portray an image of modern technology and speed during America's streamline era.

The railroad equipment within *Ballad* further reinforces the film's period-piece qualities. We see late steam and early diesel locomotives in these scenes, representing the transition from coal-powered engines to more efficient diesels during the World War II era. By the late 1950s in much of Europe and the United States, railroad companies had all but replaced their aging steam locomotives in favor of newer diesel engines. This "transition era," as railroad historians call it, was therefore well represented in *Ballad*, thanks in no small part to the museum opening its doors to the filmmakers.

Dr. Gaul's Lab and War Department

One of the more unusual filming locations was adopted for Dr. Gaul's creepy though spacious lab. Considered a part of the War Department, the lab was shot inside a relatively new crematorium in Berlin, called *Krematorium Berlin-Baumschulenweg*. First opened in 1999, Francis Lawrence says, "It's a really beautiful building and a fantastic architectural piece. It's in the middle of a graveyard. It has a really big space and then these smaller chapels where loved ones can gather, which is where we shot. They let us take over the place and turn it into Head Gamemaker Dr. Gaul's lab" (Zelmer).

With its minimalist modern concrete structure designed by German architect Fritz Eisel, one writer describes the space as "both visually stunning and emotionally evocative" (Zelmer). Eisel relied heavily on the use of concrete, glass, and steel, which are all primary construction materials within the modernist aesthetic. The unornamented, functional interior was designed to provide a dignified space for family and friends to mourn their departed loved ones. Its intentionally simplistic design is reminiscent of Japanese architect Tadao Ando's philosophy, highlighting the concept of sensation and physical experiences. His own buildings are meant to emphasize nothingness and empty spaces, thereby representing the beauty of simplicity. Similarly, Eisel is known for his own minimalist and functionalist approaches to architectural design. It is no surprise that the structure has become widely acclaimed as a regional masterpiece in modern architecture.

Unlike the crematorium's interior spaces, we do not see its exterior in the film. Rather, the *James-Simon-Galerie* (James Simon Gallery) was chosen for the outdoor shots of the Capitol's War Department. The building is named in honor of James Simon, once a prominent 19th century Jewish donor to Museum Island's collections. This was an intentional gesture to recognize many such donors whose identities had been systematically erased by the Nazis (Wainwright). The site is most prominently featured as mentors Clemensia and Coriolanus ascend the Gallery's broad staircase to its entrance above.

The art gallery is located on Berlin's Museum Island, between the reconstructed Neues Museum and one arm of the Spree River. And cattycornered across the street is the Altes Museum, which supplied the exterior front façade of the Capitol's Academy building (see below). This is the newest structure featured within the film, as the gallery was completed only in July 2019 after nine years of construction.

Aside from its function as an art gallery, the modernist structure was further designed as a visitors center to orient guests to Museum Island. Its British architect, David Chipperfield, designed the facility in the form of a white Grecian temple, highlighted by a colonnade of slender, white columns not visible in the film. The building further provides space for practical functions that could not be accommodated by the surrounding museums and is described by Chipperfield as "a sort of subway station" (Wainwright). As such, the site serves as a central entrance hub with connections to surrounding buildings including the Neues Museum and the Pergamon. As for the stairway featured in *Ballad*, it is designed to lead visitors up three flights to a kind of Grecian temple mount, consisting of an elevated plateau with a ticket desk, café, and terrace.

The Academy Lecture Hall

Coriolanus and his classmates spend some of *Ballad's* more poignant scenes inside a distinctive circular classroom with vertically tiered rows and seating. In one scene Dr. Gaul interrupts the class from above to engage in a debate about the future of the Games. Sejanus' philosophies on human rights come to light here. It is Coriolanus who most impresses Dr. Gaul, however, as she asks him to draft a proposal to make the Games more appealing to audiences. Much later in a scene derived from the book's Epilogue, we find a smug Coriolanus handing over Sejanus' personal belongings to Dean Highbottom, just prior to the dean's own untimely demise. Not just incidentally, this is likely Coriolanus' first murder by poisoning, not counting his role as accomplice to similar acts within the arena.

As for the classroom, such a place is likely unfamiliar to those expecting a more conventional, rectangular space. This is because these scenes were shot on site at the *Tieranatomische Theater* (Theater of Veterinary Medicine), a historical veterinary training facility built in 1790. Today it is found within the north campus of Berlin's Humboldt University. Its original construction had been commissioned by King Friedrich Wilhelm II as the centerpiece for a new Prussian college of veterinary medicine. Rather than focus on today's more familiar pets, the King believed the country needed a veterinary medicine school to study the diseases of cattle and horses.

The building was designed by architect Carl Gotthard Langhans, perhaps better known for designing the Brandenburg Gate. For his new anatomical theater, he designed it in tiers to allow students to gaze downward on veterinarians performing surgery. The theater's exterior and interior were both designed in the neoclassical style with references to Andrea Palladio's Renaissance-era Italian villas ("Tieranatomisches 2"). Neoclassical architecture swept across Europe during and prior to the 19th century as a revival of Classical Greek design elements. Though barely visible in the film, the theater is capped by a central dome reminiscent of Palladio's *Villa Capra*, which was often copied for similar neoclassical buildings of the time. Thomas Jefferson's home in Virginia, *Monticello*, is one of the more famous. In the theater's case the dome served a practical purpose as well. It was built atop a truss structure with windows to provide better illumination prior to electricity ("Tieranatomisches I").

Today the theater is considered the oldest surviving academic teaching building in Berlin and is a protected historic landmark. Following its restoration in 2012, it is now open to the public and still hosts occasional art and science exhibitions, not to mention the occasional movie set.

The Academy Exterior

The imposing front façade of the Capitol's Academy building provides one of *Ballad's* more impressive scenes. This is where Coriolanus and his peers spent their high-school years, including the interior of Heavensbee Hall (more below). For the Academy's exterior shots, filmmakers chose *Altes Museum* (Old Museum), built between 1823 and 1830 by architect Karl Friedrich Schinkel. It is honored as Berlin's oldest museum and serves as the geographic and architectural hub of Museum Island. Cattycornered across the street is the much newer James Simon Gallery, where the exterior of the Capitol's War Department was filmed (see above).

The museum's historic roots date to 1810 when King Friedrich Wilhelm III commissioned Wilhelm von Humboldt "to compile a public, well-selected collection of art in Berlin" ("Masterplan"). The Royal Museum—today's Altes Museum—was built to showcase "all collections of art," which included the Old Master Paintings, the Numismatic Collection, and the Collection of Classical Antiquities. After 1966 the German Democratic Republic (GDR) converted it to a museum of contemporary art. Following the reunification of East and West Germany, the Collection of Classical Antiquities has gradually moved back.

The film's panoramic exterior shots of Altes Museum reveal a quintessential example of the 19th century neoclassical style. This was when many of Europe's elite designers and architects adopted the temple-like architecture of Classical Greece and Rome. In this case the portico's slender yet massive ionic columns easily remind one of the Parthenon and related classical temples of ancient Greece. This interest coincided with the Enlightenment period, characterized by a renewed appreciation for the arts and sciences—not to mention a renewed fascination with Greek and Roman history.

Keen observers will note that filmmakers used CGI to add another massive block to the building above the columned portico. For whatever reason, they seemed to believe that the actual museum's imposing façade was not grand enough for purposes of the Capitol's posh Academy.

Heavensbee Hall

As the cameras turn to Heavensbee Hall, our characters find themselves inside a different building altogether. Early in the film, we enjoy the welcoming statements of Dr. Gaul and Dean Highbottom in advance of the reaping ceremonies. If one looks carefully behind the Dean as he shuffles through the hall, one can view a plaque and head bust honoring "Trajan Heavensbee, Father of Panem." He is no doubt an ancestor to Head Gamemaker and revolutionary, Plutarch Heavensbee, from the original series.

It is notable that the fictitious Heavensbee Hall actually serves as a hall in real life. The scene was filmed inside *Altes Stadthaus*—that is, Old City House, or City Hall. Today the restored hall serves as an event space one can rent for galas, balls, weddings, anniversaries, and related ceremonies. The Old City Hall formerly served as an administration building and is still used today by the Senate.

As for Old City Hall itself, it was originally referred to as the *Neues Stadthaus*, or New City House after its construction in 1911. Later it was appropriated by the GDR Council of Ministers with the separation of East and West Germany after World War II. At that time, the building was renamed "Old City House" to avoid confusion. The building sustained some damage during the Allied bombings of World War II, though it was most severely damaged during the culminating Battle for Berlin near the war's conclusion. When the Soviets moved in, the building was still in disrepair. The seat of government therefore moved nearby to the Fire Society Building. This is when the New City House was renamed the Old City House to avoid confusion. Reconstruction of the now-Old City House took place throughout the 1950s ("Altes").

Fans of *Ballad* will be more excited about what is found inside. Heavensbee Hall was filmed within the aforementioned *Bärensaal*, or Bear Hall, a barrel-vaulted hall towering three stories at the center of the building. The space can hold 1,500 people, and the walls are inscribed with moral sayings above the rectangular side door openings. Most notable given the hall's name, the room comes complete with a 400-kilogram (880 lb) bronze bear, the symbol of Berlin. Commissioned by the city in 1911, Georg Wrba crafted the sculpture that ultimately gave the hall its name.

After its reconstruction in the 1950s, various offices reoccupied much of the building, though Bear Hall remained unused. It was not left alone indefinitely, however. During the early 1960s the building saw extensive alterations, during which the hall was converted for use by the Council of Ministers. The capacity was thereby reduced to 300 people. The windows and arcades were closed off and replaced with wood wall moldings. A suspended ceiling was further installed to create the look of a modern office room. The bear statue was removed in 1959 and installed at the new East Berlin Zoo.

REBUILDING THE CAPITOL

These modernist renovations effectively hid the hall's historical design qualities, considered obsolete and old fashioned. It was not just the East Germans who viewed historical architecture as antiquated. Rather, this modernist trend swept across Europe, the United States, and around the world during the second half of the 20th century. New and modern was "in," while historic was "out." For its part, America lost vast swaths of perfectly good urban neighborhoods and downtowns to the bulldozers of the so-called Urban Renewal era. What wasn't torn down was plastered over with plain, modern facades that harkened a new, high-tech future.

The updates to Bear Hall reflected the fundamental tenets of the modern movement. Not until the 1970s and later decades did communities realize how much urban history and architecture was being lost. The ensuing reaction led to the blossoming historic preservation movement on both sides of the Atlantic, still going strong today.

This newfound appreciation for history became part of Bear Hall's story as well. The turning point came when negotiations were held there for eventual German reunification in 1990. This political shift was accompanied by the historic preservation movement as well. A massive restoration of Old City House and Bear Hall was accomplished over the next fifteen years. For its part, the once-elegant hall was lovingly restored and reopened on June 21, 1999, in much of its former glory. And the bronze bear for which it was named also made its return in 2001, after a copy had been made for the zoo. A replica plinth was constructed to support the statue, finally returned to its rightful home ("Altes").

That said, viewers hoping to catch a glimpse of the bear statue in the film will be disappointed. The statue has understandably been hidden, moved, or digitally erased from the Academy scenes. Still, we can easily enjoy a sense of the room's original, restored design. The tacky dropped ceiling was removed, and it seems that natural light is once again filtering down from the third-floor area (if not floodlights for filming). The side entrances and arcades are opened once again, revealing their ornate stonework.

Of course, set designers have added their own appropriate touches for the film, consisting of lengthy banners and the insignia of Panem and the Academy. In one sense, the ability to adopt this space as a likeness of Heavensbee Hall was enabled by our larger society's renewed appreciation for our past. Through such efforts of historic preservation, we can now celebrate this heritage rather than cover it up with false facades. The story of Bear Hall (i.e. Heavensbee Hall) exemplifies this trend quite well.

PART 3: The People

• CHAPTER 9 •

Wardrobe and Makeup for a Postwar Panem

In addition to the filming locations and architecture, the story of postwar Panem is further expressed through an elaborate process of costume design and makeup. For this important role costume designer Trish Summerville returned from her work on *Catching Fire* to lead the effort with *Ballad*. Asked during an interview about her return to the franchise, she recalls, "Well, Francis [Lawrence] called me and said, 'Hey, I think we're doing this again.' [*Laughs*] And what really drew me in was, this film is so completely different than the one I did. The overall look of the film is so different than *Catching Fire*. It's a much different color palette; it's a much different environment. The tone is different, and all different actors as well" (Puckett-Pope).

In follow-up conversations with director Francis Lawrence and executive producer Nina Jacobson, Summerville discussed seeking a balance with the new film. While still focused on presenting fresh ideas and designs, they also desired to satisfy the fan base. This would present a substantial challenge, given that Coriolanus and Tigris were the only characters to carry over from the original series.

All other characters—and all the actors playing them—would be new to the saga. As Summerville continues, "I was thinking of where, especially in the clothing, I could give the fans a little bit of a taste of where the Capitol's going, where the Hunger Games are going. So, I chose to do that with the characters that made sense, like Tigris, like Snow and his family—because they're having this façade of still having money and means and upholding their family heritage" (Puckett-Pope).

Differing Looks for the Capitol and Districts

In conjunction with the costuming, the actors' makeup and styling needed to fit the period themes of the film. Portraying a clear distinction between the Capitol and the districts was a particularly vital goal. The makeup design for each character needed to complement and enhance the costuming. In an interview for *On Makeup*, the film's lead makeup designer, Sherri Berman Laurence, discussed her own inspirations for the diverse array of character looks she would help create. Laurence first notes her close coordination with Francis Lawrence and Trish Summerville. Although the film is set in the future, "Francis wanted it to have a touch of period look, with a nod toward the 1940s and 1950s," recalls Laurence. She adds, "I then incorporated these elements into character-specific inspiration boards and refined and mapped out each of the character's looks" ("Makeup").

She further notes how Francis wanted District 12 to "look like old black-and-white photos of the Appalachian region in the 1930s/40s." To accomplish this, Laurence emphasized more muted colors for District 12 characters, as people were supposed to be covered with coal dust, grease, soot, and sweat. The exception was Lucy Gray, for whom Laurence was challenged to create a variety of different looks depending upon the scene and context. In a separate interview, she describes the situational needs for Lucy Gray's character:

Lucy, she has quite a few looks on this, weirdly enough. We started with the Games, so it was just her dirty and sweaty the whole time. And once we moved onto the lake scenes and stuff like that, we got to take that down and do a little more natural look... and less dirt, and a youthful look. But we also got to do some really fun looks for the Hob. She had two different performance looks, and the reaping day too. Most of the people in District 12 were always really dirty, covered in coal and soot, except for on the reaping day. It was as if they cleaned themselves up. And for me I looked at Lucy like, that was almost a performance; she knew what she was doing. And so, I gave her more of a look that day. The funny thing about that is, since we started with the Games, I had to do that look on her first, off camera, and then take her back to what it would have worn down to during the Games... But then the Hob, her two performance looks were quite fun to do. The thing about makeup in District 12, and I talked to Francis about this, they don't really have anything, and so everything she would put on herself had to come from somewhere. And so, I would create backstories for, how did this get here, and why would this color be on her. Such as, rosy lips and cheeks were from raspberries, and for one of the Hob scenes, she had a really iridescent eye shadow, and so we said she crushed up beetles and put those on her eyes. It kind of became a game with us, it was like where did this come from? So that was fun. ("Cast")

In stark contrast, Laurence's designs for Capitol characters were cleaner and sharper, despite the city's ongoing reconstruction efforts. "The Capitol was the wealthiest," Laurence says of the socioeconomic differences, "so the people were very put together. This was where the background actors had the most classic 1940-50s looks... The mentors were fresh-faced for the day-to-day, and more stylized and dressed up for the reaping day. This was their most glamorous and futuristic look" ("Makeup").

This approach to makeup coincided with Summerville's own inspirations for the dress of Capitol citizens. Costume design began in coordination with production designer Uli Hanisch to best determine the look of the Capitol during that era. Summerville begins,

> We shot in Germany, and I was really inspired by these photos from our location scouts of massive statues and the incredible buildings that made up the Academy. From these photos, I knew that I would have the liberty to work with color because I was not competing with the sets and background. We also wanted this film to have a postwar feeling as the story comes right off the heels of the rebellion. Knowing this, we wanted to describe that feeling similar to America in the 1940s and 1950s. (Williams)

With this context in mind, Summerville stuck with mainly solid colors for Capitol clothing, and without a lot of print. Her aim was to create the essence of a colder, more serious vibe. They do not have a lot of fun, she believed, and a sense of joy in the Capitol is hard to come by. Summerville explains, "Even though in the Capitol there is more money and wealth, you don't see joy or the freedom of expression. Everybody's treated as one of many and as a number, and you're all equally the same" (Williams).

With that in mind, her approach for the districts was just the opposite. Aside from the ever-present Peacekeepers, district citizens cared little about meeting the social norms and judgments imposed by their snobby Capitol counterparts. Rather, out in the districts "you get to see the lives of everyday people, outside of what the

Capitol thinks of them," says Summerville, adding, "I wanted to express these ideas in the colors of the clothing, showing the difference between the lightness and darkness of both worlds" (Williams).

If fans think this comparison between the districts and the Capitol is counter to the original films, that is no mistake. The coloration within the earlier films painted a stark contrast between the drab, depressed, and dark grays and blues of the districts, as compared with the rich, vibrant color palettes representing the Capitol and its flamboyant excesses. This contrast was made even more apparent with Effie Trinket's arrival in District 12 to oversee the reaping ceremony in *The Hunger Games*. She and her outrageous Capitol outfit were clearly out of place. As Summerville explains, her desire was to flip that around for *Ballad*. She continues:

> For this one—since it's so early, [the characters] have only seen ten Hunger Games [at this point]—I wanted to flip that, to show more life in the districts, of how joyful and how much of a community they had before the continual control of the Capitol took over. So instead of having them always in these dingy coal-mining type of clothes, we have these big scenes at the Hob where they're dancing and they're joyful and the bands are playing. Especially with Lucy Gray's character and her band, the Covey, we have a lot of color there, a lot of embroidery. For the Capitol, I kept the palette very solid tones and no prints, nothing floral in that world. [The style is] kind of communistic, very concrete, and it lends itself to the locations we were shooting in. We kept the Capitol definitely looking moneyed—you can tell that they have means, but keeping it very controlled, very classic, very contained. (Puckett-Pope)

The distinction Summerville makes between *Ballad's* Capitol and districts is an important one. In her book Collins describes a Panem that is still largely capitalist and reasonably free of oppressive state control, much unlike Katniss' time. Reflecting our own world, Collins cleverly portrays the more privileged students of the Academy as the most successful. Coriolanus' peers are the daughters and sons of prominent, monied Capitol families that have accumulated important investments and industries within the districts. The Panem of the prequel therefore remains largely a free-market society.

Beyond the Capitol, people can still move about the country on conventional railroad trains. This is portrayed well in *Ballad* with war-era railway equipment (see Chapter 8). Even the mail travels by train, just as it did throughout the United States in special *Railway Post Office* cars prior to World War II. Most important, this is how Coriolanus and his bunkmates receive Ma Plinth's precious cookies and related treats. And notably, there are no fences or walls around the districts! All of these draconian restrictions on freedom are yet to come. It is not difficult to fathom that Coriolanus will play a major role in that transition, what with his extreme control issues and all.

Fortunately, this less restrictive version of Panem was not lost on the producers of *Ballad*, and certainly not on Trish Summerville. She acknowledges this progression of Panem as we are to see it 64 years later. Asked how the film's costuming communicates such meaning, she considers,

> I think it was showing a progression of time and control with government. I mean, these stories do have a really big message in them. These books have a really big message, and we hope that the target audience, besides enjoying the story, does catch on to what these messages are. And I think in this one particularly, we had the opportunity to show joy in the districts. Lucy Gray's character is much

different than, say, Katniss, in her approach to survival, and having this band that she's a part of, and this love story unfolding in the beginning. I think it was important to convey that through the clothing, the environment, also with the hair and makeup. (Puckett-Pope)

She further acknowledges the distinctive cultural and economic qualities of the districts following the Dark Days. These aspects are also accentuated through costuming, as Summerville continues,

And then also showing the individuality of each district—because, this time, when they're in the Games, they're in their own clothing from their districts. So having them be dressed up pridefully in what I always consider, like, their Sunday best—whether you're in the movie and you're the audience of the Capitol or watching the movie as the audience, you can identify which district each person came from and you get to develop this bond. Whereas in the later films, they're all given a uniform that they have to compete in. So, I wanted to show that this is how the Games started—and where we progressed to later. (Puckett-Pope)

In highlighting the individuality of district cultures, Summerville provides some examples in a separate interview:

Each district has a different attribute, whether it be fishing or mining. So, we gave them a little feel for each district. So, Wovey comes from the fabric district, so there's a lot of buttons and ribbons sewn into her costume, so we put buttons and ribbons in her hair. Coral comes from fishing, so we gave her salty, sort-of crusty hair. Some of the actors had modern haircuts, and we didn't have time to have wigs made for them, so we just accentuated the modernness of their style. It was just nice being able to bring out their own personality with their own style, into the character. ("Cast")

Those Red Academy Uniforms

The Academy's school uniforms posed a differing set of opportunities and challenges altogether. As noted earlier, Summerville had noticed the preponderance of gray, stone, and neutral tones associated with the filming locations and architecture. She held conversations with Francis Lawrence, Uli Hanisch, and the location managers about the starkness of these environments. This encouraged her to propose designing the uniforms in a deep, saturated red. She knew that red immediately draws the eye, and that it can soak up the attention of an audience. The color would also provide a stark contrast to the otherwise gray and neutral tones of the filming environments. About this decision, she recalls, "Francis was cool with the idea and liked it. When I saw what the arena would be like, and the school and the stairs that [the characters] walk up, it's like this veining of blood going up and into the buildings and flowing out and back down" (Puckett-Pope). Overall, the color palette for all the Capitol clothing focused on red, gray, black, white, and blue undertones. Summerville and her team worked hard to assure that "every working hired hand in the Capitol" conformed to that color palette (Williams).

The uniform design further contributed to the Capitol's suppression of individuality. This mirrored the role of the Peacekeeper uniforms in Collins' postwar Panem. "The fatigues for bootcamp, you're all the same. With the school uniforms, you're all the same... Whatever gender you were, you had the same thing on," Summerville says, describing the Capitol's obsession with uniformity (Puckett-Pope). One challenge was to design a school uniform that applied to everyone, regardless of gender or other individual differences. As Summerville explains, she therefore "wanted to keep an androgynous, gender-neutral kind of look where it wasn't girls in skirts and boys in pants. In the Capitol, if you're one, you're the same; they never let you feel elevated to be special" (Williams).

Summerville's solution to devising such a conservative, regimented look was the time-honored kilt. She explains, "I loved the idea of the kilt because the kilt is a very old article of clothing that we still use in contemporary times. We've seen it every decade in some way or another" (Williams). Rather than use the full skirt all the way around, however, Summerville's modern version includes only a front and back panel.

To round out the uniforms, the shirts are simple and gray with no collars, and all the buttons display the Academy symbol. Their sports coats were likewise simple and clean, with no lapel.

Producing mass quantities of the uniform for the entire student body presented its own logistical challenges. When asked about this issue, Summerville reacted with,

> Oh my gosh. [*Laughs*] There was definitely a struggle with these uniforms and the mass amount that we had to make. Procuring enough fabric... we're talking about hundreds and hundreds of yards of fabric to make uniforms for so many students. We had to make excess uniforms so you can do all the fittings. Then you [need] extra. Plus, we had all the mentors in the uniforms, so they all had doubles of their uniforms. So, it was a lot of red fabric... It was really tricky. (Williams)

Overall, the number of costumes for the film ran into the "thousands," with the Academy uniforms constituting a large percentage of the total. And since all of the buttons required the Academy emblem, it was necessary to make and cast between 8,000 and 10,000 of them. Added to that, "If you're going to have 200 or 500 students, you have to make two to three times that many costumes because you don't know people's sizes; if you have 500 background [actors], you need about 2,000 pairs of shoes to make that work for people" (VanHoose).

• CHAPTER 10 •

The Performer: Lucy Gray Baird

A Forgotten Victor

One of the more subtle though significant references to the prequel is found in Chapter 1 of *The Hunger Games*. While describing the Games for the benefit of her readers, Katniss makes a brief reference to a previous District 12 victor. She apparently knows nothing about this individual. As the mayor begins the reaping ceremony for the 74th Games, he reads a list of previous victors from Twelve. Katniss tells us, "In seventy-four years, we have had exactly two. Only one is still alive" (*THG* 19). Right on cue, a drunk Haymitch Abernathy takes the stage to represent the more recent victor who is, at least in some capacity, still alive. Katniss must also know Lucy Gray's name as the first victor, given that the mayor reads their names each year. Further, it is now apparent that Collins was setting up the possibility for a future prequel that would not be released for another decade.

THE PERFORMER: LUCY GRAY BAIRD

The notion that Collins at least intended to write future books was confirmed during an interview for Scholastic. On the day of the prequel's release on May 19, 2020, David Levithan asked whether Collins had any sense of the identity of that first victor when she wrote *The Hunger Games*, to which she responded, "Yes, but she's evolved a lot since then" ("Scholastic"). She further reveals why few residents have heard of Lucy Gray decades later. In the same interview Collins refers to Dr. Gaul having erased "nearly all recordings" of the 10th Games. In a similar manner, the memory of Lucy Gray has been all but erased as well.

This full-blown erasure plays out during a conversation between Coriolanus and Dr. Gaul in the prequel's final chapter. Coriolanus argues that the Hunger Games are still "pointless," because "No one in Twelve even watches it." He further reveals that their Peacekeeper base in Twelve did not even have a working television. To this Dr. Gaul responds, "While that could be a problem in the future, it's a blessing this year, given that I've had to erase the whole mess." She then adds, "Every last copy gone, never to be aired again… I've a master in the vault, of course, but that's just for my own amusement" (*BSS* 509).

For Dr. Gaul, the use of student mentors and numerous other aspects of the 10th Games proved little more than an embarrassment. At best they were an experiment with mixed results. Still, Coriolanus' observation about the lack of televisions in the districts likely encouraged the future use of those giant screens placed in the public square during Katniss' Games. This would assure that the entire population would be forced to watch, if not enjoy, the show.

The Backstory of Lucy Gray Baird

As we learn from the prequel, Lucy Gray's name is derived from the poem, "Lucy Gray," by William Wordsworth. Collins deftly writes her own character's story to mirror that of Wordsworth, as his Lucy Gray likewise disappears without a trace. A more thorough discussion of the poem is found in Chapter 5, within the section, "Lucy Gray." Her surname, "Baird" is a Gaelic form of "bard," meaning a poet, minstrel or singer who tells stories through song. The Gaelic language was native to the Gaels of Scotland, and most of modern Scotland was once Gaelic speaking. The common literary language eventually spread and was shared by the Gaels of both Scotland and Ireland through much of the 17th century.

It is not an accident that Collins imbued Lucy Gray with a largely Scottish surname. Aside from the Indigenous people already there, much of the central and southern Appalachians were settled during colonial times by waves of Scottish and Irish immigrants. In a classic case of cultural diffusion, these immigrant families brought their ancestral Gaelic cultural traits and musical traditions with them when they populated the home region of District 12 (more on this in Chapter 1).

Collins' prequel is therefore rooted largely in this Appalachian tradition of Scottish and Irish balladry. It is certainly possible that some of the Covey's songs even used words derived from Gaelic traditions. As the narrator tells us, "Some of the [Covey's] numbers bordered on unintelligible, with unfamiliar words that Coriolanus struggled to get the gist of, and he remembered Lucy Gray saying that they were from another time" (*BSS* 364). During his first Hob concert, Coriolanus becomes anxious and uneasy during these songs, as he likens the Covey's high-pitched singing to mockingjays. *Welcome to the world of bluegrass music, Coryo.*

In both the book and film, Lucy Gray claims she is not originally from District 12. During her first interview with Capitol News' Lepidus Malmsey (not Lucky Flickerman as in the film), she introduces herself as Lucy Gray Baird of the Covey Bairds. She makes it clear, however, that she holds little emotional attachment to District 12, as that is not her original home. After Lepidus refers to

THE PERFORMER: LUCY GRAY BAIRD

her as "Lucy," the "tribute from District Twelve," she corrects him with a curt, "It's Lucy Gray and I'm not really from Twelve... My people are Covey. Musicians by trade. We just took a wrong turn one day and were obliged to stay." She further explains that they are from "no district in particular," as they "move from place to place as the fancy takes us" (BSS 53). This conversation from the zoo progresses similarly within *Ballad*.

Various fan theories have attempted to tease out the Covey's original home, with one educated guess being the Capitol itself. This is not unfounded due to various clues Collins drops within her narrative. For instance, Coriolanus expresses surprise at the unexpected social mannerisms of Lucy Gray and her Covey counterparts that do not easily fit the district stereotype. He even attempts to pass her off as "Capitol" to help her gain sponsors. During the pre-show with Lucky Flickerman, Coriolanus spends much of his time talking about the Covey and "emphasizing that Lucy Gray was not really district, no, not really at all." Later the narrator adds, "In fact, if you thought about it, they almost *were* Capitol... Surely people could see how at home Lucy Gray seemed in the Capitol?" (BSS 198). It is further notable that in doing so Coriolanus is acknowledging the Capitol's deep prejudices toward district residents, much like his Grandma'am's own attitudes. In this case he is not beyond using the Capitol's aggrandized sense of superiority to achieve what he wants.

Granted, such comments could be breadcrumbs referencing some as-yet unknown connection with the Capitol. But Lucy Gray's childhood home is not likely one of them. When she introduces herself for the first time during the tribute interviews, she says,

> I'm Lucy Gray Baird, of the Covey Bairds. I started writing this song back in District Twelve, before I knew what the ending would be. It's my words set to an old tune. Where I'm from, we call it a ballad. That's a song that tells a story.

And I guess this is mine. 'The Ballad of Lucy Gray Baird.' I hope you like it" (BSS 170).

Given Lucy Gray's extensive knowledge of ballads, it is only logical that Lucy Gray is likewise from somewhere else in the central or southern Appalachians. She was brought up with ballads and their related Appalachian music traditions.

The narrator says as much shortly thereafter, stating, "Coriolanus had heard her sing dozens of songs over the past few days, full of everything from the beauty of springtime to the heart-wrenching despair of losing her mama. Lullabies and toe tappers, laments and ditties" (BSS 170). And the "old tune" to which she sings her own ballad is likely an Appalachian folk song handed down through the generations, just as mountain tradition would have it. No, Lucy Gray is not Capitol. She is the epitome—the personification, even—of Appalachian musical history and folk song traditions. The current states of Tennessee or North Carolina would be credible guesses, as two possible candidates.

Producers of *Ballad* picked up on this as well, as they attempted to imbue her on-screen character with a southern Appalachian accent. This was adapted in part from Collins' own choice of language and mannerisms expressed by Lucy Gray throughout the book. To that end, Rachel Zegler was purposely coached, as one writer says, on "how clearly Appalachian Lucy was, and how her accent exists in that vernacular throughout the duration of the book, something that was destined to carry over into the music." Zegler says further, "I'm glad Francis [Lawrence] wanted to explore that— he even sent me the trailer for 'The Coal Miner's Daughter' to give me an idea about the accent" (Amorosi). And, *Coal Miner's Daughter* could not have been more appropriate as a teaching tool. The 1980 Academy Award-winning biographical musical film relates the story of country music singer Loretta Lynn, from her teen years through her rise into the country music spotlight.

THE PERFORMER: LUCY GRAY BAIRD

Beyond Zegler's efforts to capture Lucy Gray's identity, Erinn Sweet of the Urban Appalachian Community Coalition believes both of Collins' female characters—Katniss Everdeen and Lucy Gray Baird—can lead to "thought-provoking discussion on the identity of Appalachian women." Collins' fictional dystopian setting provides an opportunity to further explore how Appalachian women have contributed to regional identity and culture. "The setting of District 12, rooted in the Appalachian region," Sweet suggests, "becomes a symbol of resistance as the women of the series emerge as powerful symbols of strength and resilience." For her part, Katniss becomes a catalyst for change, questioning the Capitol's authority and inspiring others to do so through her own defiance.

Lucy Gray's approach may contrast sharply from that of Katniss, though her intent is one and the same. As Sweet explains,

> Lucy Gray's strength lies in her ability to use her creativity and charisma to navigate the Capitol's treacherous political landscape. She becomes a symbol of hope through her music, captivating both Capitol citizens and those in the districts. Lucy Gray's resilience and determination to remain true to herself, despite the Capitol's attempts to control her, mirror Katniss' defiance in the original trilogy.

Comparing Lucy Gray with Katniss

As portrayed within both the book and film, the personalities of Lucy Gray and Katniss are essentially polar opposites—at least in some fundamental ways. Collins envisioned both as agents of defiance against restrictive governments. Both are clearly survivors. Above all, they value family, home, and protecting those they love. Beyond these aspects, the similarities are few and far between. Rachel Zegler perhaps said it most succinctly: "Lucy Gray is a performer forced to fight, while Katniss is a fighter forced to perform" (Goffe). As Sophie Butcher summarizes, "Katniss provided a reluctant face of the rebellion." She was forced to smile for the cameras and often resisted public speaking unless she was thrown into real-world situations herself. In contrast, "Lucy Gray relishes the spotlight. Where Katniss was deadly with a bow, Lucy Gray uses her wiles as a weapon."

To his credit, director Francis Lawrence became well versed in the similarities and contrasts between the two characters. He explains,

> What's interesting about this, and this all comes from the book and Suzanne, is that Lucy Gray... often people compare her to Katniss, who was also a female tribute from Twelve. They are very different people. What they share in common is that they're both really intelligent, and they're both survivors. It's how they do their different things that are very, very different. Lucy Gray is a performer, she's an extrovert, she uses charm, she knows how to manipulate, she can flirt, and she's very, very smart, and quite cunning. Whereas Katniss is a little more introverted, quiet, introspective, she's a hunter, she's more capable with weapons, so very, very distinctly different kinds of characters. ("Scene")

It was this very contrast that concerned Lawrence during the film's production. He was unsure whether fans of the original series would bother to see a new Hunger Games movie without Katniss as a central character (Butcher). As for Lucy Gray, Lawrence refers to her as the "anti-Katniss," adding that "Katniss was an introvert and a survivor. She was quite quiet and stoic, you could almost say [she was] asexual. Lucy Gray is the opposite. She wears her sexuality on her sleeve, [and] she really is a performer." He adds that Lucy Gray "loves crowds. She knows how to play crowds and manipulate people" (Butcher). In a separate interview, Zegler provides further insights into her own character:

> The Hunger Games kind of started that era with *Divergent* and *Shadowhunters*; Suzanne was the first to write, this young woman who was anti-establishment, anti-government, and really standing up for what's right in a very unconventional way, without an aura of sweetness. There was nothing cordial about her either. She was very rough around the edges. Lucy Gray is such a compelling character; she's kind of a breeding ground for what Katniss becomes 65 years later. The word that comes to mind is mercurial, you never know what you're going to get with her, and I think what's so amazing about this story whether you're reading the book or watching our film. You can never really tell whose side she's on, and the way I approached her was that she was always on *her* side, her own side—her family, her friends, herself. And that's why her relationship with Coriolanus is so interesting because she starts to see what it's like to put someone else's needs before your own. And she's living with her whole heart, but when she starts to see traits in him that she may not find trustworthy, she has to put herself first and make those decisions. ("Cast")

Lucy Gray, Rousseau, and Frankenstein

To recall from the Introduction, Collins intended to explore the timeless questions of human nature through her prequel. This is no trivial undertaking, let alone accomplishing this feat in less than three hours on screen. Differing notions of what explains human beings have further led to spin-off political structures and government systems around the world. The experimental democracy of the United States is a relatively recent case in point. It follows that much of the dialogue between Coriolanus, Lucy Gray, and Sejanus is written to mirror the fundamental debates of the Western world's most influential thinkers. In her one-page epigraph, Collins provides a substantial clue as to Lucy Gray's own perspectives on life and humanity.

Lucy Gray's philosophy on life is especially highlighted in two conversations with Coriolanus in both the book and film. As the happy couple is leaving District 12 for a promising new life in the wilderness, Coriolanus mentions that people are "mostly awful." This provides an opening for Lucy Gray. She says, "People aren't so bad, really... It's what the world does to them. Like us, in the arena. We did things in there we'd never have considered if they'd just left us alone" (BSS 492). Following more dialogue, she adds, "I think there's a natural goodness built into human beings. You know when you've stepped across the line into evil, and it's your life's challenge to try and stay on the right side of that line." In the so-called "nature versus nurture" debate, she basically believes we are all born as decent and pure beings. Only later does the world potentially corrupt and eat away at that goodness.

Lucy Grays's overarching philosophy can be matched most closely with that of the Enlightenment thinker, Jean-Jacques Rousseau (1712-1778) (Frankel, "Songbirds"). In the prequel's epigraph Collins provides a quote from Rousseau's *The Social Contract* (1762): "Man is born free; and everywhere he is in chains." This succinctly states his belief that people are born with inherent goodness until rendered corrupt by society's myriad of challenges and hardships.

This line of thought translates into Rousseau's ideal form of government. His central political doctrine is that a state can be legitimate only if it is guided by the "general will" of its members. The people will enjoy the protection provided by the state while still retaining their individual freedoms. In *The Social Contract* Rousseau

THE PERFORMER: LUCY GRAY BAIRD

tackled what he considered to be the fundamental question of politics—that is, how to reconcile the freedom of the individual with the authority of the state ("Jean Jacques"). He argued that the laws of the state are ideally willed and approved by the citizens themselves. Thus, one is simply following the people's collective will by obeying the laws. As a result, the subjects of this government essentially remain free. As Frankel suggests, "The Covey model this peaceful, utopian self-rule. If Lucy Gray were to build a government, she would choose this kind" (Frankel, "Songbirds" 41-42). Since people are naturally decent, she believes they can police themselves.

Collins' epigraph also includes a quote from Mary Shelley's Frankenstein in support of Rousseau: "I thought of the promise of virtues which he had displayed on the opening of his existence and the subsequent blight of all kindly feeling by the loathing and scorn which his protectors had manifested towards him." In her book, Shelley applies Rousseau's theories by creating Frankenstein with a blank slate who has unlimited potential. While he begins his manufactured life completely benevolent and harmless, it is the incessant mistreatment and abuse from ignorant humans that turn him violent. As Frankel writes, "Certainly, the entire Hunger Games series stresses this, with characters from Peeta to Cato explaining that the games have made them killers" (Frankel, "Songbirds"). Lucy Gray demonstrates that people are inherently decent by saving Coriolanus not once, but twice—inside the tribute truck and during the arena bombing. Though genuinely grateful, Coriolanus remains puzzled and wonders why she didn't simply escape from the arena when given the chance.

Lucy Gray's behavior counters Coriolanus' belief that people are self-centered and therefore need to be forcefully controlled. Rousseau's connection between individual freedom of choice and the innate decency of humans is critical to his argument against authoritarian government. To renounce freedom in favor of another person's authority is contrary to one's morality ("Jean Jacques").

Nonetheless, Coriolanus ultimately comes to prefer the strict authoritarian controls promoted by Thomas Hobbes, as we will explore in Chapter 11.

A Rousseau-Plutarch Connection

Rousseau's belief in the fundamental goodness of humans was partly a product of his upbringing. With his mother having died just after childbirth, he was raised by his father until age 10. He recalled a haphazard education from his father, though it involved the ingraining of republican patriotism. He absorbed histories of ancient republican governing systems including one written by none other than the Classical Greek philosopher, Plutarch himself. It is no mistake that Collins' leading revolutionary character in her original series is named Plutarch Heavensbee, who expounded on his own plans for a democratic Panem. Near the end of *Catching Fire*, we are informed that a plan for overthrow had already been in the making for several years, well before Katniss emerged out of the woods to promote the cause.

In a roundabout way, then, Rousseau was influenced by Plutarch's ancient essays and philosophical writings that had been rediscovered by Europe's Enlightenment-era thinkers. At one point in Plutarch's own life, he directed a school with a varied curriculum in which topics of morality and ethics remained central. He was particularly devoted to preserving free will, not unlike Plutarch Heavensbee and the real philosopher, Rousseau. Notably for purposes here, Plutarch's most widely translated work in Europe was his *Parallel Lives*, in which he features the noble deeds and characters of Greek and Roman government officials, soldiers, and orators (Walbank). In this famous biography, he paired each of his Roman subjects with a similar Greek counterpart. One goal was to encourage mutual respect between the Greeks and Romans. Some of his featured individuals included Brutus, Caesar, Cato, Coriolanus, Romulus and others whom Collins adopted for her own series.

Plutarch's work was translated into English by Sir Thomas North in 1579. North's translation became the primary source for William Shakespeare's Roman history plays and influenced the development of his conception of the tragic hero. This means that Plutarch's historical writings are imbued within eighteen characters within Collins' original series, since they are pulled directly from those timeless Shakespeare plays. And apparently Shakespeare was quite impressed with North's translations, because he lifted entire passages with only minor changes (Walbank).

It turns out that the Classical Plutarch had earned many followers and admirers during his lengthy life. He became a celebrity of the Roman Empire. His public duties eventually took him to Rome where he lectured on philosophy and made numerous friends as well. He was further recognized by the emperors Trajan and Hadrian, with Trajan having bestowed the high honour of *ornamenta consularia* upon him. Trajan is considered to be the second of the "Five Good Emperors" from 98-117 CE. He was one of Rome's more philanthropic rulers who oversaw extensive public works projects and led Rome to its greatest territorial extent.

This would otherwise be considered historical minutiae, except for one curious thing. Heavensbee Hall was of course named for an ancestor of Plutarch Heavensbee. As noted in Chapter 8, keen observers of the film can peak behind Dean Highbottom to see a plaque honoring "Trajan Heavensbee: Father of Panem." In the spirit of the historical Trajan, perhaps this Heavensbee was a more benevolent leader himself, or so we would like to think.

A Prequel Love Story?

The nature of the ill-fated relationship between Lucy Gray and Coriolanus remains a mystery, as Suzanne Collins certainly intended. There is little clarity to be had on this topic in either the book or film. One thing is for sure—this is no Katniss and Peeta reboot. In their scenario, Peeta had unquestionably loved Katniss since well before the 74th Games. But it was unrequited love, as Katniss did not feel similarly until much later in the series. Rather, they were forced to present an inauthentic relationship for the Reality TV show they were tied into.

In one respect, the relationship between Lucy Gray and Coriolanus can be described as authentic and mutual. Both clearly develop true feelings for one another, though to what extent is left open to interpretation. The pair kisses several times in the book, and not just for the cameras. That said, to what extent is their love real and long-lasting? One could easily apply Peeta's inventive game with Katniss, "Real or not real." The question surrounds the ambiguity of their mutual feelings, and how those feelings might be subservient to their true intentions.

Executive producer Nina Jacobson preferred to leave the nature of their relationship uncertain as well. In crafting their characters for the film, she explains,

> I hope audiences will have different ideas about, are they in love, are they not in love? Is it real, is it not real? When does it feel real, when does it not feel real? Especially because they meet in a performance. They connect through a performance, realizing that they both have this ability to wear these masks, and to put them to service for survival, which they both are very familiar with. ("Nina")

Because their budding relationship was questionable by design, the casting for their characters was particularly challenging. For Coriolanus' part, his character was "neither villain nor hero at this moment, and both villain and hero at this moment. It is about that tension and nuance," adds Jacobson. And as for Lucy Gray, "She's a complex character, there's a lot of give and take between these two characters" ("Nina"). The challenge was to provide a balanced approach to the characters and their verbal and nonverbal interactions within the film adaptation.

To better understand their cinematic relationship, both producers and actors provide their own perspectives on the issue. Francis Lawrence suggests that Katniss' draw to Peeta had been based largely on "shared trauma," adding that, "You go through an experience together and feel more understood by that person than anybody else." This is a similar scenario with respect to Lucy Gray and Coriolanus, he contends. With them, "There's this mutual need. He needs her to win and survive so *he* wins. She needs him to help her win and survive so *she* survives... There's manipulation on both sides" ("Olivia").

In a separate interview, Lawrence emphasizes how their ambiguous relationship serves as one of the core aspects of the film. He further shares his own role with molding that relationship:

> It was really fun to play with the relationship and the mystery of the relationship. Because the two have mutual needs for each other. Tom [Blyth] wants her to listen to him and to win, because if she does, he does. She obviously needs him; he's her mentor. She needs him to try to win because that way she actually survives. So, there's this mutual need, but there's always a bit of a mystery of whether or not their feelings for each other are true. ("Scene")

There is little additional clarity to be gained from the actors themselves. While being interviewed together, both Zegler and Blyth were asked directly whether their respective characters are in love. In response, both remained non-committal, perhaps even unsure. Of course, this only heightened the vagueness that producers were aiming for. Blyth finally offers some insightful thoughts on the matter: "If I had to pick one, I would say they are in love for a short time, a short and sweet time, but is it love or circumstance? Is it born out of circumstance and out of need for each other, and then the question is, what even is love? Does love have to be this pure thing that comes out of nowhere, or is it sometimes out of circumstance or what one person needs from another? So, I would say, 'yes, but'" [*laughter*] ("The Hunger"). His last two words likely serve as good a summary as any.

Portraying Lucy Gray in *Ballad*

Collins' mysterious character of Lucy Gray Baird is played by the American actress and singer, Rachel Zegler. Unlike many of her counterparts, Zegler did not need to audition, but was offered the role by director Francis Lawrence. In some ways she had been preparing for such a role since childhood. Born on May 3, 2001, the New Jersey native was named after Rachel Green, the fictional character from the hit TV show, *Friends*. Her mother is of Columbian descent, as Rachel's maternal grandmother had emigrated from Columbia to the United States in the 1960s. Her father is of Polish descent. Prior to becoming a global sensation, Zegler gained experience with singing and acting in several high school musicals, including as Belle in *Beauty and the Beast*, Ariel in *The Little Mermaid*, and Princess Fiona in *Shrek the Musical*.

Zegler's first big break came in January 2018 when director Steven Spielberg posted an open casting call for his new adaptation of *West Side Story*. At 16 years old, Zegler sent in a video featuring her renditions of "Tonight" and "I Feel Pretty." The rest, as they say, is history. She was selected out of over 30,000 applicants to play the role of Maria, marking her debut on the big screen. She ultimately won a Golden Globe Award for Best Actress—Motion Picture

THE PERFORMER: LUCY GRAY BAIRD

Comedy or Musical. She thus became the first actress of Columbian descent and the youngest actress to win in that category.

Upon being offered the role of Lucy Gray Baird, Zegler initially turned it down. She had met Francis Lawrence in London to discuss the role, when she realized how far she was from home. She further learned that filming for *Ballad* would require substantial time in Germany and Poland. Uncomfortable with the notion of being away from friends and family for so long, she initially said "no" (El-Mahmoud). The fact that she had already been away for so long while filming for *Snow White* did not help. Consequently, her enthusiasm for playing the role of Lucy Gray was greatly minimized.

Despite all that, Lawrence refused to give up. Knowing she had a boyfriend, he offered to fly him in to join her on set, along with members of her family. Given the timing with the Pandemic, he further promised not to quarantine her. None of this was enough, however, and for the time being she stuck with her decision. Meanwhile the search for someone to play Lucy Gray dragged on, and both Lawrence and Nina Jacobson grew concerned. Jacobson explains, "We auditioned a zillion people and there are a lot of wildly talented people out there, but this is such a specific character. When she sings, it has to be jaw-dropping; anything short of that won't deliver" (Amorosi).

Eventually, Lawrence was assisting with auditions to cast the role of Sejanus Plinth, Coriolanus' presumed best friend. The role ultimately went to actor Josh Andrés Rivera, who had played opposite Zegler in *West Side Story*. In a funny coincidence, he also happened to be Zegler's boyfriend. Lawrence had no idea about this connection until he noticed Zegler starting to reconsider the offer. In a video interview about his casting decisions, Lawrence recalls, "My assistant was like, 'Do you know who that is?' and I go, 'Yeah, he was in *West Side Story*'. She says, 'That's Rachel's boyfriend'" ("The Ballad"). With this new knowledge, Lawrence held out hope that she would still take the role. Now Rivera would need to be in Europe as well.

Jacobson was likewise in the dark about the duo's relationship. She recalls that Rivera "had this amazing audition. I didn't realize he was Rachel's boyfriend—I just thought he was the guy who came in and gave us a great audition." With this turn of events, Zegler and her team reconsidered her initial decision. Jacobson says, "We got the call [from her team]: 'Is it too late?'" (Amorosi). Zegler finally accepted the role and regretted her initial decision to refuse it. Had Rivera somehow not been cast as Sejanus, it is very possible we would have witnessed a very different Lucy Gray Baird singing all those ballads.

One additional step remained in the casting process. Lawrence and his team devised a "chemistry test" between Zegler and Blyth to better determine how they might interact with one another. Even over Zoom, this first encounter sealed the deal. Lawrence recalls, "We all wanted to be mindful of her musical theater background and make sure we got that authenticity in her singing… As soon as she came on the Zoom test with her and Tom, I had her sing an *a cappella* version of 'Wildwood Flower' to Tom. And she just nailed it. It was slow, emotional, and she had a little dialect happening. It was so, so good" (Amorosi).

In the end Lawrence felt relieved that his insistence to cast Zegler was vindicated, as he happily recalled later:

> Choosing Rachel, she was my first choice to play Lucy Gray. I'd seen her in *West Side Story*, she's a very talented actor. I knew that she could sort-of play all the different facets that we needed for Lucy Gray; there's also music, which is a big element in this movie, and Rachel has an amazing voice, which made the songs fantastic. But what I really like is that Rachel as an actor, and Lucy Gray specifically, is not really built to be in an arena and

fighting. And so, I like that sort of fish-out-of-water feel that she [brings]. And especially in [her] kind of rainbow dress that's so specific to her, kind of stands out in this arena filled with dirt and dust and rubble. ("Scene")

Prepping for *Ballad*

For Zegler to prepare her simultaneous roles of singing and acting was no walk in the park. In a rare move for modern Hollywood films, Zegler chose to sing live on set, rather than quietly mouth over her vocals (this aspect is discussed more in Chapter 3). For inspiration she turned to the classic Hollywood films, something she always tries to do when studying for her roles. Her appreciation for these older movies was nurtured, she believes, from being raised on the classic film network, *Turner Classic Movies*. The channel was seemingly always on at her home. She says, "I really do love revisiting those when I'm prepping, but also just when I'm learning" (Lopez).

For her role in *Ballad*, Zegler focused on the acting style of Audrey Hepburn, and more specifically her 1963 performance in *Charade*. In one interview, Zegler describes Hepburn in that role as "a little kooky, she's a little ditzy but also very grounded and sure of herself." Hepburn is further motivated for self-preservation throughout the film, not unlike Zegler's character of Lucy Gray. *Charade* can also be classified as both a comedy and a mystery, a combination that Zegler took to heart. This became important when studying how to interact with Tom Blyth's character, Coriolanus Snow. She explains, "The way that [Lucy Gray] is able to flip-flop and play the game, and Coriolanus doesn't even realize that he's being played, and the audience doesn't either" (Lopez). One is left to ponder what the audience is missing as well.

Zegler further appreciates the genuine acting efforts of her predecessors, prior to the advent of CGI (computer-generated imagery). Without CGI the acting performances stood out more.

Zegler explains, "There's such an emphasis on performance in those movies. There was no spectacle back then. When it was stripped down to a two-camera job, and you really only have Gregory Peck giving his all on camera. It really just shows you how much of your soul an actor had to wear on their sleeve back then" (Lopez).

Of course, one is reminded of the old adage, *be careful what you wish for*. When asked whether the music or the physical acting was more demanding, she answered immediately: "Definitely the action bits, are so much more than I've ever had to do before. Other movies I've had stunts that I simply wasn't allowed to do," she says, adding, "This one was, 95 percent I did all my own stunts, and it was without much preparation. It was a lot of care, a lot of patience from the people around me" ("What Fans").

The most challenging action sequence was, not surprisingly, the so-called bloodbath at the beginning of the Games. She explains, "it was a lot of camera choreography, and God bless our crew, they were just pushing me out of the way to make sure I didn't... die in the process." To this Tom Blyth—who was also present for the interview—responded that watching Zegler run through the forest in high heels was "pretty intense, too." This reminded Zegler, "All of it was in heels, that was really the thing. Trish Summerville said, 'No flats and no zippers.' Those were tied up every day" ("What Fans").

Creating the Look of Lucy Gray

Much like the film, the book introduces us to Lucy Gray as the mayor calls her name at the reaping. The narrator tells us, "Lucy Gray Baird stood upright in a dress made of a rainbow of ruffles, now raggedy but once fancy. Her dark, curly hair was pulled up and woven with limp wildflowers. Her colorful ensemble drew the eye..." (*BSS* 24). As Lucy Gray takes the stage in front of the Justice Building, Coriolanus senses something recognizable with her outfit, something "vaguely familiar but disturbing about her." Her dress is then described in more detail, with its rows of "raspberry pink, royal blue, and daffodil yellow ruffles" (*BSS* 25). One of the female mentors remarks, "She's like a circus performer." This jogs Coriolanus' memory of the circus from his childhood.

The mentor's "circus" comment is adjusted for the film and voiced by Arachne Crane (Lilly Cooper). During the reaping ceremony she asks no one in particular, "What is that dress? Is she some sort of clown?" At this point it becomes clear that the production team has made a good-faith effort to reproduce Lucy Gray's outfit. Prior to the release of *Ballad*, her dress was perhaps the most popular subject of fan art. The backstory of Rachel Zegler's own costume design is perhaps just as enticing as the dress itself.

The task of reproducing Lucy Gray's iconic outfit fell squarely on costume designer Trish Summerville. No stranger to the Hunger Games franchise, she had enjoyed the same role for *Catching Fire*. Her first goal was to lay out a plan for the costume and how it might come together. In an interview for *The Art of Costume*, Summerville first acknowledged her ongoing appreciation of the fan base. "Because of that," she says, "I did want to be true, as seen on the page. When I first read 'rainbow ruffle dress,' it spun around in my head. What could that be?" (Williams). The outfit also needed pockets for storing items such as Coriolanus' gifts.

Summerville explained her vision in a separate interview: "With Lucy, I wanted her to be more of that vaudeville, carefree musical entertainer... You see that in her peasant blouses and the cinched-in waist. [She's] always in a dress, very feminine, and very done up" (Lapid). She further envisioned the dress with "dusty, muted tones," she explains, "because it's also Lucy Gray's mother's dress, so it couldn't be too fresh and vibrant." This particular goal required numerous fabrics and several versions to see what colors worked best together (Dominick, "Here are").

She further aimed to creatively tie the dress back to Katniss' costuming in *Catching Fire*, which she had also designed. "With that,

I chose to do this corset shape that mimics the same corset shape of Katniss' Mockingjay dress, the blue dress where she spins, and the wings come out" (Williams). Summerville was referring to her featured creations from ten years earlier, when Katniss' wedding dress was stunningly transformed into a mockingjay.

Summerville's nods to Katniss did not stop there. The corset was hand painted by her team in Berlin to give it more of an aged, rugged look. In one of the most subtle Easter eggs, the hand-painted blooms on the front are the flowers of katniss (white) and primrose (violet) plants. The corset's color palette continued from there, with yellow and green snakes painted around the chest and down the back to reflect her own identity as a sort-of snake charmer.

Achieving the final design for the dress did not come easily. The list of requirements was extensive for this particular piece. She explains that the dress was "definitely something I started with in the beginning, because it was a big tackle" (Puckett-Pope). Working at the outset with an illustrator, Summerville pulled in various fabrics and did some fabric testing and swatching. With "quite a few" illustrations in front of her, Summerville still did not feel comfortable with what she was seeing. She could not yet confidently say, "Oh, that's it!" She then took a break from the project and turned to Tigris before returning later to Lucy Gray. About this unplanned break, she elaborates, "I had two different illustrators working, going back and forth with different characters because of our timeframe. And I decided I wanted to lean a bit more into the Katniss feel... so doing the corset and figuring out if we could do embroidery or hand-painting on the corset" (Puckett-Pope).

She additionally consulted with Francis Lawrence for input on the sample illustrations. One primary challenge was to please numerous stakeholders, as she explains:

> That's the beauty about reading and having books is you can conjure up your imagery in your head for each reader

THE PERFORMER: LUCY GRAY BAIRD

as to what it should be. It was a lot of boxes to check over; trying to stay true to Suzanne Collins' vision and what she's written in the book, giving something to the fans that would be visually appealing, and hopefully would please a lot of people, and pleasing Francis and giving him something that he saw and conjured in his head, and then, definitely making myself happy because I'm the one who has to live with it. (Tangcay)

Although Lawrence was leaning toward one design, Summerville remained skeptical. She thus made the painful decision to reboot and start from scratch. For his part, Lawrence knew the importance of getting the dress right for the film. He explains how Lucy Gray's dress was an iconic and vital piece of the story line:

Trish [Summerville] and I started talking about it, and talked about how the dress is passed down, it was her mother's, it's passed down to her. Trish wanted to design something that felt authentic to the location of District 12, to the idea that she's sort of part of this traveling troupe of musicians and performers... But Trish also knew that we were going to be doing a lot of different things. [Lucy Gray's] going to have to run around, to roll around in the dirt, she's going to have to be able to move freely, so a lot of this was practical design of the dress. Trish had to be smart so that it would work in sequences like this. ("Scene")

Given Lawrence's focus on practicality, it was vital for the dress to be durable as well as aesthetically appropriate. Designing the iconic rainbow-colored tulle skirt was particularly challenging when faced with this added criterion. Lucy Gray would find herself—and her colorful skirt—in the midst of the grimy and bloody arena.

Summerville explains, "For the tulle skirt, I was figuring out what I could do to show a rainbow that would also work functionally because she has to do so many stunts... She's in this dress for a very, very long time" (Williams).

When asked facetiously whether they made 200 such dresses, Summerville explained how they accomplished this goal:

> I wish we could have had the time and money to make two hundred of that dress! [*laughs*] We had between eight and ten. On the top layer, it was tulle made into hand-cut ruffles and sheared. We were looking for fabrics that we could use that had a bit of stretch and give to it because of all the action she would have to do, so the dress wouldn't just tear every time. That helped us with that top layer, and we rigged it where each piece was separate and snapped together so that if she did rip some of the top skirt, we could switch. We also had pre-made strips of each color of the tulle handy in case one ripped off; we could stitch it back on. It was definitely a project of love. (Williams)

To build the skirt, Summerville acquired seemingly mountains of fabric and tulle that had stretch, as well as every possible color to prevent the need for dying every ruffle. She worked closely with Kellie De Pietro at Los Angeles' Western Costume Company and the cutting room team on precisely how to layer the dress, determine the scale of the ruffles, and how many ruffles should be included. The corset and blouse were built by Lea Chaudat in Berlin, including the corset's meticulous hand painting job. While Summerville may not have assembled a full 200 dresses, she still required a combination of eight to ten pieces of the outfit's every layer to assure that Rachel Zegler would not run short (Tangcay).

With this lengthy list of complexities in mind, Summerville provides further insight on the building process:

THE PERFORMER: LUCY GRAY BAIRD

With the skirt, I really love dégradé and ombre kind of fabrics. I wanted it to be dusted down and not too bright... And knowing it was a lineage heritage piece that had been passed down through Lucy Gray's family, it couldn't be brand new. So, we swatched tons of fabrics and came up with the idea of toile, because it has some stretch and give for all the stunts and crawling she has to do. We got a swatch card from Western Costume of every color toile in the world and then started laying them out to see what was the most complementary and how many of those we could fit in. We then configured what the size of each ruffle could be, how many ruffles we could have, and then did the under layers of the skirt with some metallics, so that we could get shine through it. We put bloomers under her dress, which could also hide pads. So, it did take a lot of thought. We ended up making about eight to ten [versions] of the dress, for all the stunts and all the aging. It was a big undertaking, but I think it looks really beautiful. (Puckett-Pope)

• CHAPTER 11 •

Coriolanus: Snow Lands on Top

At the core of both the book and film is a villain origin story, comparable to the likes of *Joker* (2019) and the *Star Wars* prequels. Admittedly the Hunger Games fandom was not clamoring for the backstory of a young Coriolanus when Scholastic trumpeted the pending prequel in 2019. *Why not tell the story of Haymitch or Finnick or Mags*, many fans of the original series asked. No matter. As one might expect from the desk of Suzanne Collins, there are grander reasons behind her inspirations, characters, and messaging, as further explored above in the Introduction.

To think of *Ballad* merely as the superficial story of Coriolanus risks overlooking numerous layers of meaning. Despite what Coriolanus may think, it's not all about him. Rather, his own character arc allows Collins to explore humanity's biggest questions. And whether one accepts a story about the future President Snow or not, Collins persists with her messaging. Her allegory encourages us to reflect on our human state of nature, and who we are as a species.

Coinciding with the day of the prequel's release on May 19, 2020, Scholastic provided its own rare interview with Suzanne Collins.

Her comments offered some welcome insight into the character of young Coriolanus. Asked by Scholastic's David Levithan how Collins envisioned him as a teenager, she responds,

> Well, I thought about Wordsworth's line, "The child is the father of man." The groundwork for the aging President Snow of the trilogy was laid in childhood. Then there's Locke, who's all over this book, with his theory of tabula rasa, or blank slate, in which we're all products of our experiences. Snow's authoritarian convictions grew out of the experiences of his childhood, as did his complicated relationships with mockingjays, food, the Hunger Games, District 12, District 13, and women. So, you rewind and plant the seeds.
>
> But given all that, you still need to leave room for Snow's personality. Is he a product of nature or nurture? Everyone of his generation experienced trauma, loss, and deprivation. And yet Sejanus, Tigris, Lucy Gray, and Lysistrata turned out very differently.
>
> For whatever reason, Snow has a very controlling personality. Then he experiences one of the most out-of-control emotions, falling in love. It turns out to be a bad combination. ("Scholastic")

Coriolanus and Thomas Hobbes

Beyond these insights, Collins deftly leaves it to us to match her main characters with the worldviews of specific Enlightenment philosophers. A substantial clue is found in her prequel's epigraph, just prior to the book's opening chapter. The opening quote is by philosopher Thomas Hobbes from his *Leviathan* (1651): *"Hereby it is manifest, that during the time men live without a common Power to keep them all in awe, they are in that condition which is called Warre; and such a warre, as is of every man, against every man."* Cutting to the chase here, Coriolanus can be considered Hobbes reincarnate—a veritable avatar of Hobbesian thinking on the state of humanity. And in his time Hobbes believed that humanity's normal state was one of perpetual war. Not fun. And definitely not candy, to quote *Ballad's* own Lucky Flickerman.

To better understand Coriolanus, then, we must turn to Hobbes, whose upbringing was shaped by the incessant brutality of the English Civil War. His own childhood was fundamentally affected by observing his country's political disintegration. He came to believe that even the most oppressive government would be favorable to the horrors and chaos produced by civil war. He further argued that continued stability could only be guaranteed if people agreed to refrain from undermining the regime. Perhaps most apropos for Coriolanus, Hobbes pressed for a reciprocal relationship between political obedience and peace.

To emphasize his point, Hobbes invited his contemporaries to consider what life would be like in a state of nature—or said another way, a society without a centralized government ("Hobbes's"). Is this not the fundamental reasoning President Snow offers to the districts within the original series? In return for providing so-called peace and security for the districts, as his propaganda video projects, the districts supply resources the Capitol needs. This basic thinking represents a colonial economic system. Extractive resources like lumber, coal, and grain flow from the exploited colonies (e.g. colonial America) to the colonizing power (e.g. Britain) for the manufacturing of everyday products. In the real world, at least some of those products filter back to the colonies for purchase in peripheral markets. Not so much in Panem's districts, however.

As one might expect, Hobbes' preference for an authoritarian state did not sit well with England's common folk. He spent a decade in exile in Paris, having left England in 1640 and not returning until 1651. His exile was related to the ongoing civil war and his stalwart perspectives on the conflict. Because he supported the royalists, Hobbes may have feared punishment due to his persistent defense of absolute sovereignty. He wrote *Leviathan* while finishing his sojourn in France, and it was published the year of his return to England in 1651 ("Thomas").

Hobbes became famous for his elaborate writings on what came to be known as *social contract theory*. Essentially, he justified political principles around which a population should unite to govern themselves. Most famously, he applied his theory of the social contract to his astonishing conclusion that citizens should limit their freedoms and submit to an absolute sovereign power. Rather than take him seriously, however, his perspective has often been used as a foil to argue for more democratic political systems ("Hobbes's").

Strangely, Hobbes somehow left a giant loophole within his social contract theory. That is, he reserves the right of a government's subjects—its people—to disobey the state's commands when deemed necessary. *Say what?* The people retain the right, he argues, to defend themselves against a sovereign power—that is, to resist, rebel, and disobey—when their lives are in danger, or when their families or even their honor are at stake. Those who have studied Hobbes have been understandably intrigued, if not puzzled, with what he calls the "true liberties of subjects." During his own time, Bishop Bramhall even perceived *Leviathan* as no less than a "Rebell's Catechism." More recent commentators have viewed this as the Achilles' heel of Hobbes' theory ("Hobbes's").

Perhaps had the younger Snow studied Hobbes more thoroughly, he may have taken this important qualification to heart. Katniss and her rebel followers sure did.

Coming full circle, Dr. Gaul reframes Hobbes' core beliefs as the trifecta of *chaos*, *control*, and *contract*. Coriolanus struggles with these concepts off and on throughout much of the prequel. As a follow-up to his essay on what he liked about the war, Dr. Gaul asks Coriolanus to elaborate on the value of control. Coriolanus tells her, "Chaos happens. What else is there to say?" to which Gaul responds, "Oh, a good deal, I think. Start with that. Chaos. No control, no law, no government at all. Like being in the arena. Where do we go from there? What sort of agreement is necessary if we're to live in peace? What sort of social contract is required for survival?" (*BSS* 244).

As readers attempt to follow his thinking, we thereby witness the young Snow's education in Hobbesian theory. Within his final essay to Dr. Gaul, Coriolanus concludes, "Without the control to enforce the contract, chaos reigned. The power that controlled needed to be greater than the people—otherwise, they would challenge it. The only entity capable of this was the Capitol" (*BSS* 292).

Upon returning from his adventures in District 12, he encounters Dr. Gaul for a follow-up conversation. She asks, "Did you think about the Hunger Games?" Elaborating from his earlier thoughts, he says, "They're not just to punish the districts, they're part of the eternal war... And they're a reminder of what we did to each other, what we have the potential to do again, because of who we are." Dr. Gaul then asks who we are, to which he responds, "Creatures who need the Capitol to survive" (*BSS* 508-9). And right there is the Hobbesian perspective undressed.

The Meaning of *Coriolanus*

Given his character's ties to Hobbes, we can better understand why Collins named him Coriolanus. Despite what readers may believe, she is not simply challenging our pronunciation skills. It is helpful to keep in mind that Collins pulled heavily from Shakespeare's own plays focused on the Roman Empire. No less than nine major characters in the original series referenced Shakespeare's *Julius*

Caesar alone, including Brutus, Cinna, Portia, Purnia, Flavius, Messala, Cato, Claudius, and of course, Caesar.

In a similar vein, she purposely named the future autocrat after the lead character in Shakespeare's play, *Coriolanus*. The play is set during the early Roman Republic with elected officials. It opens with rioting because Gaius Marcius Coriolanus is withholding grain from the plebeians, or commoners, while the patricians (aristocrats) are accused of hoarding. He believes the commoners do not deserve the grain since they are not in the military. As Valerie Estelle Frankel supposes, this could easily be the situation of Panem's districts demanding food and justice (Frankel, "Katniss"). Though a celebrated warrior, the Roman Coriolanus fails to win the popular election and is subsequently banished to the provinces in disgrace.

Regardless, he later becomes the ruling Consul after an impressive victory in battle. At his appointment, however, his tribune Brutus reminds Coriolanus how he had previously insulted the people. Now suitably enraged, Coriolanus speaks passionately about how the lower classes should be ruled by the patricians in the first place, thereby denouncing democratic government. He then declares war on his birth city of Rome, perfectly content with killing his fellow citizens out of vengeance. As Frankel observes, "He is no more the hero than Snow is—he's a thoroughly despicable figure who exists only to terrorize the citizens. Eventually, as with President Snow, the Romans execute him for his treachery" (Frankel, "Katniss").

The prequel builds on these parallels with Shakespeare—even better than the original series, Frankel contends (Frankel, "Songbirds"). In one parallel related to Gaius Coriolanus' great military victory, the people propose to make him Consul. To do this, however, he must lower himself and go into the streets to solicit votes from the commoners. The idea disgusts him, as he views himself as superior to the plebeians. This attitude of superiority and disdain for the district commoners carries over to young Snow.

As one case in point, the book's opening paragraph reveals Coriolanus refusing to waste one drop of broth. "It was one of a long list of precautions he took to mask the fact that his family... was as poor as district scum" (*BSS* 3). Then later, upon seeing the tributes spill out of the train, we learn, "a wave of pity and revulsion swept through him. They really were creatures from another world. A hopeless, brutish world" (*BSS* 41). His deeply prejudiced Grandma'am only reinforces this attitude, continuously branding the districts as an uncivilized *other*. They are brutish and "barbaric" as compared to the more classy and properly civilized Capitol citizenry (*BSS* 77). Of course, she never questions who contributed to their plight in the first place.

A Childhood Nickname

What does not appear in Shakespeare's play is Coriolanus Snow's cute nickname, Coryo. Tigris is the first to address him this way, though not until Chapter 3. "Imagine how terrified she must be, Coryo," she tells him while discussing Lucy Gray's pending arrival at the train station. The nickname appears in the book and film alike and is usually reserved for Tigris (*BSS* 37). Though we are not told directly, the nickname is likely credited to her imagination during childhood. The narrator tells us in the first chapter that the name *Grandma'am* "was another nickname coined by little Tigris" (*BSS* 11). "Coryo" is likely the other.

Later we learn more when Coriolanus saves Sejanus from the arena. Still winded and panting outside, Sejanus apologies to "Coryo" for the trouble he caused. The narrator says, "Coryo was a nickname for old friends. For family. For people Coriolanus loved. And this was the moment Sejanus decided to try it out? If he'd had the energy, Coriolanus would have reached over and strangled him" (*BSS* 240). This dispels the errant thinking that Sejanus coined the nickname first. Further, the nickname is clearly old and dates back to the cousins' childhoods, providing more circumstantial evidence that the nickname is owed to Tigris.

The Family Surname

Compared to his Shakespeare-derived first name, the surname *Snow* is almost anticlimactic. It does come with multiple, perhaps loaded meanings depending upon one's preferred connection. Frankel says adroitly, "Actual snow is of course frigid and can kill, in the same way katniss can nourish" (Frankel, "Katniss"). He is also an emotionally cold person. Beyond these literal associations with frozen precipitation, the colloquial phrase, "to snow" someone refers to a deception or double cross. In a more distant association with military history, author V. Arrow informs that "SNOW" was the codename of a Welsh mole during World War II who specialized in bugging his enemies, mirroring the Capitol's President Snow and his authoritarian regime. For their part, Coriolanus and his family use the play on words to invent their own feel-good slogan of superiority, "Snow lands on top."

Tom Blyth: Becoming Coriolanus

Unlike Rachel Zegler, who was actively courted to play Lucy Gray, Tom Blyth persevered through a more traditional auditioning process. The road to landing such a prominent role is challenging in its own right, and Blyth recalls it being "long and arduous." He adds, "It was definitely not at a point in my career where anyone was offering me stuff without auditioning" ("The Ballad"). When someone suggested he could potentially play a younger Snow, he wasted no time and submitted an audition video. It was that video which first placed Blyth on the radar of director Francis Lawrence, who recalls, "Tom, kind of honestly came out of the blue for me. I was not aware of his TV show [*Billy the Kid*], not aware of him and his work. He read for the part, and I was in Germany scouting [locations], and his tape came in and I was just blown away. We had seen some pretty good people, but he just blew everybody out of the water" (Dominick, "I Genuinely"). From this point Blyth provided some solo reads with fellow actors who were also being considered. Only after additional "chemistry reads" was he finally awarded the role.

Born in Nottingham, England in 1995, Tom Blyth began his professional acting career at age 15 in films such as *Robin Hood* (2010). He graduated from the prestigious Juilliard School in New York City in 2020, after which he landed roles in *Benediction* (2021), the HBO series *The Gilded Age* (2022), and the lead role in the Epix series, *Billy the Kid* (2022). That same year he was cast as Coriolanus Snow for *Ballad*.

In one interview, Blyth hinted at some adversity he faced prior to being accepted into Juilliard. Following his role in a play at the TV Workshop in Nottingham, he struggled with low energy and a short voice. He realized that if he was going to pursue professional acting in Broadway-type productions, serious additional training would be necessary. At 21 he applied to a variety of British schools, though one educational institution stood out. He explains, "I also couldn't get my mind off Juilliard which is the school I'd read about when I was a kid, and I knew that some of my [favorite] actors like Oscar Isaac and Adam Driver went there." Following his instincts, he used some "birthday" money and paid for a flight to audition there in 2016. He now adds, "There's no other reason I'd have been in New York if it wasn't for Juilliard, but I'm staying here for now because of ongoing work" (Goldstein).

Upon his casting as Coriolanus, Blyth remained concerned about following in the footsteps of esteemed actor Donald Sutherland. He had played President Snow in the original films. However, Lawrence was less concerned about emulating a younger version of

Sutherland. In fact, the director actively discouraged Blyth from focusing on Sutherland's distinct persona and mannerisms. Lawrence bluntly recalls, "Didn't want him to study Donald. Didn't want him to pretend to be Donald in any way. I wanted him to own the character, we're meeting the guy at a very young age, not fully formed. Wanted him to play the way he would play it" (Campione).

That said, Blyth's physical appearance provided a reasonable likeness to a younger Sutherland. In the same interview, Lawrence admits, "There are physical sides of him that you can believe that he can grow up into the Snow we know" (Campione). In a separate interview he elaborates, "Tom had the great blue eyes that you sort of believe could be Donald Sutherland's later. He's great at his craft. He's Juilliard trained. I knew he could do everything emotionally we needed him to do on this character's journey. But he was also very sophisticated and intelligent. So, to believably be the guy that turns into Donald Sutherland, you have to have that kind of intelligence and sophistication" (Dominick, "I Genuinely").

Blyth's physical features and acting prowess were supplemented with some rather unnatural hair styling and makeup efforts. His hair provided unique challenges on its own. According to hair designer Nikki Gooley,

> Tom's very dark-haired; we needed to make him lighter. And he was this young, careless, sort of wayward teenager. Hair could be more carefree at that point. Then the buzz cut—we had to bleach his hair probably every ten days to maintain the color, which was a real challenge because he's in every scene, so it was difficult getting time with him to bleach for an hour and a half, or however long it took. And the final sequences, months later, he's at university, so we gave him a 1940s style look, still incorporating some of the curl in his hair but making him look a little more grown up. ("Cast")

BEHIND THE BALLADS

A Shirt with Tesserae

And of course, the creation of Coriolanus' look involved costuming as well. Aside from his Academy uniform discussed in Chapter 9, the most noteworthy garment was his button-down dress shirt inherited from his father. In the book and film alike, Tigris rushes in to show Coriolanus how she modified the shirt in preparation for the reaping ceremonies. In the book we are told, "It was gorgeous. No, even better, it was classy. The thick linen was neither the original white nor the yellow of age, but a delicious cream. The cuffs and collar had been replaced with black velvet, and the buttons were gold and ebony cubes. Tesserae. Each had two tiny holes drilled through it for the thread" (*BSS* 9). While Tigris excitedly tells Coryo about her creative accomplishment, we learn that the tesserae had been pried from a cabinet interior in the maid's bathroom.

About recreating the shirt, costume designer Trish Summerville recalls, "I found organza fabric that had a black pinstripe and a white raised stripe through it. I thought that would be something she could take and add a tuxedo bib to the front of a shirt that would spruce up his existing shirt." And Summerville's team did not take the tesserae lightly. She adds, "We built the buttons. Our patina team in Berlin cast the buttons for us and hand painted [them]. I took those buttons to Uli Hanisch, the production designer, so that he could put them in the tiles in the wall and Snow's bathroom" (Tangcay).

In this context, *tesserae* are defined as small, square tiles of stone or glass, often used in mosaics. *Tesserae* is the Latin plural of *tessera*, a single tile, the likes of which were also popularly crafted out of bone or wood in ancient Greece and Rome. The word derives from the Greek *tesseres*, meaning four, or four-sided. Given Collins' prolific borrowing of historical references from the Romans, this is likely the inspiration for tesserae within her prequel.

This may also be a callback, or Easter egg, to her original series, in which the meaning of tesserae is very different. Somehow, we go from bathroom tiles to the unjust welfare system imposed on the districts during Katniss' time. One may recall the pressure placed on poorer families, like that of the Everdeens, to enter their children's names more times to receive *tesserae*, or additional rations each year. Early in *The Hunger Games*, Katniss tells us, "Each tessera is worth a meager year's supply of grain and oil for one person." Later she adds, "I've listened to [Gale] rant about how the tesserae are just another tool to cause misery in our districts. A way to plant hatred between the starving workers of the Seam and those who can generally count on supper and thereby ensure we will never trust one another" (*THG* 14).

Why Collins chose this term to describe this rationing system remains a mystery (at least to this author), though modern-day Italians can refer to *tesserae* as entrance tickets purchased for public dinners or related events. This is still a far cry from its more literal reference to mosaic tiles. While beyond the scope of this book, V. Arrow devotes a full chapter in her interpretive guide, *The Panem Companion*, to untangle the unjust socioeconomic underpinnings of tesserae as referenced in the original series.

A Sympathetic Character?

Aside from hair and wardrobe, Snow's character development was particularly challenging. Screenwriters sought a balance with respect to the amount of sympathy viewers should feel for him. Not only were they cognizant of working in Donald Sutherland's dominant shadow. They were further challenged to decide how much sympathy Coriolanus deserved as compared to his character in the book. One perspective is provided by Francis Lawrence, who quickly admitted to this issue:

> Yeah, that's the trick in the movie. I think that was the thing, the real challenge that we all felt we had in the

adaptation. And when you read the book, you're very much in his head, so you get a lot more than we can actually show. So, we had to figure out how to dramatize and visualize that character journey. We knew we had a challenge with the fans of the books in the series... [Fans] know that he's the villain and we have to get them as an audience to be behind him, to root for him, to empathize with him. Tom certainly helped with that, but I think the story itself and our characterization of him did [as well]. But we also had to work [on] his ambition, and his greed, and his need for power, and the darkness that is fighting within him. We had to weave that in... so that you get to the end, and you understand why he turns when he turns. (Stedman)

Lawrence's favorite portrayal of Coriolanus' transition to darkness consists of the forest sequence. During an interview for *The Hollywood Reporter*, Brian Davids mentions the boldness of a franchise movie to end with some version of a mental breakdown for its lead character, as a truly psychological ending. To this Lawrence responds,

> I love that sequence. It's my favorite sequence in the movie. It's where we really see Snow go through this series of emotions for the first time and descend into the darkness that we know will come with the philosophies of the later Snow. And I just love doing sequences like this because it has very little dialogue. It's very visual. It was a great day in the forest, and the light was beautiful, but Tom's performance was amazing. So, to just watch him go through the fear of the snakebite and the anger of being betrayed to the grief of being left, darkness settles in, and he realizes, "If I can't trust the last person on this earth that

I thought I could trust, then Gaul must be right." And to sell all of that with just performance was really beautiful and really satisfying to shoot. Yeah, it's by far my favorite sequence in the movie.

The question of whether Coriolanus deserves sympathy is one of the story's fundamental issues—within the book and film alike. It is also one which will invite further interpretation and debate for time unending. Disclaimers aside, the film's Coriolanus appears to have been scripted as less dark and troubled than his counterpart in the book. The production team apparently created more of a villain origin story than what Collins may have intended. That is, the cinematic Coriolanus may follow the more familiar "villain's journey," starting with more innocent and affable qualities than we might otherwise imagine.

This appears to be supported by the actor who plays Coriolanus himself. When asked in an interview to discuss the character he portrays, Tom Blyth responds,

> Coriolanus at this point in his life is still relatively innocent. He's not undergone the kind of transformation to become the future president of Panem, the future tyrant of Panem. He is, at this point in the story, still like a cousin-slash-brother to Tigris; he's a grandson to Grandma'am, he's still got love in his heart, he's not lost hope yet. And for me that was what was so interesting about playing him; it was kind of like getting to lift the lid and getting to look at him before he undergoes that transformation. I think that's what's exciting for the fans too, is getting to, like, see a character they think they know and kind of have their expectations challenged a little bit. ("What Fans")

Blyth then digs deeper to describe his character's story arc as a series of personal choices—choices sometimes made quite impulsively. He continues,

> I feel like, watching Coryo go through this movie is like watching him at the most pivotal point of this 'Choose your own path' story. And he keeps kind of choosing this slightly more murky, more complicated path every time, which is the most interesting one, but also the most heartbreaking one. For me, getting to play that is always fascinating, getting to play that kind of duality of a person, and I think like, me as an actor as well as the audience are kind of rooting for him—even though we know where he ends up, which is the amazing thing about this story... you know where he ends up, and yet you can watch this and still be rooting for him to make the right choice and do the right thing, and then—when he may or may not—you're kind of heartbroken, with Tigris, with Grandma'am, with Lucy Gray.

Coriolanus Versus Anakin

Whether intended or not, it was almost too easy for reviewers to make comparisons between Coriolanus and Anakin Skywalker from the *Star Wars* prequels. Anakin of course emerges to become the villainous Darth Vader. Viewers of *Ballad* could be forgiven for their puzzlement over exactly which of these two characters they were watching. It is also admittedly difficult to not view Coriolanus as headed to the "dark side."

Star Wars references aside, more favorable writeups have recognized something beyond this superficial comparison. Jim Hunter writes that *Ballad* "becomes a story about descent into fascism and how people can be kind and affectionate in everyday interactions but retain political points of view that end up being fascistic and genocidal." He then suggests, "For all the villain origin stories we've seen... the one that feels most grounded in a tragic, Shakespearean character arc is [*Ballad*]." He then correctly enlightens readers, "Not for nothing, Coriolanus Snow shares a name with the title character of Shakespeare's play, *Coriolanus*, a story about a Roman general resisting the spread of democracy."

In his own review, Mark Meszoros even titles his article, "The Villain's Journey." He still highlights a "few key differences: First, 'Ballad' does not appear to be the first in a trilogy of prequels" but is more of a "standalone story." He continues, "Also, it's a better movie. Instead of backstory of fallen Jedi Anakin Skywalker, we get the origin of Coriolanus Snow, future tyrannical president of Panem and persistent thorn in the side of 'Hunger Games' franchise protagonist Katniss Everdeen."

Other reviews of Coriolanus' character are less enthusiastic. After describing for his readership how screenwriters Michael Lesslie and Michael Arndt "divide this one into three parts," Joey Morona suggests this "gives the film an epic feel" despite pushing the runtime to just under 2 hours, 40 minutes. He then continues with his own *Star Wars* comparisons:

> The issue is that the movie doesn't just want to be one of the 'Star Wars' prequels, telling the origin story of its OG villain, it wants to be the entire prequel trilogy at once... But there's a bigger problem. His name is Coriolanus Snow. Lawrence & Co. would like you to believe Coryo is their Anakin Skywalker: clever, cocky, ambitious, broken, but deep down a good person. The film constantly dangles that proverbial other shoe—the one thing that turns him to the dark side—like a carrot in front of the audience. But what if he's Darth Vader from the jump?"

To Morona's insightful question, Suzanne Collins might say "Yes, he *is* Darth Vader from the jump"—though perhaps with qualifications. In her aforementioned interview for *Scholastic*, she tells us there is something different with his personality from the onset, as compared to his kinder, more empathetic peers like Tigris. This distinction is not so clear in the film. This is due in part to the inability to reveal Coriolanus' internal thought processes on screen. This dilemma plagued the original series as well, perhaps even more so with its first-person narrative. This is in contrast to the prequel, written in the third-person perspective through an anonymous narrator.

Whether *Ballad* producers expected such easy comparisons with Anakin Skywalker is unclear. That said, Lawrence does provide some insight into his own thinking on the matter. Although admitting that Dr. Gaul, for example, has a "sinister underpinning," he has never been known to simply view his antagonists as villains. Lawrence explains, "Even going back to Donald playing Snow, a lot of people would say that he's villainous and evil, but Donald and I never really thought of him that way. I know *objectively* the character is, but these characters have to believe in their philosophies" (Wang, "Director").

With respect to Dr. Gaul, he continues, "And so, she's a real believer in a specific philosophy. She truly believes that at our core, humans are savage, and that's why we need the Games. That's why people need to be ruled with an iron fist." This seems to contradict how executive producer Nina Jacobson perceives Snow's character, describing him as "neither villain nor hero at this moment, and both villain and hero at this moment. It is about that tension and nuance" ("Nina"). It is of course left to readers and viewers alike to determine our own answers to the "Is he a villain?" question.

Coriolanus in the Novel

Collins' original intention for the younger Snow is less debatable. Although her litany of subtle clues may "snow" some readers on the first round, a careful inspection reveals a particularly troubling Coriolanus from the onset. And these clues take us far beyond his more overt class consciousness and learned prejudice toward the districts. One of the first indicators of his personality is actually quite prominent. While fretting over the status of his shirt in the book's opening scene, we are told:

> The shirt. The shirt. His mind could fixate on a problem like that—anything, really—and not let go. As if controlling one element of his world would keep him from ruin. It was a bad habit that blinded him to other things that could harm him. A tendency toward obsession was hardwired into his brain and would likely be his undoing if he couldn't learn to outsmart it. (*BSS* 7)

This passage provides serious foreshadowing of his own personal obsession with Katniss in the original series, as it does with his own budding obsession with maintaining control. Then we have the affable, upbeat Tigris with her continuous counseling on how to be more grateful and thankful. As Grandma'am pins a rose to his shirt, Tigris says, "It does look elegant. You know what her roses mean to her. Thank her" (*BSS* 12). He further projects a personal façade of superiority through his manipulative charm. We are told, "his only real currency was charm, which he spread liberally as he made his way through the crowd" (*BSS* 15).

Other clues to his personality are more subtle. It is possible, for instance, to view his younger self as kind and decent, as opposed to his childhood classmates who were making Sejanus' life a "living hell." More accurately, Coriolanus had simply ignored him. "If the other Capitol children took this to mean that baiting the district brat was beneath him, Sejanus took it as decency. Neither take was quite accurate, but both reinforced the image of Coriolanus as a class act" (*BSS* 17).

We soon learn of Coriolanus' challenge with feeling empathy, or trying to imagine himself in the shoes of others. Once again it is Tigris who coaches him in preparation for his risky venture to meet Lucy Gray. "The cousins agreed that he needed to make a good first impression on the girl," and Coriolanus agreed that greeting her at the station "would give him a jump on the assignment, as well as an opportunity to win her trust." He is already setting up to manipulate Lucy Gray for his own benefit. Then Tigris counsels, "Imagine how terrified she must be, Coryo... How alone she must feel. If it was me, anything you could do to make me feel like you cared about me would go a long way" (*BSS* 37-38). Such thinking did not come naturally to Coryo, even at this point.

Something else is a little off with Coriolanus' emotions—that is, his inability to grieve, or mourn the loss of others. Granted, the book's Coriolanus is at first horrified by the sudden murder of Arachne Crane at the zoo, as is Tom Blyth's portrayal in the film. Beyond this commonality, the film captures little of what happens next. His initial reaction was to "recoil like the others" who had dropped back out of shock (*BSS* 100). It was Lucy Gray who hissed, "Help her!" At which point he "remembered the cameras streaming live to the Capitol audience. Not wanting to be seen "cringing and clinging," he only then forces himself to approach Arachne's ailing body to assist. He may end up assisting in some ambiguous way, though it is not due to genuine altruism or compassion.

This episode at the zoo sets up Dr. Gaul's test of Clemensia Dovecote with her colorful snakes. Unlike Coriolanus, Clemensia is too distraught to assist with the proposal they had agreed to work on together. "It was not until Coriolanus had walked Clemensia home that they remembered the assignment Dr. Gaul had given them," we are told. Clemensia says, "Surely, she won't still expect it... I couldn't do it tonight. I couldn't possibly think about it. You know, without Arachne" (BSS 102-3). Arriving home, Coriolanus finds Grandma'am "in a state," and Tigris is weeping. Finally, he ends up sobbing in the shower, but it passes quickly. We are told, "he wasn't sure if it had to do with sorrow over her death or unhappiness over his own difficulties. Probably some of both." Nonetheless, he decides to "take a shot at the proposal." He does offer the credible thought that working through the project would help calm him. Then we learn an added benefit, that he preferred working in solitude. He had no wish to consider "the thoughts of his classmates diplomatically" (BSS 103).

And so it was. While his family, friends, and classmates worked through grief and shock, Coriolanus wrote up an assigned proposal so as not to displease Dr. Gaul.

He further tends to think the worst of people, first presuming that the snake thrown down Mayfair's dress was venomous. Later he questions Sejanus' motives when offering sandwiches to the tributes in the monkey cage. He asks, "What was Sejanus up to? Was he trying to outdo him and steal the day's thunder?" His mind kept going down this darker rabbit hole, considering that Sejanus was strategically stealing his idea of coming to the zoo and then "dressing it up" in a way that he could "never compete with" (BSS 66).

Of course, a completely innocent Sejanus then sees Coriolanus and enthusiastically gestures for him to join in. Already in Chapter 5, therefore, we can detect a serious contrast between their respective personalities and outlooks on life. We further learn that "Coriolanus didn't like sharing the spotlight, but Sejanus' presence could protect him" (BSS 66). Using people for his own benefit was already a natural character trait for the young Snow.

Still, Coriolanus does retain some redeeming qualities as a teenager. While he and Lucy Gray are discussing their respective wartime experiences, he admits, "Look, I'm sorry. I'll find you some food. You shouldn't have to perform for it." He then passes a folded handkerchief through the bars, perceived as an innocent gesture of kindness at the moment. Lucy Gray reacts with a dark humor that Katniss might appreciate. Taking the handkerchief, she responds, "Thanks. I left mine at home" (*BSS* 69). Although signaling a naive insensitivity to the vast inequities between the Capitol and districts, not all is lost with our apparent villain-to-be.

That said, Part 1 of the prequel already paints a disturbing if subtle picture as the examples above indicate. Coriolanus is distrustful, manipulative, cunning, overly proud, prejudiced, negative, a kiss-up, and lacking in empathy. Moreover, he is averse to sharing the spotlight and despises collaborative team projects. He further resents Sejanus, and (checking notes)—oh yes—is already hopelessly obsessive and controlling. Not a good look.

It turns out that, from a mental health perspective, the young Snow is already demonstrating sociopathic tendencies. As Elizabeth Hardy writes, "Thanks to Collins' wonderful writing, readers know early on that Snow is a sociopath who justifies his increasingly immoral decisions as being necessary, someone else's fault, or well-intentioned. However, in the film, Snow seems far less Machiavellian" (Hardy, "Hollywood").

Sociopathy is another term for antisocial personality disorder (ASPD), a mental health condition that can cause harmful behaviors without a sense of remorse. The most common traits of sociopathy include not understanding the difference between right and wrong, disregarding the feelings or emotions of others, violation of the rights of others through dishonest actions, and difficulty recognizing emotion or appreciating the negative aspects of their behaviors. Other common sociopathic traits include manipulation, arrogance, impulsiveness, risk-taking, and callousness ("How"). All of these traits are observable within the prequel's Coriolanus, though few appear overtly in the film's first act.

A Façade of Friendship

The friendship between Coriolanus and Sejanus may appear on the surface as genuine and reciprocal. After all, Coriolanus does rescue Sejanus from one self-inflicted predicament after another. While visiting the Snow's apartment, Ma (Mrs.) Plinth admits to Tigris, "Your cousin's his only friend" (*BSS* 221). But this is merely a ruse on Coriolanus' part. He has essentially snowed the Plinths into believing he is a meaningful friend to their wayward son. More truthful is that Coriolanus always identifies an underlying motive for bailing Sejanus out of trouble. He additionally reveals no issue or compunction with taking advantage of the Plinth family's good fortune when opportunities arise.

While Coriolanus is dissuading Sejanus from martyring himself in the arena, Sejanus reveals distress over his father's habit of buying favors. He tells Coriolanus, "He'll buy you if you let him. Or at least compensate you for trying to help me." To this, Coriolanus first thinks, *"Buy away,"* considering next year's tuition payment. Instead, he covers and tells Sejanus, "You're my friend. He doesn't need to pay me to help you" (*BSS* 234). Later Coriolanus even visits Mr. Plinth at his family home, hoping for precisely that type of compensation. To his chagrin, he is only given a cordial drink and a terse conversation before being turned away.

We learn just what a good friend Coriolanus was at the prequel's final hanging tree scene. Sejanus' untimely end befits a typical Shakespearean tragedy. Coriolanus had made the conscious choice to interfere with Sejanus' plans that had ultimately sent him to the noose. And not unlike Prim from the original series, Sejanus aspired to be a medic and was cut down prematurely before reaching that honorable goal. While wrestling with his inner emotions over Sejanus' death, a little voice inside Coriolanus keeps asking, *"What choice did you have?"* He concludes that he had no choice at all; Sejanus had been bent on self-destruction. Immediately afterwards he fumbles through Sejanus' personal effects, and he just can't resist a few bites of Ma Plinth's delicious, left-over cookies (BSS 472).

Contributing to Coriolanus' attitude is a persistent sense of resentment toward Sejanus and his family. This resentment is in turn rooted in the Capitol's disdain for all things district. Early in the book we learn, "For Coriolanus, the Plinths and their kind were a threat to all he held dear. The newly rich climbers in the Capitol were chipping away at the old order simply by virtue of their presence. It was particularly vexing because the bulk of the Snow family fortune had also been invested in munitions—but in District 13." After that district's apparent nuclear destruction, the Capitol's military manufacturing had shifted to District 2 and had "fallen right into the Plinths' laps" (BSS 17).

This fact provides some fitting irony, though Coriolanus remains oblivious within the prequel. When weapons manufacturing shifted to District 2, the Snows lost their fortune while the Plinths profited grandly. Adding insult to injury, much of District 2's weaponry was used against District 13 during the First Rebellion. Imagine the day Coriolanus discovers that "District 13 is alive and well"—as Katniss was supposed to tell us in *Mockingjay, Part 1*—and that he had personally been snowed himself. Indeed, he and his family had suffered throughout the war and his meager childhood for nothing.

The profound level of Coriolanus' resentment is revealed when he considers Sejanus' idea to trade tributes. Having weighed the pros and cons in his head, he finally rejects the idea specifically because of his attitude toward the Plinths. The narrator tells us that, with Lucy Gray as his tribute,

> He had something Sejanus Plinth wanted, and wanted badly. Sejanus had already usurped his position, his inheritance, his clothes, his candy, his sandwiches, and the privilege due a Snow. Now he was coming for his apartment, his spot at the University, his very future, and

had the gaul to be resentful of his good fortune... If having Marcus as a tribute made Sejanus squirm, then good. Let him squirm. Lucy Gray was one thing belonging to Coriolanus that he would never, ever get. (BSS 74-75)

Such attitudes preclude even a possibility of forming a genuine friendship with Sejanus. Though he personally benefits from upholding that impression in public, he reverses course with Dr. Gaul—or at least tries to do so. Dr. Gaul asks him, "What's going on with your friend?" Coriolanus responds, "He's not really . . . that." Even Dr. Gaul doesn't believe him. He contemplates that his civility to Sejanus had obviously been misread. "Really, they were hardly more than acquaintances," the narrator tells us (BSS 224).

When Coriolanus learns why Sejanus had broken into the arena, he is beside himself with disgust. Mrs. Plinth had explained how it was a cultural custom in District 2 to dust breadcrumbs on the body of someone who dies. This is what Sejanus was doing with Marcus. In response, Coriolanus feels embarrassed for Mrs. Plinth. Then he thinks, "If you ever needed proof of the districts' backwardness, there you had it. Primitive people with their primitive customs. How much bread had they wasted with this nonsense?... He had a sinking feeling that his supposed friendship was going to come back to haunt him" (BSS 224). He was right, of course. Things would not turn out so well, at least for one of them.

Those Repelling Mockingjays

One of the more telling indicators of Coriolanus' need for control is found in his ongoing—and rather amusing—aversion to mockingjays. This is not so apparent in the film, where his disgust for the talkative birds is relegated to various nonverbal cues. Most dramatically, we see him shooting his rifle indiscriminately at the pesky creatures during the forest sequence. In the book we learn more about how his hatred for mockingjays develops, and for what reasons.

Upon arriving for the hanging of Arlo Chance, Coriolanus experiences his first dose of District 12's chaotic natural environment. "Thick trees, vines, and underbrush grew every which way. The disorder alone felt disturbing. And who knew what sort of creatures inhabited it? The medley of buzzing, humming, and rustling set him on edge. What a racket the birds here made!" (*BSS* 348). The birds likely include mockingjays. After Arlo is hung, his final words are, *"Run! Run, Lil! Ru—!"* which reverberate through the trees (*BSS* 350). The mockingjays seemingly engulf Coriolanus and attack him audibly from behind.

Eventually the birds transform Arlo's cry "into something almost melodic." Now practically horrified at what he was hearing, a fellow soldier grumbles, "Mockingjays... Stinking mutts" (*BSS* 351-2). Then he recalls talking to Lucy Gray prior to the interviews, when she had quipped, "The show's not over until the mockingjay sings." Of course, she was referring to the District 12 hangings such as this one—the Capitol's own spectacle of oppression. Now able to recognize the distinctive black bird with "dazzling white" patches under its wings, the narrator says, "Coriolanus felt sure he'd spotted his first mockingjay, and he disliked the thing on site" (*BSS* 352). To satiate his personal need to control his environment, Coriolanus considers that, when he becomes an officer, he could organize a hunting party to clear the woods of the pesky creatures. He then convinces himself that there is no need to wait. "Surely, no one liked the birds," he tells himself (*BSS* 353).

During his first Hob concert performed by the Covey—whose name refers to a flock of birds—he ends up enjoying some of their catchy numbers more than others. For some songs, "the five Covey seemed to turn in on themselves, swaying and building complicated harmonies with their voices." As discussed more in Chapter 4, Coriolanus was experiencing his first taste of traditional

Appalachian bluegrass music. No matter, we are told that "Coriolanus didn't care for it; the sound unsettled him. He sat through at least three songs of this kind before he realized it reminded him of the mockingjays" (BSS 365).

Then during a scientific outing with Dr. K., Coriolanus finds an opportunity to learn more about jabberjays and their recent mockingjay offspring. Dr. K. admits she is still learning about them, suggesting that if they manage to reproduce, "what's one more songbird?" (BSS 417). Though he eventually agrees they are probably harmless, he realizes that he didn't mind the jabberjays—"they seemed rather interesting from a military standpoint," he considers. But the mockingjays were simply repelling, for some reason he could not fathom. "He distrusted their spontaneous creation. Nature running amok. They should die out, and die out soon," he declares to himself.

In that scene Collins encourages us to make the connection with Coriolanus' abhorrence of chaos. While the jabberjays provide a metaphor for proper authoritarian control, the mockingjays are uncontrollable. They represent the very chaos he clamors to eradicate in his life. One might consider how, some six decades later, these chaotic songbirds return to haunt him once again. This time it is our favorite mockingjay personified—the heroine of District 12, Katniss Everdeen.

Cousin Tigris: An Alternative Voice

Like Coriolanus, his cousin Tigris lost both parents during the war. Both orphans were taken in by their determined grandmother, or "Grandma'am," as Tigris nicknamed her when she was little. The girl had felt that titles like Grandma and Nana were not regal enough for the Snow family matriarch. We originally met a much older Tigris in *Mockingjay*, when she decides to hide Katniss and her Star Squad in her used clothing shop. When interpreting her name, author Valerie

Estelle Frankel informs us that the historical Plutarch had described the Tigris River and Alexander the Great's campaign to conquer the surrounding Mesopotamian kingdoms (Frankel, "Katniss"). *Mesopotamia* means "land between the rivers—namely, the Tigris and Euphrates. Thus, the Tigris watershed ends up harboring Rome's enemies, much as our beloved character Tigris assists the rebellion by helping Katniss.

In a more convenient connotation, Tigris can refer to the animal itself. Frankel explains, "Tigers themselves symbolize swiftness and cunning. They camouflage and no one knows where they are until they pounce" (Frankel, "Katniss"). Likewise, Tigris gives Katniss' team various outfits for camouflage as they make their way into the city center. Sadly, her body becomes grossly deformed and disguised with tattoos that make her resemble her namesake.

Flashing back to the prequel, a younger and more optimistic Tigris clings to the belief that Coriolanus is redeemable and can become a better human being. As the older cousin, she plays the role of Mom by suggesting how he should behave or react in various situations. More to the point, she is the voice of empathy and kindness, countering the pessimistic Hobbesian viewpoints of Dr. Gaul. Her advice to Coriolanus begins when she instructs him to thank Grandma'am for one of her precious roses. At this point he was smarting from being pierced by a rose thorn. Mildly aggravated, he contemplates how the old woman was giving him opportunities to practice self-control (*BSS* 12). It is Tigris who reminds him of his manners and how to be grateful.

Tigris had already shifted into a motherly role by the youthful age of eight. With their cook having died of the flu, "It fell to eight-year-old Tigris to boil the beans to the thick stew, then the soup, then the watery broth, which was to sustain them throughout the war" (*BSS* 33). For her part, Grandma'am had not learned her way around a kitchen; she and the family had once relied heavily on servants. Later we find Tigris helping the teenage Coriolanus think through a strategy to meet Lucy Gray for the first time. "The cousins agreed that he needed to make a good first impression on the girl so that she would be willing to work with him. He should treat her not as a condemned prisoner, but as a guest" (*BSS* 37).

This leads into Tigris' now-famous line aimed at helping Coryo become more empathetic. In the book she tells him, "Imagine how terrified she must be, Coryo... How alone she must feel. If it was me, anything you could do to make me feel like you cared about me would go a long way. No, more than that. Like I was of value. Take her something, even a token, that lets her know you value her" (*BSS* 37-38). This leads Coriolanus to consider his grandmother's roses, and the rest is history. Of course, much of this scene is adapted for the film and becomes one of Tigris' (Hunter Schafer's) more memorable moments in *Ballad*.

More to the point, it is the persistence of voices like that of Tigris that attempt to counter Dr. Gaul's darker counseling. Tigris attempts to convey a sense of empathy, to have him think about what the other person might be feeling or dealing with. Later her cooking skills come in handy for this purpose as well, as she cooks some homemade food for Lucy Gray. She had made bread pudding, hot from the oven and drizzled with corn syrup. When Coryo tells her it "looks amazing" because it was one of his favorites, she says, "And there's plenty, so you can take a piece to Lucy Gray. She said she liked sweet things—and I doubt there are many left in her future!" (*BSS* 79). Not only does she become emotional over Lucy Gray's plight, but she is the one teaching Coriolanus how to consider his tribute's situation for himself.

The lessons continue to add up, though to little avail. As Coriolanus is fuming over Lucy Gray's ballad addressed to her former boyfriend, Tigris reminds him, "We all did things we're not proud of." She tells Coryo that Lucy Gray has probably been fending for herself since losing her parents. When he attempts to make light of Tigris' own past, she snaps back, "We all did [things we're not proud of]. Maybe you were too little to remember. Maybe you didn't know how bad it really was." He retorts that it's all he can remember, to which she replies, "Then be kind, Coryo... And try not to look down on people who had to choose between death and disgrace" (*BSS* 176). After mulling her arguments, he only becomes more concerned with what Tigris might have done in the past. He finally tells himself that he really does not want to know about Lucy Gray's own personal history.

The role of young Tigris in *Ballad* was awarded to the acclaimed up-and-coming actress, Hunter Schafer. Born in Trenton, New Jersey in 1998, Schafer had already become a model and actress at the time she secured the part of Tigris. Her debut came in the HBO teen drama series, *Euphoria* (2019-present), portraying a transgender high school student named Jules. *Time* Magazine recognized her in its *Next* list of 100 emerging leaders shaping our future. As of this writing Schafer was also in production of the Neon film, *Cuckoo*.

When crafting Tigris' character, director Francis Lawrence explained they were seeking a balance between the Tigris from *Mockingjay - Part 2* and her younger self. He elaborates, "One thing we have to do with Hunter is to keep the sweet youthfulness about her, while still doing something a little different and avant-garde. It's not over the top. We didn't want to lean into what Tigris becomes, but just provide a nod to it" (Dominick, "Here are").

To create her trademark look for *Ballad*, costume designer Trish Summerville teamed up with makeup artist Sherri Laurence and hair designer Nikki Gooley. Summerville says, "I'm a big fan of 1940s' silhouettes, so I leaned into that... We had a very contained color palette with the film, and I wanted Tigris' colors and shapes to be really exaggerated since she is the most fashionable person in the film" (Dominick, "Here are"). In a separate interview Summerville explains how her team treated Tigris' costume, knowing she would become *the* stylist for Panem:

Right. Could there be another Tigris? (i.e. Hunter Schafer) No. That was really a joy. She's so lovely, and we could have dressed her endlessly. Every single thing we put on... how can we work in another costume? With her costumes, I was inspired by Lilli Ann, a fashion designer really prominent in the 40s. We wanted to go with some of those silhouettes where there was the extreme peplum and a strong shoulder with a very narrow skirt. We were staying true to that 40s feel with also a 40s or 50s Balenciaga shoulder.

For her piece worn to The Hunger Games, I wanted to show a bit of fraying by sewing the seams on the outside. It looks like she's maintaining it. She's repurposing pieces because she is talented and is a designer in her own right. Tigris is able to keep the family looking presentable when they're really struggling inside. There is a bit of discoloration to her look. It's faded. So, we airbrushed all the edges and airbrushed a darker fuchsia tone along the seams. It was a very subtle process, and the team did such a beautiful, beautiful job. I tried to keep her in a happier tone because she is trying to remain hopeful, and she's always optimistic. But also, she is terrified of what's happening in the world and like you said, her clothing is her armor. It's how she can protect herself and then present something that's not really happening internally for her. Her costumes were really important. As a little teaser, we're working on a collaboration for wearable streetwear merchandise and jewelry that we're doing as a nod to the film. It'll also be nice to see what the fans think of that! (Williams)

Despite her tireless optimism and counseling of Coriolanus to be better, her despair by the end of Ballad is finally complete. She reveals her growing disapproval of her ambitious cousin, telling him tersely that he looks just like his father. As media and fans alike have pointed out, this is no compliment. She had tried to turn Coriolanus away from the hate that had driven his father, but to no avail. Having failed, she realizes this as Coriolanus prepares to move upwards under the capable guidance of one Dr. Volumnia Gaul.

Snow's Nemesis: Dean Casca Highbottom

Casca Highbottom shares his first name with his historical counterpart, Publius Servilius Casca Longus, one of Julius Caesar's assassins who struck the first blow. He was also a main character in Shakespeare's play, *Julius Caesar*, which also served as the inspiration for numerous characters in Collins' original series. Like the historical Casca, this one is devoted to bringing down the Snow family, though he is rather less successful.

His last name is a reference to the disease of alcoholism. A high-bottom alcoholic is defined as a higher functioning alcoholic, someone who manages to maintain a normal daily life while still challenged with drinking (Leipholtz). They are apt to be in a deeper state of denial, dedicated to normalizing their excessive drinking habit while maintaining a job or career, family, and home life. They tend to convince themselves that their drinking habit is not a concern to worry about.

This attitude is represented handily by Dean Highbottom. He tells stories of getting drunk with Coriolanus' father, Crassus, during their college days. After the first annual Hunger Games that he helped invent, Highbottom became further addicted to *morphling*, the same pain-killing drug the Capitol uses in the original series. This is, of course, Collins' adaptation of the real painkiller, morphine.

The backstory to why Dean Highbottom despises Coriolanus is told in successive pieces throughout the book. Casca had attended the university with Crassus. They became best friends, often hanging out at Pluribus Bell's nightclub. Neither Pluribus nor the nightclub are featured in the film, leaving out this part of the story. Casca also studied under Dr. Gaul, though he loathed her and nearly failed her class. Dr. Gaul's final assignment was to create a punishment for their enemies so extreme that they would never be able to forget their wrongdoing. Crassus and Casca were paired up for the project.

As Dean Highbottom explains to Coriolanus in the Epilogue, "It was like a puzzle, which I excel at, and like all good creations, absurdly simple at its core. The Hunger Games. The evilest impulse, cleverly packaged into a sporting event. An entertainment. I was drunk and your father got me drunker still, playing on my vanity as I fleshed the thing out, assuring me it was just a private joke." Awaking the next morning, Casca was horrified at what he had created, intending to destroy his notes. It was too late, however, as Crassus had already given it to Dr. Gaul without his permission. The Dean continues, "He wanted the grade, you see. I never forgave him" (BSS 514). And thus we finally learn why the Dean felt so much animosity toward the Snow family, and—not just incidentally—how the Hunger Games actually began.

Adding insult to injury, Dr. Gaul pulled out Casca's proposal after the war and introduced him to Panem as the architect of the Hunger Games. It was that night when he tried morphling for the first time, leading to a dependency. Although he presumed the Games would die out, the opposite occurred. He says, "Dr. Gaul took it and ran, and she has dragged me along with it for the last ten years." Though some minor details and dialogue are altered for the film, much of this story remains intact at the end of *Ballad*.

In the end the Dean falls victim to poisoning at the hands of Coriolanus, thereby foretelling his signature method of murder. Shakespeare would be proud.

Playing the role of Casca Highbottom in *Ballad* is one of the production's veteran actors, Peter Dinklage. He is best known for his acclaimed role as Trion Lannister in the HBO hit series, *Game of Thrones* (2011-2019). For that role Dinklage won the Primetime Emmy Award for Outstanding Supporting Actor in a Drama Series a record four times.

Standing four feet, five inches tall, Dinklage has a common form of dwarfism known as achondroplasia. His celebrity status has allowed him to raise social awareness about the condition. He initially had a difficult time finding acting work that did not involve stereotypical roles of elves and leprechauns. While first studying acting at Bennington College, he had performed in various amateur stage productions. He made his first film debut in the black comedy film, *Living in Oblivion* (1995) before starring in his first breakthrough role in the 2003 comedy-drama, *The Station Agent* (2003).

For his role in *Ballad*, Francis Lawrence knew Dinklage would be perfect as Dean Highbottom. Consequently, no audition was necessary. Speaking about his character, Dinklage says, "Highbottom—he's a brilliant man, but he's realized that he's made a terrible mistake. It's sort of like he didn't think through the consequences of it. He didn't fully understand or think about the consequences of his creation" ("Cast").

All told, Casca Highbottom is the epitome of a tragic literary figure and, all told, he was a pretty decent fellow. Much like Haymitch Abernathy before him (or after him, as the case may be), his substance abuse was a way to numb the pain from extreme injustices and trauma in his life, over which he had little control. For this reason—again like Haymitch—Casca proves to be one of the saga's more stigmatized and misunderstood characters.

Close-Ups of Coriolanus (and Friends)

If Coriolanus sometimes appears in *Ballad* to be right up against the camera lens, this is no illusion. In some scenes Tom Blyth is literally inches from the camera. One distinct aspect of *Ballad's* cinematography as compared to earlier films was the heavy reliance on newer, wide lenses for many of the closeup scenes. If hand-held, shaky action shots defined the first Hunger Games film as directed by Gary Ross, the prequel film takes its cinematography in a whole new direction. The updated technology of these modern camera lenses allowed director Francis Lawrence to apply more of his own creative license. In describing his favored approach to filming, Lawrence explains, "What I always like to do is try to be as intimate with the characters as possible. I like using wider lenses because you can be up closer to people, and you don't feel too distanced from everybody. But at the same time when you use a wider lens you've still got a sense of geography and a sense of space" ("Director").

His own visual style has grown in tandem with his go-to cinematographer Jo Willems, with whom he has produced more than 100 music videos, numerous TV and film projects, and of course the previous three Hunger Games films. Their shared affinity for wide-angle lenses has been enabled in part by the continued advances in camera technologies. He explains further:

> We've been growing our visual style together a little bit. We've been using larger format digital cameras with larger format sensors, which have a different lens package. We were using these really wide lenses, but they're rectilinear, so you can shoot up close to people and not distort like normal fisheyes would. They're just built differently now. Plus, you have the large format sensor, and that really changes the way things look and feel. In that scene in the forest, the camera was probably an inch

and a half or two inches away from Tom's face. And so, the depth of field is very shallow, but the clarity is perfect. So, it's all tack sharp, and if you choose the right time of day with the light in the right spot and you prep it just right, all the things line up. (Davids)

• CHAPTER 12 •

Sejanus Plinth: Up on a Pedestal

For those who thrive on complex character development, it would be unwise to look past Sejanus Plinth. In certain ways he may present more of a mystery than Coriolanus and Lucy Gray combined. Is he likeable, honorable, wise, and altruistic, or is he immature, spoiled, naive, and thoughtless? Readers of Sejanus can, and do, argue justifiably for one extreme or the other. Given the complexity that is the human mind, the answer most likely lies somewhere in the murky middle.

Before Coriolanus confronts any of Sejanus' personality traits, however, he is already plenty resentful of him and his family. Sejanus' apparent friendship with Coriolanus is decidedly one-sided, as discussed in Chapter 11. Still, this does not prevent Coriolanus from kissing up to the Plinths and benefitting from their genuine kindness and deep pockets. Having sided with the Capitol during the war, the Plinths from District 2 were awarded rare Capitol citizenship, earning them instant privileges that the Capitol's "old money" families had spent generations accumulating. The Plinths eventually moved to the Capitol when Sejanus was eight.

SEJANUS PLINTH

We further learn that upon leaving District 2, family and friends cut them off in disgust for abandoning their roots. And there were no new friends to be made in the Capitol, either, thereby rendering the family effectively isolated. Sejanus' father, Strabo, "still thinks it was the right thing to do," Ma Plinth says, adding, "No kind of future in Two. His way of protecting us. His way of keeping Sejanus from the Games" (*BSS* 226). Upon learning this, Coriolanus picks up on the fitting irony. Sejanus had just broken into the arena to pay respects to Marcus before attempting to martyr himself.

While discussing options to extract Sejanus from the arena, Coriolanus suggests that Ma Plinth should be the one to do the honors. But she rejects the idea, saying, "I don't know if I can... Him so upset and all. I can try, but he'll have to think it's the right thing to do." This is a critical line to best understand Sejanus as a person. Coriolanus considers Ma's point as well. He then realizes that "doing the right thing had always defined Sejanus' actions, his determination to do the right thing." This never impressed Coriolanus, however, as he thinks, "Frankly, [Sejanus] could be insufferable with those superior little comments of his" (BSS 227). Rather than commending his so-called friend for his decency toward others, Coriolanus only looks down on him with condescending disdain.

On the flip side, Sejanus does not consider potential consequences to his decisions. His influential father, Strabo, had bailed him out of precarious situations and poor decisions since he was a child. Only after considering his actions does Sejanus realize how he has affected others. One can certainly sympathize with Coriolanus in this respect, who tires of Sejanus' continuous need to apologize. For instance, after discussing Sejanus' idea for trading their tributes (not in the film), Sejanus later states, "I shouldn't have asked. I never even considered I might be making things difficult for you" (*BSS* 76). In another scene, we find Sejanus and Coriolanus panting outside the arena after their dramatic escape. At which point, Sejanus says, "I'm so sorry, Coryo... I'm so sorry" (*BSS* 240). Of course, this pattern of behavior and thoughtlessness continues well into District 12. Although one can understand this frustration, it is Coriolanus who is later faced with his own moral decision on how best to handle Sejanus' rebellious escapades.

Sejanus in Rome

The complicated friendship between these two teenage boys—lest we forget they are precisely that—was apparently written by Suzanne Collins as yet another parallel to Roman history. As Valerie Estelle Frankel explains, "Lucius Aelius Sejanus was historically from the lower part of Rome's upper class, yet he became the confidante and best friend of Emperor Tiberius. Lucius thus gained power through the emperor, just as our Sejanus does through Snow. Lucius went on to achieve numerous social reforms while purging many people from the opposing party. As an idealist, this too is Sejanus' goal, though he never enjoys the chance to make a meaningful difference" (Frankel, "Songbirds"). Also like his Roman counterpart, Sejanus was executed for treason ("Sejanus").

The Plinth family name also suggests Roman connotations. A *plinth* is defined as a pedestal that supports meaningful cultural objects such as statues or columns, dating back to ancient Classical times. A plinth could be interpreted as a metaphor for Strabo Plinth's social climbing and personal ambition (Frankel, "Songbirds"). An alternative association views Strabo's munitions manufacturing as having supported the Capitol during the First Rebellion ("Sejanus"). Yet a third option is to think of Sejanus being placed on a veritable pedestal by his parents, especially Strabo who bails him out of challenging situations. The name Strabo is symbolic in its own right. The Roman Strabo was a wealthy philosopher who made his mark while the Empire was just beginning. He formed an alliance with the

Roman leadership and was suitably rewarded for doing so (Frankel, "Songbirds").

Sejanus and John Locke

We gain more insights into Sejanus' character through his belief system. In her novel's epigraph, Collins provides a quote from Enlightenment thinker John Locke (1632-1704): *"The state of nature has a law of nature to govern it, which obliges every one: and reason, which is that law, teaches all mankind, who will but consult it, that being all equal and independent, no one ought to harm another in his life, health, liberty, or possessions..." (Second Treatise of Government*, 1689). As Locke's quote attests, the natural condition of humans is characterized by freedom and equality. To preserve one's liberty, health, and property is a natural-born right that everyone enjoys.

However, Locke further recognized that natural law was insufficient to protect people's lives and property. A set of common laws is also necessary, created through a voluntary "social contract" in which the people willingly give up some power to a central government. Should the government not fulfill its obligation, the people have a natural right to form a new one. Consequently, the public holds the right to resist authority. No less than America's Founding Fathers took Locke's philosophies to heart as they proceeded with their own populous rebellion. Thomas Jefferson and his peers embraced Locke's fundamental ideas and inscribed them into the Declaration of Independence.

During the 17th and 18th centuries it was common for philosophers to write about natural rights theory and the notion of the *social contract*. Natural rights are those that humans are said to enjoy before a centralized government comes into being. For instance, we all have the right to struggle for our own survival, just like other animals. This is Locke's fundamental view as well. To explain the importance of government, Locke proposes that living conditions in the state of nature are unsatisfactory. In turn, people agree to transfer some of their natural-born rights to a central government to protect people's lives, liberty, and property ("John"). This essentially describes the notion of *social contract theory*.

Although government is necessary to uphold the people's will, Locke spends much of his writing in opposition to authoritarianism. Rather, sovereignty resides in the people. He was radical for his time in further calling for the separation of Church and State in his *Letter Concerning Toleration*. Locke preferred that each of us use our own reasoning to search for truth rather than simply accepting the opinions of so-called authorities ("John").

With his unwavering concern for human rights, Sejanus becomes the unwitting personification of John Locke and his worldview. We first witness this parallel when an emotional Sejanus explains why he had suggested trading tributes—that is, Marcus for Lucy Gray. He erupts, "It's just this whole Hunger Games thing is making me crazy! I mean, what are we doing? Putting kids in an arena to kill each other? It feels wrong on so many levels. Animals protect their young, right? And so do we. We try to protect children! It's built into us as human beings. Who really wants to do this? It's unnatural!" (*BSS* 76).

Later he courageously lashes out at Dr. Gaul, arguing, "You've no right to starve people, to punish them for no reason. No right to take away their life and freedom. Those are things everyone is born with, and they're not yours for the taking. Winning a war doesn't give you that right. Having more weapons doesn't give you that right. Being from the Capitol doesn't give you that right. Nothing does" (*BSS* 160). The film's Sejanus includes a variation on this powerful statement. He adds that Panem's government exists to protect everyone—district and Capitol citizen alike. Either way, Sejanus' notion of inalienable rights could have easily been voiced by John Locke himself.

Portraying Sejanus Plinth

The actor Josh Andrés Rivera was awarded the role of *Ballad's* Sejanus. Aside from his own success with the traditional audition process, he helped convince Rachel Zegler to finally accept the role of Lucy Gray Baird. It was only after being cast as Sejanus that film producers learned he was Zegler's boyfriend (see Chapter 10). In another connection, Rivera had played the part of Chino in Spielberg's Oscar-winning adaptation of *West Side Story*, opposite Zegler herself. Before that he was a series lead in the HBO Max pilot, *Vegas High*. Perhaps more notably, Rivera performed in *Hamilton* with the hit musical's original company on its first national tour. When asked to describe Sejanus as a character, Rivera offers,

> He's a man of heart, wears his heart on his sleeve. He's got really, really strong convictions. He's originally district and was able to come to the Capitol because his dad made a lot of money and became rich enough to move... And because of that there's a fair amount of resentment that he has for his environment, and I think because of that he's able to [recognize] that Coriolanus is not the polished, wealthy sort of paragon that he tries to pretend to be, and there's kind of a relationship that gets built from that, and he just really believes in the good of humanity. ("What Fans")

Unfortunately for Sejanus and for everyone he tried to defend, the aspiring medic never had a chance to help improve society. He dies in a Shakespearean-style tragedy, in which he ends up becoming too much of a threat to Coriolanus' bright future. Thinking rationally about having sent his apparent friend to the gallows, Coriolanus begins to justify his decision before moving on with his life:

Without him, Sejanus would have died in the arena, prey to the pack of tributes who had tried to kill them as they fled. Technically, Coriolanus had given him a few more weeks of life and a second chance, an opportunity to mend his ways. But he hadn't. Couldn't. Didn't care to. He was what he was. Maybe the wilderness would have been best for him. Poor Sejanus. Poor sensitive, foolish, dead Sejanus (*BSS* 472).

• CHAPTER 13 •

Dr. Volumnia Gaul

Described as a "small, stooped old woman with frizzy gray hair," Dr. Volumnia Gaul is introduced in the book much later than the film. Following Coriolanus' first escapade at the zoo, he is escorted back to the Academy and taken directly to the high biology lab. Upon entry, Coriolanus finds Dr. Gaul fussing with a caged rabbit, his first experience with one of her genetic mutations. In this case her otherwise cuddly creature has a jaw with the strength of a pit bull. Of course, this is a predecessor to the future, more advanced mutts encountered during Katniss' Games. The rabbit further leads to one of Dr. Gaul's favorite tag lines, "Hippity, hoppity!" which did not make it into the screenplay (*BSS* 57).

At this point readers learn that Gaul is the Head Gamemaker and "mastermind" of the Capitol's experimental weapons division. Coriolanus also recalls that she teaches a class at the University, though it was rare for her to show up like this at the Academy. He had also been unnerved by the creepy woman since childhood.

This is when Dr. Gaul reveals her quirky rhyming habit, of which only two instances are written into the film. She says to Coriolanus, "Hippity, hoppity, how was the zoo? You fell in a cage and your tribute did, too!" (*BSS* 58). Now smiling, he looks over to Dean Highbottom for guidance on how to react. Getting nothing, Coriolanus stumbles through an extension of the rhyme, saying "We did. We fell in a cage," to which she encourages him on. He responds, "And ... we ... landed onstage?" Dr. Gaul excitedly agrees and says, "You're good at games. Maybe one day you'll be a Gamemaker" (*BSS* 58-59). This latter exchange was adapted for the film when Dr. Gaul visits the Academy classroom. Their dialogue may confuse viewers at first, as there is no prior context as to why he decides to complete her thought. Beyond this, she attempts only one additional rhyme in *Ballad*, when Coriolanus returns in shock from saving Sejanus. In this case he refuses to play along.

Aside from reciting children's rhymes, we ultimately learn that Dr. Gaul is quietly grooming Coriolanus for his own glorious future in Panem. She instills within his suggestive brain a dark, pessimistic Hobbesian worldview. Coriolanus may indeed be the personification of Enlightenment thinker Thomas Hobbes, as discussed in Chapter 11. But it is Dr. Gaul who serves as Coriolanus' own personal mentor, coaching him on the supposed brutal nature of human beings. This is made most apparent when Coriolanus and Dr. Gaul discuss his killing of Bobbin in the arena. Using the incident as a lesson, she explains in the book, "What happened in the arena? That's humanity undressed. The tributes. And you, too. How quickly civilization disappears. All your fine manners, education, family background, everything you pride yourself on, stripped away in the blink of an eye, revealing everything you actually are. A boy with a club who beats another boy to death. That's mankind in its natural state" (*BSS* 243).

This dialogue is largely adapted for the film. Later she connects her philosophy with governance. She asks, "Who are human beings? Because who we are determines the type of governing we need" (*BSS* 243). Like Thomas Hobbes before her, Dr. Gaul eventually teaches Coriolanus that only the control provided by an authoritarian government can adequately maintain the peace. Otherwise, chaos reigns, reflecting—as she argues—humanity undressed.

Still unconvinced, the book's Coriolanus laughs and asks, "Are we really as bad as all that?" Following more dialogue, he later snaps, "I think I wouldn't have beaten anyone to death if you hadn't stuck me in that arena!" This logic is correct. At this point his thinking leans more toward that of Lucy Gray, who believes people should simply be left alone in their free, natural state to make their own decisions. What Dr. Gaul does not care to understand is that it is the circumstances people are forced to confront that make them do terrible things, not necessarily human nature in itself. This is the fundamental flaw in Dr. Gaul's thinking.

We learn later that she began her career as a medical doctor, in obstetrics. After telling him this, Coriolanus thinks somewhat humorously, *"How awful... To have you be the first person in the world a baby sees."* She then explains, "Wasn't really for me... Parents always want reassurances you can't give. About the futures their children face. How could I possibly know what they'd encounter?" (BSS 241-242).

It turns out in the end that many of Coriolanus' adventures throughout the prequel were a series of tests and lessons arranged by Dr. Gaul. After debriefing his experiences in District 12, she surprises him by saying, "It seems you've learned a lot on your summer vacation, Mr. Snow." Upon expressing his confusion, she adds, "Well, what were you going to do here? Laze around the Capitol, combing out your curls? I thought a summer with the Peacekeepers would be far more educational" (BSS 510). At which point, she provides him with an honorable discharge, along with the news that he will study under her at the University. And thus, Snow finally does land on top, and the future president is off and running.

DR. VOLUMNIA GAUL

Liar, Liar, Pants on...

Credit for Coriolanus' aversion to lying—arguably not a bad trait—likewise goes to Dr. Gaul. Near the beginning of *Catching Fire*, President Snow visits Katniss' home and says, "I think we'll make this whole situation a lot simpler by agreeing not to lie to each other... What do you think?" (*CF* 19). Katniss agrees. Later in *Mockingjay* this uneasy pact resurfaces while he is held prisoner in his own mansion. He categorically denies having bombed the children with the parachutes, and readers are compelled to believe him. "We both know that I'm not above killing children," he tells her, "but I'm not wasteful." He further states that he was about to issue a full surrender before the parachutes fell (*MJ* 356). This is critical news for Katniss, all but convinced he is telling the truth. Collins had foreshadowed this scene through President Snow's earlier visit to Katniss' home. We are thus left with the inconvenient conclusion that President Coin and the rebels are responsible for this final atrocity.

It turns out that it was Dr. Gaul who first taught Coriolanus to never lie. Following the snake attack on Clemensia, she asks in the book if Coriolanus wrote the proposal alone. He affirms that he did, thinking, "There was no point in lying. Lying had probably killed Clemensia. Obviously he was dealing with a lunatic who should be handled with extreme care." Dr. Gaul shoots back, "Good. The truth, finally. I've no use for liars. What are lies but attempts to conceal some sort of weakness? If I see that side of you again, I'll cut you off. If Dean Highbottom punishes you for it, I won't stand in his way. Are we clear?" (*BSS* 114). This is likely Collins' way to reveal the source of Coriolanus' proclivity for truth-telling. It further strengthens Snow's claim that he did not unleash the parachute bombs at the end of *Mockingjay*.

Volumnia Gaul and Shakespeare

Dr. Gaul's view of humanity further sheds light on the meaning behind her name. In Shakespeare's play, *Coriolanus*—for whom the future President Snow is named—Volumnia is his mother. During the play, Coriolanus is easily swayed by his "bloodthirsty military stage mom," who encourages him to succeed in the military and to later pursue a political position. While delighting in her son's exploits in battle, she is also a practical politician who ultimately dissuades her vengeful son to not attack Rome itself (Miller).

Likewise, Dr. Gaul directs her own protégé to join the Peacekeepers for "summer vacation" and will no doubt continue to shape his aspirations at the University. As for her last name, Gaul refers to a historical area of western Europe—much of modern-day France—that was conquered by Rome's Julius Caesar as the empire was expanding. Like Panem's districts, the Gauls were characterized as savages, as their Gallic armies had invaded and sacked Roman cities in the past. A similar tit-for-tat, vengeful relationship is paralleled with the tensions between the Capitol and the districts—one which Dr. Gaul only provokes further.

To invoke another play on words, she had a lot of *Gaul*, but not all of it. District 12 would continue to evade the Capitol's oversight, eventually leading to the efforts of one Katniss Everdeen to take full advantage of that malfunctioning district fence.

Portraying Dr. Gaul

The process of casting Volumnia Gaul for *Ballad* had a rather unconventional beginning. Director Francis Lawrence happened to see a meme posted on Instagram by the legendary actress, Viola Davis. He recalls, "It was a piece of fan art, and somebody had photoshopped, I think, an image of her standing by a window. It may be a still from *The Help*, but she had this sort of sinister little smile, and they had made a fake horror poster as if she was the villain in this. I was like, you know what, she may be really good for this." Continuing, he adds, "She has this gravitas, but she could be playful and quirky and get all of that. It'd be very different for her. I don't think we've seen her do this kind of thing a lot... We wanted to create a very different kind of character in terms of powerful women in these stories." In contrast with the District 13 president Alma Coin from *Mockingjay*, who was portrayed as a leader corrupted by power, Lawrence says Gaul is a "very strong believer in a specific philosophy and is grooming Snow in that direction" (Wang, "Director").

When asked whether Viola Davis was his first choice for the role, Lawrence recalled,

> Yeah, Viola was definitely my first choice. She and I have a little bit of a relationship because we've been developing a project together. I wanted her to do this. I called her. She obviously knew of the Hunger Games but wasn't too educated in it. So, we had a long conversation about the books, the movies, the cast that's involved and why they're involved, the themes. Then into her character, and her character is tied to the themes of this book. And I had some references to talk about. But I also pitched her. I thought she'd think it was really fun to do something wildly different from what she's done before. (Stedman)

Davis was subsequently invited to play the role without an initial audition. And although she accepted with little added encouragement, she admits to an ulterior motive. She explains, "I'm just going to say it. I wanted to impress my 13-year-old daughter" ("The Ballad"). The role provided an opportunity to step out of her comfort zone, as she typically takes on roles of loving, motherly characters.

Davis thus found herself pulled into the Hunger Games realm in the midst of a celebrated and productive acting career. Having graduated from the Julliard School in 1993, she is one of the few performers to have been recognized with all four major awards—an Emmy, Grammy, an Oscar, and a Tony, known colloquially as an EGOT. Moreover, she is the sole Black actress to achieve the "Triple Crown" of acting (an Oscar, Emmy, and a Tony), along with five Screen Actors Guild (SAG) Awards. Added to that, in both 2012 and 2017 *Time* named her one of the world's top 100 most influential people. In 2020 she was ranked in the *New York Times* as ninth on its list of greatest actors of the 20th century. In the time-honored Hollywood tradition that celebrates such accomplishments, Davis was presented with the 2,597th star on the Hollywood Walk of Fame in 2017 by her co-star and friend, Meryl Streep.

Achieving such success by her late 50s had never been a sure thing. She had been born on her grandmother's farm in 1965 on the Singleton Plantation in St. Matthews, South Carolina. The second of six children, her parents moved with Viola and two older siblings to Rhode Island, leaving her other siblings with grandparents. Her mother found various work as a maid, factory worker, and homemaker, though she was also a staunch participant of the Civil Rights Movement. When Viola was only two, she was taken to jail with her mother, who had been arrested during a civil rights protest. She also recalls having grown up in a continuous state of poverty and dysfunction, living in apartments that were rat-infested and condemned.

More recently Davis has collaborated with the *Hunger Is* campaign, devoted to eradicating childhood hunger across America. Speaking about her work, Davis emphasizes that one in five children in the United States goes to bed hungry, and that she was one of those kids. She recalls having done everything imaginable to secure enough food on a day-to-day basis, including stealing from local stores and rummaging through garbage cans ("Viola").

DR. VOLUMNIA GAUL

In preparing Davis for her antagonistic role in *Ballad*, Lawrence explains that he partially based her character on the whimsical candy maker, Willy Wanka. He says of Wanka from the 1971 film, "There was this wild, kind of quirky creativity and joy in creativity that character had, but with this kind of sinister underpinning. I have to admit, I was a bit nervous to tell [Viola] that reference. But she got it immediately, luckily" (VanHoose). He further explains his view on whether Dr. Gaul is a villain, saying that her character "may appear to be sort of the villain in this, but she actually really believes in these things and thinks it's the right thing to do."

Gaul's Wardrobe and Makeup

The near-herculean efforts with Davis' costuming and makeup were second to none. One of her character's most striking features was actually her idea—namely, her different-colored eyes. As the film's makeup artist, Sherri Laurence explains, Davis believed her irises should be different hues. With all the close-up shots of Dr. Gaul's menacing gazes, contrasting eye colors might suggest one too many lab experiments gone wrong (Moore). The makeup team landed on a "hazy," dark brown color for one eye, with the other a "piercing blue." Davis wore specially designed contacts to portray the different colors, giving an aged look to the brown eye and an icy blue appearance for the other. The makeup and prosthetics teams also worked to age her appearance through distinct facial scars. Similarly, Davis' weathered skin was crafted to suggest a life of scarring and disfigurements sustained from dangerous lab experiments.

A comparable backstory is provided by costume designer Trish Summerville, who explains, "Her hands are destroyed from all the experiments she works on. I always wanted to have her hands covered in every scene." This explains her blood-red latex gloves that become a quintessential addition to her overall costume (Moore).

Keeping with the theme of blood, Gaul's lab coat was designed from duchess silk which was then washed to "get this kind of veining through it," Summerville explains, adding that it was then dyed in red. "I like using red in that stark, cold environment—it empowers the presence of Dr. Gaul" (Dominick, "Here are"). The result is the appearance of blood-red veins on the lab coat, with blood having continuously washed down from the top before fading near the bottom. As a metaphor, the coat can be interpreted as Gaul's bloodthirsty influences washing over the white (Coriolanus) Snow beneath her.

And what about that hair? Hair designer Nikki Gooley looked to the 1940s for inspiration and eventually landed on a "beautiful silver-gray afro" that "blended with the eccentricity of the character and her colorfulness." Gooley adds, "Her character's very big and strong, so it made sense to have a big wiry kind of hair. And it also suited Viola as well, I think" (VanHoose).

In an interview for *The Art of Costume*, Summerville was asked to elaborate on the creation of her outfits for the film. She says,

> Yeah! I knew [Dr. Gaul] was someone that I could make a bit more progressive because of her exposure to the world and being a scientist. There is a cultivation of progression in her costume and character. For her character, the location was very important. Set decoration brought all of this amazing shelving, creatures, columns, and light! However, I wanted to stick with that red color we talked about in the [Academy] uniforms. The color was intimidating! There is a scene where she is sewing up [Coriolanus'] shoulder with those red latex gloves. I loved how that would look. Francis kept making references to her as a Gene Wilder in *Willy Wonka & the Chocolate Factory* type! I leaned into that.

I also leaned into this idea of a mad scientist with a bit of Dr. Frankenstein. There's that serious level as well, but she's also quite playful. Viola Davis was just really brilliant to dress because she does let you do anything. She just starts transforming into this character. She was just a joy to work with and looked phenomenal. She had just come off of doing *The Woman King*. Her artists in makeup and hair were phenomenal. I really love her character and how much presence she commands. Everyone is afraid of her. (Williams)

Summerville adds that she wanted the costumes for Davis to stand out from those of other characters through the use of multiple colors. Perhaps makeup artist Sherri Laurence summed up Dr. Gaul's appearance best. She says, "Between the hair, the costume, that eye, it really just took her to a scary place. Then you throw in her acting—I mean, come on. You could have heard a pin drop when she would walk [on set]" (VanHoose). In an interview for *The Tonight Show* with Jimmy Fallon (November 14 2023), Davis mentioned that four hours were necessary to fully apply her costume and makeup. She noted that her fake nose was particularly challenging to peel off.

Who Bombed the Arena?

The screenplay for *Ballad* confirms that district rebels were behind the arena bombing. We are even told that a rebel group took responsibility for the incident. This narrative continues to shape the film's storyline, as an enraged Dr. Gaul promises swift revenge toward the districts. To send a message that nobody should mess with the Capitol—or her Games—she sends in her terrarium of rainbow snakes to snuff out all remaining tributes, including Lucy Gray. Only a unified student protest led by Tigris begins to alter her thinking, followed by some wise words from Coriolanus. Of course, she finally relents and allows Lucy Gray to escape as the victor of the 10th Games.

This alternative plot comes as a substantial surprise to readers of the prequel. Many have expressed puzzlement as to why screenwriters and producers took this approach. Readers cite multiple reasons for their confusion. First, the book's Dr. Gaul does not try to prevent Lucy Gray from winning, nor from escaping the arena at the end. Instead, the snake sequence occurs in the midst of the Games. As Lucy Gray wraps up "The Old Therebefore," multiple tributes remain alive, and the fighting continues apace.

Moreover, Collins' narrative does nothing to clarify just who bombed the arena. Even while debris is still raining down from the explosions, Coriolanus keenly realizes there had been no hovercraft to drop the bombs. He thus concludes the bombs must have been planted in advance. He further detects smoke, meaning the bombs were incendiary. In a darkly humorous, if telling line, the narrator says, "He had a vague thought that this would not be conducive to [Lucy Gray's] singing" (*BSS* 140). While gaining his composure with Lucy Gray—after she saves him—he further notices the pattern in which the bombs had been planted. They were placed in intervals around the arena, with the "mother lode" exploding at the entrance.

Readers are then presented with some rather ambiguous dialogue: "What had happened—at least what the Capitol News claimed had happened—frightened citizens with both its immediate fallout and its ramifications for the future. They didn't know who set the bombs—rebels, yes, but from where?" (*BSS* 143). The narrator then speculates that it could have been any of the twelve districts, or a ragtag bunch escaped from District 13, or even a leftover cell in the Capitol. The bottom line is that nobody knows. The bombs could have been placed six days or six months beforehand since the arena is always locked and ignored. Thus, the "timeline for the crime was baffling" (*BSS* 142). Two tributes from District 6 were killed, which "caused little concern," but the Ring twins had perished, and three

DR. VOLUMNIA GAUL

mentors were hospitalized, including Coriolanus (*BSS* 143-4). One later succumbs to his injuries.

Back at home, Tigris and Coriolanus argue with Grandma'am over the incident. At this point Suzanne Collins deploys the older woman as a foil, allowing her grandchildren to provide alternative viewpoints. Grandma'am says, "I suppose [the districts] see the arena as a symbol." She further presumes the districts saw the bombing on television and are no doubt celebrating over it. But then Tigris pushes back, retorting, "But they say hardly anyone in the districts saw it, Grandma'am... The people there don't like to watch the Hunger Games coverage" (*BSS* 145). This exchange seems to imply that the district rebel theory does not hold water.

Later still, Dr. Gaul is being interviewed by Lucky Flickerman during the Games. He asks, "[W]here are the tributes this year? Usually they're easier to spot." To this Dr. Gaul responds, "Perhaps you've forgotten about the recent bombing... In previous years, the areas open to the tributes were largely restricted to the field and the stands, but last week's attack opened up any number of cracks and crevices, providing easy access to the labyrinth of tunnels inside the walls of the arena. It's a whole new Games, first finding another tribute, and then ferreting them out of some very dark corners." Lucky responds, "So we might have seen the last of some tributes?" To which Dr. Gaul responds, "Don't worry. When they get hungry, they'll start poking their heads out... That's another game changer. With the audience providing food, the Games could last indefinitely" (*BSS* 213).

Is this the sound of someone who is devastated because her precious arena has been blown apart by a rebel faction? Added to that, it seems very strange indeed that no rebel group ever takes responsibility. In fact, readers learn absolutely nothing more about it, leaving the incident's cause as a loose end.

An alternative theory posits that Dr. Gaul herself was solely responsible for the bombing. As head of the war department, she could easily muster the labor and technologies to stage a grand explosion. She also knew precisely when to set off the bombs to suit her personal interests. Would a rebel faction have known about the first annual arena walkthrough far enough in advance? It is likely no coincidence that Panem's leadership was seriously considering the cancellation of the Games. Dr. Gaul and her counterparts were desperate to make the Games more appealing for Capitol audiences. What better way to do so by providing a more interesting and engaging arena landscape? Overall, Dr. Gaul seemed quite pleased with the results. We further know she is not beyond sacrificing tributes—and perhaps even mentors—to promote her cause. In the end, she uses the event to promote her Hobbesian worldview of "humanity undressed," while instantly improving the spectacle of the Games. From her perspective, what was there to lose?

• CHAPTER 14 •

Lucretius "Lucky" Flickerman

Beyond the characters of Coriolanus and Tigris, Suzanne Collins provides clues in her prequel to the ancestors of a handful of trilogy favorites. We are thus introduced to Hilarious Heavensbee and Heavensbee Hall, Livia Cardew, Arachne Crane, and—of course—Lucretius "Lucky" Flickerman. It is not unreasonable to presume that Lucky is the father of Caesar Flickerman, the effective overlord of the airwaves during Katniss' time. This notion is supported by the film, when Lucky calls a restaurant to make reservations for two people and a highchair which, viewers have all but concluded, must be little Caesar's.

Known in the Capitol as the "clownish, Capitol TV weatherman," Lucky was first tapped to run the tribute interviews and was subsequently named as host of the 10th Games (*BSS* 185). We do not meet Lucky in the book until Chapter 11, for the kickoff of *A Night of Interviews*. This is because news reporter Lepidus Malmsey is covering the Capitol Zoo action, not Lucky as we see in the film. We first read about Lucky as he welcomes the audience to a "brand-new Hunger Games for a brand-new decade" (*BSS* 167). For the first time, he explains, every Capitol citizen could now participate by sponsoring the tribute of their choice. This is described as "a new wrinkle" by the narrator, likely a subtle nod to Plutarch Heavensbee's own "wrinkle" in *Mockingjay*. Lucky further explains that citizens can now send in money to feed a tribute, or to place a bet on one.

Other than reading the cue cards, Lucky discovers he has too much downtime during these televised events. He thus provides impromptu entertainment with various magic tricks and, later, with his parrot, Jubilee. The responsibility of hosting proves to be a challenge; he is largely out of his comfort zone as Capitol weatherman. The narrator explains, "Having a full-time host for the Games was new territory, and he struggled to create the role" (*BSS* 211). Though he stumbles through the process with only his wits and magic tricks, Dr. Gaul eventually decides his skills are worth keeping in the future. She tells Coriolanus, "Not a total loss. I think we'll bring Flickerman back next year" (*BSS* 509). This is how Lucky's future role is secured, along with that of his heir.

The Naming of an Amoral Character

That Lucky is not the most moralistic or empathetic individual is a gross understatement. In fact, such sentiments are all but nonexistent within his character. With respect to the tributes, he is thoroughly desensitized to their plight and the prescribed violence that ensues. During the pre-show at the TV studio, Dean Highbottom is explaining to Lucky how the Capitol student mentors had "begun with certain prejudices against their district counterparts," but many had developed a new appreciation for them. Lucky reacts indignantly, asking, "But surely, you're not comparing our children to theirs? One look tells you ours are a superior breed." Easily taking the moral high ground, the Dean shoots back, "One look tells you ours have had more food, nicer clothing, and better dental care." He adds that this sort of hubris almost caused the

Capitol to lose the war. Not knowing how to respond, the shallow Lucky Flickerman simply replies, "Fascinating" (BSS 198).

The film's Lucky Flickerman (Jason Schwartzman) is correctly cast as an amoral character who feels little sympathy or regard for the districts or their tributes. He serves as the movie's comic relief, though he is also the epitome of human desensitization that Suzanne Collins warns us about. Audiences can therefore feel awkward, not quite comfortable with laughing at his tasteless jokes at the expense of disadvantaged victims. While chuckling at his creative one-liners, they are often cringeworthy as well.

The family's surname, Flickerman, holds multiple if related references. For one, a dramatic documentary about someone's life is known as a "flickerman" (Frankel, "Songbirds"). The name further evokes images of the city lights and possibly refers to a "flick," a colloquial name for a movie or film. His nickname, Lucky, signifies a sense of fortune or happiness, which is echoed in the names of other *Ballad* characters as well, such as Hilarious. He also finds himself in the lucky position of Capitol weatherman and amateur entertainer, having already become something of a public figure. It is this initial fame that launches him into the Games. Like the younger mentors, all of them were luckily born well prior to the war, when life in the Capitol was presumably pretty good.

It is difficult not to further associate "Lucky" with the Capitol's infamous tag line, "May the odds be ever in your favor." Quite simply, the generic phrase is a ponderous if cute way to wish someone "Good luck." No less than three instances of this phrase—or derivatives of it—appear subtly throughout the prequel. The producers of *Ballad* took note as well; they have Lucky telling Lucy Gray after her interview, "I don't love your odds, but may they be in your favor." All of this suggests that Collins intended Lucky to play with this phrase prior to its widespread use in Katniss' time.

His first name, Lucretius, once again points back to a Classical Roman precedent, if not a Shakespearean variation of it. His name is traceable to one Titus Lucretius Carus, a Roman poet and philosopher. He was the author of a six-book didactic poem on Epicurean physics usually translated as *The Nature of Things* or *On the Nature of the Universe*. This ultimately inspired many additional works such as *The Aeneid*. In parallel fashion, it is Lucky Flickerman's inaugural broadcast that sets the stage for future Games (Frankel, "Songbirds").

Portraying Lucky

Regardless of whether one guffaws or cringes—or both—at Lucky's insensitivity, the esteemed actor and musician Jason Schwartzman fills the role admirably. Schwartzman hails from a family of actors and entertainers, including his actress mother, Talia Shire (nee Coppola) and his film-producer father, Jack Schwartzman. Prior to launching his acting career, he served as drummer and songwriter for the band, Phantom Planet. He is also an accomplished composer, having written the musical scores and theme songs for numerous films and television shows. Following his acting debut in *Rushmore* (1998), he has played roles in six additional Wes Anderson films such as *The Grand Budapest Hotel* (2014). His most recent appearance alongside *Ballad* was in *Asteroid City* (2023).

The main challenge for crafting Lucky's onscreen character was to strike a balance between humor and distaste. At once Lucky elicits multiple and opposing emotions from *Ballad* audiences. His is a brilliant juxtaposition that rides a fine line of appropriateness. Are we supposed to laugh at his references to "ill Dill" and shocks of "Ooohh!" as a tribute falls? Such reactions may be more appropriate on competitive shows like NBC's *American Ninja Warrior*. Either way, as viewers we are forced to confront our own sentiments while moving through the 10th Games, with or without a carefree Lucky at the helm.

Addressing this careful balancing act, director Francis Lawrence explains, "And so almost now everything you see are improv lines that are based on all the research that we did and the talking that we did, and weren't actually scripted. And I will say we probably have another two or three hours-worth of Jason's stuff" (Stedman). This allowed producers to pick and choose from Schwartzman's lines to achieve such a balance. Lawrence continues, "And we had to find that right line of when something's emotional or moving or intense, is it appropriate to go to a joke?... That was a little tricky, but really fun, too, because we had so much material from him" (Stedman).

This largely explains why very few of Lucky's lines in *Ballad* can be found in the book. This includes his new tag line, "That's what happens when you do stuff." In one sense, his character was given permission to come alive and expand beyond Collins' original narrative. Despite Lucky's diverse set of entertainment and celebrity skills, Schwartzman required additional preparation and practice to master the role. Lawrence explains,

> I will say that I'm a huge fan of Jason. Jason was my first choice for the role and loved him since *Rushmore*, and he was excited to be a part of it and signed on. And as soon as he did, I called and I said, "Look, I think that your role's been underwritten and there's so much more meat on the bone. And can I enlist you to help work with me and the writer to just create more?" And he worked so hard at researching the character weatherman, and news reporters, and vaudevillian magicians and late-night TV show hosts. And to find these quirks and little elements that start to feel like the birth of the Stanley Tucci character, but also really worked on improvising a lot of things. (Stedman)

After signing on, Schwartzman jumped in to research the character's multiple professions and hobbies for the film. He further learned some simple magic tricks to accompany his hosting gig for the Games. For this part, he worked with an established magician, Tobias Dostal to learn some necessary skills for the role ("The Ballad").

Unlike more scripted characters with little room for improvisation, Schwartzman was given an atypical amount of freedom to do his own thing. He explains,

> I love the movies, but I love the story. I love everything about it, but I really wanted to work with Francis Lawrence. And I wanted to work in this way, which was that he basically had this idea that, for my character, he said, 'Why don't we just work up a bunch of material, you'll have freedom to come up with it, and each day we'll kind of, we'll figure out what works. And so, Michael Lesslie, the writer and I got to sit down for a month, and we wrote pages and pages of material, and it was so silly; we were punch drunk, like so tired. But it was so fun to do it and present it to Francis. I've never worked in that way before. He knows this world so... this is his world. He was looking for things, and he would just pick and choose, and it was so cool to watch him do that, because it was 'yes, of course, that was the right thing to choose'... It was amazing. ("Jason")

Beyond his improvised lines, Schwartzman's costuming and makeup played a sizeable role in Lucky's transformation into a Hunger Games celebrity. Whereas he appears more buffoonish and awkward at the beginning, his confidence and professionalism improve gradually by the end of the Games. This subtle makeover may escape viewers the first time. Lucky's rise to stardom is marked by shifting outfits and hairstyles while proceeding through the film. At the outset he is given a drab look before easing into the role of a TV celebrity. He starts out with bushier eyebrows, pale and natural skin, and a plain mustache. Gradually he appears with more pancake makeup and bronzer along with stained lips. Even his eyebrows were plucked into a pointed shape ("Makeup").

About his everchanging outfits, costume designer Trish Summerville explains, "As Lucky's work covering the Games on television progresses, so does his ego and excitement, so I wanted his hair to start getting a little higher and his mustache to become fancier." His costuming complemented these changes. She elaborates, "With his wardrobe, it's a slow progression of him dressing fancier and fancier, and by the finale, Lucky's in a tuxedo with tails" (Dominick, "Here are"). It turns out that, in his case as well, that's what happens when you do stuff. You gain confidence—along with the approval of Dr. Gaul.

• CHAPTER 15 •

Of Mentors and Tributes

The idea to assign 24 promising Academy seniors as mentors for the 10th Games was yet another one of Dr. Gaul's experiments. Billed as the "finest secondary school in the Capitol," the Academy educated the "offspring of the prominent, wealthy, and influential," not unlike the prestigious boarding schools of our own world. The final senior project required them to serve as mentors in the Games. Of course, this sets up Coriolanus' entire story arc in both book and film. The narrator tells us, "If he gave an impressive performance as a mentor, with his outstanding academic record, Coriolanus should be awarded a monetary prize substantial enough to cover his tuition at the University" (BSS 13). Unlike in the film, the book's students are already well aware of their new project as the story begins.

It turns out that assigning students as mentors was a one-time trial. Dr. Gaul admits later to Coriolanus that it was a mistake to involve the students at all. "Especially when they started dropping like flies. Presented the Capitol as far too vulnerable," she explains (*BSS* 508). She was apparently less concerned with their own lives than she was assuring the Capitol upheld its image of strength.

OF MENTORS AND TRIBUTES

Casting for Inclusivity

In casting both mentors and tributes for *Ballad*, producers purposely sought new talent, often elevating up-and-coming actors to the big screen. Director Francis Lawrence explains, "The casting process was really exciting. I mean, I will say sort of the background to it. Nina and I wanted to do what was done with the original movies, which is, bring this core of people that are relatively unknown, fresh talent to the front, and then mix them with veteran legacy actors. So that's why we have Viola Davis, Peter Dinkage, Jason Schwartzman" (Dominick, "I Genuinely").

Assembling an inclusive cast was one of their foremost goals. Whereas in the original series the tributes were treated like royalty and costumed as such, the prequel strips away much of that spectacle. All that remains is the raw, underlying violence and injustice of the Games. To say the tributes are treated inhumanely by the Capitol would be an understatement. They are denied food, healthcare, and decent sleep, and they are thrown into the arena with whatever they wore from their reaping ceremonies. As we learn, numerous tributes die prior to the start of the Games—either through the Capitol's direct involvement or indirect negligence.

The producers saw this messaging as an opportunity to accentuate the Capitol's brutality through an inclusive casting process. They discovered actors with a wide range of ethnic, racial, and physically challenged backgrounds (Ulatowski). In an interview with Francis Lawrence, Kevin Polowy notes that casting someone with Down syndrome (Sophia Sanchez) was "a refreshing choice" that is not often seen in Hollywood. To this Lawrence elaborates,

> I wanted to be sure there was plenty of diversity, and I don't just mean ethnic diversity; there's all kinds. I wanted this to be more raw, more authentic. I also wanted to show, that if you are a young child and you have

tuberculosis and your name was chosen, you're going in. If you're a young child with Down syndrome and your name is chosen, you're going in. There is no mercy for anybody... and so, I just found that really interesting, to have, you know, Knox [Gibson], who's missing an arm, he goes in. Sophia [Sanchez], who has Down, she's going in. ("Sofia")

According to Rachel Ulatowski, it is the film's strong disability representation that sets it apart from the book. The diverse cast makes the story more realistic, as Lawrence suggests above. She also cites the example of actress Sofia Sanchez, who has been an unwavering advocate for Down syndrome since she was seven. Her character, Wovey was not described this way in the book. Sanchez's message to *Ballad* viewers was, "It's no big deal if you have [Down syndrome], or if you don't have it. We can all be different. And we can all be included" (Ulatowski).

Sanchez was joined on set by Australian actor Knox Gibson, an amputee, who plays the role of Bobbin from District 8. Gibson reflects, "Bobbin doesn't have a limb difference in the book. The limb difference [in the film] is just incidental to the character. I don't wear a prosthetic or anything. It's not explained, It's just that he's an amputee, that's all." Similarly, German actor Kjell Brutcheidt was cast as Tanner, a tribute from District 10. He has an eye condition in real life, which appears front and center in the film. As with the others, there is no CGI altering his image. Ulatowski offers, "when you think about it, isn't it a bit unlikely that all these tributes, chosen at random, would all be able bodied? This batch of tributes feels more like what the reality would be at some of these Games, especially because there's no evidence the Capitol distinguishes between tributes."

OF MENTORS AND TRIBUTES

The 10th Games: Film Versus Books

At the sound of the *gong*—as referred to in the book—*Ballad* viewers are met with some recognizable features from the prequel and original trilogy alike. Still, any similarities represent broad brush strokes, given the still-elementary technologies and limited development of the Games at this point. Tributes begin on individual pads equidistant from the center, where many of the weapons are placed. In this more rudimentary case, tributes are simply directed to stand on their spots until the bell sounds, upon threat of being shot by a Peacekeeper. Lucy Gray uses this imagery for a line within her own "Ballad of Lucy Gray Baird," singing, "For when the bell rings, lover, you're on your own."

The central pile of rubble in the bombed-out arena was, as Francis Lawrence envisioned, "probably the beginning for the idea of the cornucopia that's set in the center of the Games after this," he tells us ("Scene"). The debris further includes a haphazardly balanced set of building ruins upon which Marcus' abused body is hung. This stage set is meant to represent the more professionally constructed pair of twenty-foot-high steel poles in the book's open-air arena. A crossbeam of similar length, though only six inches wide, connects them (*BSS* 205). In both book and film, this is where we see Lamina climb and set up temporary refuge after mercifully killing Marcus and releasing his body. Likewise, her ultimate fate comes at the hands of a pack of tributes who climb both posts simultaneously to assure there is no escape. This is arguably one of the more heart-wrenching and violent sequences of the 10th Games—certainly within the book and even more vividly portrayed in the film. Only adding to the suspense is the building crescendo of James Newton Howard's dramatic symphonic score.

The requisite "bloodbath" likewise occurs with the sound of the gong, during which numerous tributes lose their lives. Lucy Gray somehow manages to escape while wading aimlessly into the fight to find her district counterpart, Jessup Diggs. In the book as in the film, many of the tributes scatter elsewhere. "Most fled to the gates that led to the tunnels, several of which had been blown open by the latest bombing." As a probable callback to Katniss' 74th Games, we see Coriolanus think *"Run! Get out of there!"* as he urges Lucy Gray to avoid the fight (BSS 207). This is little different from Haymitch's wise advice for Katniss to do the same, even though she is heavily tempted by the bow and arrows. And like Katniss, Lucy Gray ignores the advice, more determined to protect Jessup. Haymitch might ask, *Why don't they ever listen?*

After this point, film producers take more liberties to reinvent the story in various ways, sometimes diverging widely from the book. Lucy Gray's climactic snake-charming sequence in the film, for instance, occurs at the conclusion of the Games. Whereas, in the book numerous tributes remain alive to battle onward. This and other departures are all well and good to condense the complexity of the film. But it also means the details of who kills who, what they die from, and in what sequential order, show little similarity as translated from book to screen.

This is just as true with the mentors and their own backstories. For starters, it is worth mentioning that it is the book's mentor, Gaius Breen, who succumbs to his injuries from the arena bombing. Instead, the film has President Ravinstill's son, Felix, dying instead. Furthermore, Felix in the book is President Ravinstill's grandnephew, not his son. Of course, this twist by the screenwriters allows Dr. Gaul to rage against the districts and to justify having her snake mutts finish off the remaining tributes.

Beyond this specific adjustment, several fundamental departures from the novel warrant further discussion below.

OF MENTORS AND TRIBUTES

The Curiosities of Clemensia Dovecote

A more substantial plot shift for the film involves poor Clemensia Dovecote (Ashley Liao). Her character arguably suffers not one, but two injustices with her transition to the big screen. First, she simply disappears after the snake bite, with Dr. Gaul having caught her in a lie about co-writing the proposal. While we do see the presumed antidote administered quickly thereafter, we never hear or see from Clemensia again. This is counter to the book, where she returns to mentor Reaper through much of the Games, albeit greatly traumatized and with scaly skin to boot.

The second mystery involves her extreme personality makeover from book to screen. The movie's Clemensia is overtly self-serving and conniving, and she even curries favor with Coriolanus the first time we see them together. She says, "Just don't forget, I was your class partner while you're gloating over the Plinth Prize," as they enter Heavensbee Hall. In contrast, the book's "Clemmie" could be interpreted as a different person altogether. She is written as one of the nicer, more professional, and empathetic mentors. She even approaches the thoughtfulness of Lysistrata Vickers, perhaps the Academy's model of human decency and compassion. With the class brainstorming ideas on how to improve viewership, the narrator notes that Clemensia "was popular with both students and faculty, and her niceness excused a lot" (*BSS* 81). In this case her transgression involved little more than speaking in class out of turn.

More important, she is no fan of the Games. "The real problem is, it's sickening to watch," she says. "So people avoid it" (*BSS* 81). Even her own name suggests her character's intended traits. *Clemensia* is likely derived from the concept of clemency, a disposition to be merciful in judgment, or as an instance of leniency. Likewise, she also closely resembles the name, Clementia, the Roman goddess of clemency or mercy.

Her last name only reinforces this interpretation. *Dovecote* refers to a raised, compartmented structure or house for domestic pigeons or doves. According to Great Britain's National Trust, the use of dovecotes can be traced in England back to the eleventh century. Until the 1800s keeping one of these elaborate apartment buildings for birds was a privilege reserved for the aristocratic elite. Thus, they were usually found around castles or great houses. Aside from the connotation of the dove as a symbol for peace, Clemensia's last name may also indicate her own family's elite status within the Capitol.

What might throw off readers is when Clemensia refuses to assist her assigned tribute, Reaper, throughout much of the Games. She abstains from sending him food in the arena because, in her eyes, he has done nothing noteworthy to earn it. The point here is that such behavior was distinctly out of character, something noted by her peers. Even Coriolanus acknowledges her surprising conduct. He immediately attributes her harsh attitude to a probable side effect of the antidote, not to mention her angst from a prolonged and likely inhumane isolation from family and friends. Clearly, such unkindness is not in her nature. The extent of her trauma is further indicated from a horrific flashback as the snakes are released into the arena. To his credit, Coriolanus kindly provides reassurance that she is safe.

Readers receive a positive first impression of Clemensia when she arrives with Coriolanus for the tribute assignments. We learn she is the daughter of the energies secretary and that, "Unlike Livia [Cardew], Clemensia received news of her good fortune with tact... as she studiously made note of her tribute in her binder" (*BSS* 21). Later she expresses her thought that betting on tributes would be "gruesome." She asks Coriolanus if he was serious about the idea of placing bets. After responding in the affirmative, she simply shakes her head in exasperation (*BSS* 82-83). None of this survives into the film.

Most blatantly, Clemensia's episode with Dr. Gaul was seriously altered from the book's storyline. It is her own human decency that explains why she did not help write the proposal in the first place. Like other peers, she spent the night processing Arachne's death, despite the circumstances surrounding it. The next day, Clemensia snaps at Coriolanus, "I can't believe you wrote up some proposal while Arachne's body was still warm! I cried all night long" (*BSS* 108). Furthermore, it was Coriolanus' idea to submit it for the group, without putting anyone's names on it. She finally acquiesces to his apparent thoughtfulness, though she tells him, "But I wish I'd at least had a chance to read it" (*BSS* 109). Coriolanus' own ambition has thus put Clemensia in a bind, and she feels dragged along without an earlier opportunity for input. In one sense, she feels put on the spot. It is therefore Coriolanus who is the less thoughtful and sympathetic of the pair.

This is reinforced when Dr. Gaul asks if they brought a copy of the proposal. Not knowing how to respond, Clemensia looks "expectantly" to him for guidance. The narrator tells us, "He wasn't thrilled with Clemensia laying it at his door, when she'd been too shaky to even help write the thing. Especially since she was one of his most formidable competitors for the Academy prizes" (*BSS* 111). Not only does he view her as a rival for something he feels is rightfully his, but now he has the gaul (pun intended) to blame her for grieving a longtime classmate. It just wasn't convenient for him.

Finally, Coriolanus is the first to dip his hand into the snake terrarium, not Clemensia as we see in the film. This gives her more confidence in doing so herself. Speaking of the snakes, he even tells her, "I don't think they even noticed me" (*BSS* 112). It is only when she has already touched the paper inside that Dr. Gaul explains the snakes' association with scent. By then it is too late, as she has no chance to reconsider her decision to follow Coriolanus' lead. One is left to ponder why the screenwriters and producers portrayed both this event and her personality in such distorted ways.

Arachne Crane: After the Crime

A similar curiosity surrounds the film's version of Arachne Crane (Lilly Cooper), who is presumably an indirect ancestor to the future Gamemaker, Seneca Crane. Although she is provided with few redeeming qualities in either book or film, her story simply ends with her own murder at the hands of tribute Brandy—whether seemingly deserved or not. Though her death is the last we see or hear of her in the film, the aftermath of her character's storyline continues onward in the book. Despite Coriolanus' distaste for his classmate—not to mention her arrogant foolishness—he reflects on having known Arachne since childhood and had thus accepted her as extended family. This only deepens the mystery as to why he generally lacks an emotional feeling of loss following her death, unlike many of his peers.

Beyond this context, the book's storyline continues with an elaborate funeral and procession in her name, during which the Capitol paints Coriolanus and Arachne as virtual heroes. The funeral and associated events provide an opportunity to demonstrate the Capitol's blatant propaganda and distortion of the truth once again. Government leaders conveniently ignore Arachne's insensitive behavior, which is what ultimately gets her killed. For Coriolanus' part, it was Lucy Gray who told him to go help his dying classmate. He ultimately tries to do so, quite reluctantly. In the end, neither Arachne nor Coriolanus can rightfully claim the heroic status bestowed upon them.

A Defiant Reaper

In another notable shift in *Ballad*, viewers watch as Reaper (Dimitri Abold) gives up his body to the onslaught of Dr. Gaul's snakes. This is his way of outwardly defying the Capitol and not giving in to expectations of a state-sponsored system of oppression. His personal rebellion resembles that of Peeta, who did not want the Games to change who he was. Earlier, Reaper steals the Panem flag (*Horrors!*) to respectfully cover the deceased tributes, after which he turns to the camera and asks twice, "Are you going to punish me now?!"

As intimidating as Abold's character seems, the book's Reaper is generally merciful and kind. He carries his ailing District 11 counterpart, Dill, and lays her down on a charred piece of wood to warm her up in the sun. As she succumbs to tuberculosis, he points up to the sun in a likely attempt to soothe her, much as Peeta had done with the Morphling tribute in *Catching Fire*. Later he notices that Lamina has the opposite problem, desperately needing protection from the sun. After agreeing to a trade, he promptly cuts through the national flag to fashion a sunshade for Lamina. In this way, the national symbol of oppression and control—as the districts see it— is transformed into a humane instrument of relative kindness (*BSS* 272). Of course, Capitol citizens, including Academy students, are aghast at the afront to their national symbol. What escapes all of them in their abject disgust is that the tributes have no reason to care about their lofty values of misplaced nationalism.

The book's Reaper plays something of the role of Cato in the 74th Games. Like Cato, Reaper is considered the strongest tribute, and he finds ways to stay alive until the end. Finally, Lucy Gray eggs him on with her own veritable game of, well, Capture the Flag. She essentially runs him to death as he desperately tries to cover the bodies in his makeshift morgue. In his last act he appears to drink from a poisoned puddle of water, bringing him down for good. Only then is the book's Lucy Gray declared the winner—with no dispute from Dr. Gaul. In contrast, *Ballad* viewers know it is the snake mutts that take out the few remaining tributes in the film. The last to perish is not Reaper, but Coral (see below). This sets up Lucy Gray's showstopper, "The Old Therebefore." Thus, Reaper plays significant roles in film and book alike, though their respective characters move through the Games in distinctly different ways.

A Merciful End for Wovey

No doubt, one of *Ballad's* most endearing, lovable characters is little Wovey (Sofia Sanchez). Much like Reaper, the film's Wovey takes an alternative path through the Games. Along with Bobbin, Wovey's name reflects the textile industry. In the film she is clearly cast to remind us of Rue. Upon entering the arena to begin the Games, Wovey longingly holds hands with Lucy Gray. And back in the Capitol Zoo, Lucy Gray admits in both book and film that Wovey reminds her of her younger cousin, Maude Ivory—much in the same way Rue reminds Katniss of Prim. The film's Wovey even tells us she is a good climber, though she is not from District 11.

In Collins' own narrative, Wovey dies a terrible, painful death from drinking water laced with rat poison. Lucy Gray admits as much to Coriolanus back in District 12 (she had been gunning for Coral, she says). Instead, the screenwriters decided to have Dill's character fill that role. We thus see a sequestered Lucy Gray in silent agony over her deathly mistake. In turn, this allows Wovey to, well, die another day, and in another way. The substitution affords Wovey a more merciful end, as she is allowed to perish quickly and unknowingly from an avalanche of rainbow snakes. Screenwriters likely made this change to take mercy on *Ballad* viewers as well; death by rainbow snakes is decidedly more acceptable for Wovey fans. No matter, her passing still proved heart-wrenching as fans have attested across the internet. Not candy, indeed. Down goes Wovey.

Wovey is played by fourteen-year-old Sofia Sanchez, the first actor with Down syndrome to appear in a major movie franchise. Sanchez is also a tireless advocate for raising awareness about the genetic condition, having authored two books on the topic to date. Her first was *You Are Enough*, followed by *You Are Loved: A Book About*

Families ("Local"). As for landing the role in *Ballad*, executive producer Nina Jacobson recalls, "Sofia came in and had a great audition. And she's also a super charismatic kid; it's really hard not to fall in love with her" ("Sofia").

Credit for discovering Sanchez's acting talents goes to her former kindergarten teacher. Sanchez had played the lead in the *Gingerbread Man* play, and her teacher said, "I think she's got something." She proceeded to steal the show, and her mother was convinced to pursue this direction further. Sanchez has since appeared in commercials, has become a school cheerleader, and was recently crowned Princess at her high school in the Sacramento, California area. When asked during an interview whether she was a Hunger Games fan, she shot back, "I *am* a Hunger Games fan! Are you kidding me?" ("Sofia"). *Ask a silly question.*

The Rise of Coral

In both book and film, District 4's Coral dies being overrun by Dr. Gaul's snake assault. Beyond this similarity, the book's Coral remains a minor character relegated to the background through much of the Games. She seemingly lurks on the sidelines until she joins Mizzen and Tanner in chasing Sejanus and Coriolanus from the arena. Similarly, Coral's eventual death is much less dramatic than the event we see on screen. As the narrator tells us, Mizzen escapes the snakes and climbs one of the two poles to the top, from where he "witnessed Coral's frantic, but blissfully short, end" (*BSS* 300). Coral is then all but forgotten as Lucy Gray launches into her own musical number, "The Old Therebefore." Lucky Flickerman congratulates Dr. Gaul on her own dramatic show, and the Games press onward.

For purposes of *Ballad*, producers have greatly elevated Coral's role. Other than Lucy Gray, Coral is the last to perish, thereby paralleling Cato's character arc from the 74th Games. Prior to her final moments, Coral forms a Career-type alliance and viciously pursues Lucy Gray. In another Cato-like move, she turns on a weaker ally, Tanner, and murders him with her trident—a weapon equivalent to Cato's mighty sword. Movie reviewers noted her role as well. As Justin Clark writes, "A particularly bloodthirsty tribute named Coral (Mackenzie Lansing) emerges as a terrifying, tooth-gnashing slasher villain."

Despite this horror-film image, viewers are also afforded a glimpse of her more human side. Producers allow Coral two moments for her sense of humanity to briefly surface. As Lucy Gray slams the massive grate on Coral's hand, her childlike emotions return to reveal a rare moment of vulnerability. When her allies draw close, however, she quickly recovers her façade of toughness. More poignant are her final words as the snakes subsume her body. In a very Cato-like moment, she pleads with Lucy Gray, "It's not fair, it's not. I can't have killed them all for nothing." Viewers are thereby reminded once again who the real enemy is. Coral, too, is a victim of the Capitol's draconian, unrelenting revenge against the districts.

Perhaps no one was more surprised at Coral's rise to stardom than the actress who plays her. In a spirited interview for the Hunger Games podcast, *Into the Arena*, Mackenzie Lansing explains how, prior to being cast, she had not yet read the prequel. She had seen the prior movies and maybe read the first book, but she knew little about the film for which she was auditioning. During the casting process movies are sometimes given codenames—thereby providing little information about the project. Although Lansing admits she could have figured it out, she explains, "But I purposely don't do that, because I don't want it to get in my head, and I get nervous." For auditions, Lancing thus focuses on the scene and what the character wants and needs to do, without knowing much about the larger context. She adds, "It was only around the callback that I started to know it was a franchise, something big. But when I booked it, my manager, Patrick called me, and he said, 'You're going to be in the

Hunger Games!' and I was like, 'Did I audition for the Hunger Games?' and he was like, 'Yes! The audition you did with Francis Lawrence.'" She therefore knew little about Coral and the principal role she would play as District 4 tribute. "I don't know if I would have booked it if I had full consciousness of what I was getting myself into," she laughs ("Episode").

Having learned she was cast as Coral, Lansing remained in the dark about the extent of her role. At this point she read the prequel at the same time the scripts were being solidified. There was still little indication, therefore, about how much screentime she would receive. She explained that her management company also represents Tom Blyth, who plays Coriolanus. Still not knowing much about Coral's role, Lansing's manager called Blyth for helpful input about whether Coral's character was worthwhile. Lansing continues,

> And Tom said, 'Oh, no, it's a big part,' way more than the scene they originally gave me led us to believe... I think Francis likes to take people who are sort of up-and-coming or unknown, so I think there was some intentionality around that for some of the roles, not letting everybody know how big they were going to be. So, I really didn't know. And even when I got the script, the script kept getting reworked... Even then, as an actor, I think you try to curb your expectations. For me, I kept trying to tell myself, to protect myself, that you're not in it that much, small role, you're having a great time, you got to go to Berlin... That's great. Who cares if you end up not even in the movie anymore, this is great. ("Episode")

Further, Lansing did not attend any of the pre-screenings, largely due to schedule conflicts. Her first time seeing the final film, therefore, was during the London premier. "I was like the only one," she exclaimed. "Everyone else had seen it like eleven times." Then the reality started to sink in. "[We] watched the movie, the credits rolled, and [we] were like gripping hands and crying because this is big! I didn't know. So that all really took me by surprise."

According to Lansing's perspective on Coral and District 4, the tributes from the so-called Career districts have not yet started to volunteer during the 10th Games. The notion of the District 1, 2, and 4 Careers had not yet become solidified. She explains,

> I did a lot of research on child soldiers, because to me that's kind of like what they are. But to me, Coral has only been brainwashed to a point. That's why we still see vulnerability from her in moments. Because she can turn her empathy off, but that doesn't mean it's not there at all... For Coral, do you fight the system from within, or from the outside? And I think for Coral, she considers herself a realist, and she's like, 'Look, I can't change that any of this is happening, and I think it's horrific, but if I have to do it, to stay alive and to get home, I'm going to do it.' So, I think [for] her, it's fighting from within, rather than Reaper, just refusing to even play. ("Episode")

Speaking about Coral's final line, Lansing explains the scene was not originally scripted. In part due to conversations between Lansing, writer Michael Lesslie, and director Francis Lawrence, they ultimately decided to add her final plea to Lucy Gray. "And I was so happy when they did," she recalls, "because, to me I was already working with the idea that there had to be a heart somewhere under there, and that doesn't justify anything that she does, but the bottom line is, when she says, 'I can't have killed them all for nothing,' by that point she knows Lucy can't save her... There's a million snakes coming up her back, she's not an idiot. There's nothing Lucy can do to save her at that point. So, I think she's using her last seconds of being alive to reconnect with being a real person and to show that she's human... I was very happy that it was added to the script later" ("Episode").

Lansing further confirms that her character's apparent parallels with Cato were intentionally designed. When asked to compare their final moments alive, she offers,

> I think, obviously it's very intentional, and Francis is very thoughtful about making sure that all of these movies connect and leaving Easter eggs and things like that, so he was talking about that on set, about these two things paralleling each other, thinking about the Career districts still growing. Cato's exact line, it's like, 'I'm dead anyway, I always was.' So that's him, years into the future. That gives you an indication of how the Career districts have evolved, that he literally hasn't had a moment of being a child, or being really connected to humanity, and he knows it... Versus Coral, who still has some of that left, it hasn't been beaten out of her, there's still remorse. ("Episode")

Future Books or Movies?

One pressing question is whether Suzanne Collins plans to write another follow-up book to *Ballad*. Or, whether Lionsgate plans to produce another film—with or without Collins' blessings. In short, what's coming next? The short answer to this is that nobody except the author herself really knows. What does seem apparent for now is that the prequel book and film are together a "rare one-off." Executive producer Nina Jacobson tells us that the story was not intended as a trilogy-starter or a "continuity revival." That said, Jacobson remains hopeful that future one-off books and films will appear. She says truthfully, "Do I think she will write more books in the [Panem] world? I do, and I hope she will. Do I have any idea what they'll be? Not really!" ("New").

Producers of *Ballad* make it clear that the creation of future Hunger Games films is dependent entirely on whether Suzanne Collins decides to add to her saga. It is easy to imagine that Hollywood could take the reins and launch its own series or sequels. However, franchise producers and filmmakers have clarified that no new films will be produced without new source material from Collins. In one interview, Francis Lawrence agreed when asked what it would take for him to direct a follow-up prequel or sequel. After clarifying there are no current plans for such productions, he likewise emphasized the need for Collins to provide another book before anyone thinks about adding another film. He adds, "If Suzanne has another thematic idea that she feels fits into the world of Panem—whether with new people or familiar characters—I'd be interested in being a part of it" (Wagner).

Until then, all fans can do now is retain hope that the odds of her doing so remain ever in our favor.

APPENDIX

Twenty Callbacks and Easter Eggs in *Ballad*

Both Suzanne Collins and the producers of *Ballad* embedded countless references pointing back in some way to the original series. Some originate with the author herself, while others are the product of the *Ballad* production team's collective creativity.

While all of them reference something meaningful from the past, callbacks and Easter eggs are not the same thing. A callback can be described as a relevant and overt reference to something we saw or read previously. They often remind us of audio-visual or narrative elements that can come from the likes of former plot events, dialogue, scenes, jokes, episodes, books, or films to remind audiences of a previous emotional reaction. One prominent example in both the prequel and *Ballad* is when Lucy Gray references the katniss plant while relaxing with the Covey at the lake.

In contrast, Easter eggs are, as the name implies, hidden or subtle references not intended to be blatant or obvious, such as the katniss and primrose flowers painted onto Lucy Gray's corset (see Chapter 10). They are unannounced or largely ignored by the actors and storyline, just waiting for viewers to discover them. The following list includes a variety of callbacks and Easter eggs that are intentionally subtle or blatantly obvious—or often somewhere in between. Keen viewers of *Ballad* will certainly discover more such references beyond this list, which can be interpreted as a place to start. The references below are in roughly sequential order as they appear in *Ballad*.

CALLBACKS AND EASTER EGGS

- **A Different Form of Tesserae:** In one of *Ballad*'s early scenes, Tigris proudly displays her creative modifications to Coriolanus' dress shirt once worn by his father. As in the book, we learn that the buttons have been fashioned from *tesserae*, consisting of gold and ebony cubes. Each has two holes drilled through it for the threads (*BSS* 9). Given such a rare, little-known term, it is difficult to imagine that "tesserae" shows up coincidentally in both the prequel and the first *Hunger Games* novel. The question remains as to how Suzanne Collins made the leap from decorative bathroom tiles to the unjust welfare system imposed on the districts within her first book (more on this in Chapter 11).

- **A Favorite Dish:** As the mentors gather in Heavensbee Hall to watch the reapings, several of them gather to socialize and enjoy some *hors d'oevres*. Felix Ravenstill exclaims, "Have you tried this lamb? It's scandalous." This is the only specific food mentioned during the scene, making it a likely reference to Katniss' own favorite dish in the Capitol, lamb stew.

- **Trajan Heavensbee:** Heavensbee Hall was of course named for an ancestor of Plutarch Heavensbee. However, there are additional layers of meaning here than what easily meets the eye. While Dean Highbottom explains the Games prior to the reaping ceremonies, one can barely discern a plaque in the rear of the hall honoring "Trajan Heavensbee: Father of Panem." It turns out that the actual Greek philosopher and historian, Plutarch, had earned many followers and admirers during his lengthy life and was eventually recognized by the emperors Trajan and Hadrian, with Trajan having bestowed the high honour of *ornamenta consularia* upon him. It is thus no mistake that *Ballad* producers bestowed Panem's own Trajan as the nation's founder, given his historical connections to, and admiration for, Plutarch (more on Trajan, Plutarch, and Heavensbee Hall in Chapters 8 and 10).

- **A Hand-painted Corset:** Costume designer Trish Summerville admits she designed a few Easter eggs into Lucy Gray's colorful corset, which she wears over the top of her distinctive rainbow dress. First, she designed the corset with the same shape as the one she added to Katniss' famous blue mockingjay dress in *Catching Fire*. Further, Lucy Gray's corset is hand-painted with snakes to represent her kinship with that form of reptile, while the front was purposely painted with katniss and primrose flowers (more on Lucy Gray's dress in Chapter 10).

- **A Sarcastic Bow:** During the District 12 reaping ceremony, Lucy Gray finishes singing and performs a prolonged, sarcastic bow or curtsy with her arms extended outwards. This scene was purposely added by director Francis Lawrence on the day of filming to replicate a similar bow that Katniss took in *The Hunger Games* after shooting an arrow at the Gamemakers. Lawrence imagined that this "sort of bow curtsy" could have been handed down to Katniss as a clearly irreverent act (more on this in Chapter 5, "Nothing You Can Take from Me").

- **Our Best Customers:** At the conclusion of her reaping song, "Nothing You Can Take from Me," Lucy Gray defiantly drops the mic and curtsies to the crowd (see above). Less obvious is when she dejectedly says, "Come on, boys." She directs this to the Peacekeepers guarding her as she sullenly walks off stage. Somehow, she has managed to earn enough respect from the Peacekeepers to refer to them as an equal. The callback—if the appropriate term here—is explained in the book more so than the film. During a conversation with Coriolanus, Lucy Gray explains that the "Peacekeepers let us keep our instruments when they rounded us up. They're some of our best customers" (*BSS* 87). This is clearly evident during the Covey's performances at the Hob, within the book and film alike. It is this "customers" remark that serves as the true callback. Katniss uses a similar phrase in the first novel when she is describing her trading habits at the Hob and around town. She explains that most of the Peacekeepers "turn a blind eye to the few of us who hunt because they're as hungry for fresh meat as anybody is. In fact, they're among our best customers" (HG 5). Both scenarios reveal how the lines have been blurred between government authority and District 12 citizens. The Capitol has thereby let its guard down in this peripheral place, allowing one Katniss Everdeen to eventually take advantage of that ill-maintained fence.

- **Holding Hands:** After Lucy Gray tells a nervous Coriolanus to "own it" after falling into the monkey cage, he takes her hand and walks over to Lucky Flickerman to introduce themselves. Lucky notices this quickly, saying, "That's something you don't see every day, they're holding hands." Likewise, it was equally rare to see two tributes from the same district holding hands during the Tribute Parade in *The Hunger Games*, when Caesar Flickerman highlighted Katniss and Peeta doing just that.

- **Coriolanus and Baked Goods:** When meeting Lucy Gray at the zoo, Coriolanus brings her some cafeteria food. She suspects that he has not eaten much, either, at which point she offers him back one of his cookies. After an unconvincing refusal, he accepts the gift and eats along with her. This may be a callback to when Coriolanus enjoyed Peeta's cookies at Katniss' home in *Catching Fire*. His weakness for homemade baked goods is evident elsewhere in the prequel, if not the film. He cannot resist Ma Plinth's cooking, nor Sejanus' left-over cookies after he is hung.

- **Wovey and Rue:** During a conversation at the zoo, Lucy Gray mentions how the District 8 tribute, Wovey, reminds her of her cousin, Maude Ivory. She tells Coriolanus at the zoo, "That little one, she's so sweet, so young. Something about her reminds me of my cousin, Maude Ivory." At this point she displays a pang of homesickness while missing her Covey family. Later we see Wovey looking up to Lucy Gray and taking her hand as they enter the arena to begin the Games. In the original series and films, District 11's Rue plays a similar role. Katniss admits that Rue reminds her of her sister, Prim, and even strikes up an alliance and friendship with her.

- **A Nod to Effie Trinket:** In preparation for the start of the 10th Games, Lucky Flickerman proudly instructs the mentors, "Keep your chins down, heads up, shoulders back. And smile; it's why we have teeth." This scene is reminiscent of similar (if ignored) advice provided by Effie Trinket during the Victory Tour. As she leads Katniss and Peeta up the walkway to the presidential palace, she commands, "Eyes bright, chins up, smiles on. I'm talking to you, Katniss." In both cases instructions are being given to elicit an effective presence in front of the cameras.

- **What are you doing? Run!** As the gong sounds to commence the 10th Games, the book's Coriolanus thinks *Run, get out of there!* as he urges Lucy Gray to follow his earlier instructions. This scene translates to *Ballad* with Coriolanus uttering "Run!" while watching Lucy Gray contemplate what to do. She ultimately does not listen, of course, soon finding herself in the mayhem of the so-called bloodbath while desperately trying to find Jessup. This sequence may seem familiar, as it closely parallels the experience of Haymitch and Katniss at the start of the 74th Games. Likewise, Haymitch had instructed Katniss to run away and go find water. Instead, Katniss is distracted by a set of bow and arrows within visual range while also looking around for Peeta. The only reason she does not make a beeline for the Cornucopia is because Peeta shakes his head, thereby confusing her. Later, we see a hallucinatory Katniss being directed by Peeta to run once again, as the Career pack is on its way.

- **Untouched Bow and Arrows:** When Coriolanus sneaks into the arena for a second time—in this case to save Sejanus—he briefly spots a set of bow and arrows sitting untouched by the tributes. This is one of the film's clearest references to the future heroine from District 12, who would certainly not have passed up this opportunity 64 years later. Ironically, a similar set of bow and arrows would contribute to toppling Snow's regime once and for all.

- **Little Caesar:** In the prequel we are introduced to the ancestors of characters from the original series, including Hilarious Heavensbee, Livia Cardew, Arachne Crane, and—of course—Lucretius "Lucky" Flickerman. It is not unreasonable to presume that Lucky is Caesar's father. This is suggested further in *Ballad*, when Lucky calls a restaurant to make reservations for two people and a highchair.

- **Reaper Channels Katniss and Peeta:** Despite his exterior façade of intimidation, Reaper proves to be one of the kinder and merciful tributes within the prequel. The novel's Reaper plays something of the role of Cato from the 74th Games, though in *Ballad* the role of leading antagonistic tribute is given to Coral instead. In the book Reaper cares for the other District 11 tribute, Dill, who is suffering from tuberculosis. He lays her down on a charred piece of wood to warm her up in the sun. This act of kindness might remind one of Peeta's similar effort to soothe the female Morphling tribute at the end of her life in *Catching Fire*. In *Ballad*, Reaper more resembles Katniss when she is grieving over the death of Rue. He steals the Panem flag to cover the deceased tributes as a sign of respect, after which he turns to the camera and asks defiantly, "Are you going to punish me now?" In a similar act of defiance Katniss turned to the cameras after Rue's death to give the District 12 salute (more on Reaper and Coral in Chapter 15).

- **Coral as Cato:** In the original Hunger Games film, Cato displays a lingering sense of humanity prior to his death at the hands of Katniss and Peeta, claiming that he has always been dead anyway. It is an emotional moment that is not included in the original book. In *Ballad*, the District 4 tribute, Coral, is purposely elevated to assume Cato's role in the 10th Games. And much like Cato, the producers allow her own humanity to rise to the surface, as she, too, prepares to die. As Coral is gradually subsumed by the rainbow snakes, she reaches out to Lucy Gray and pleads, "It's not fair, it's not. I can't have killed them all for nothing." Much like through Cato's final words, we are reminded once again of the oppressive injustice of the Capitol and how the tributes are forced to fight one another against their will (more about Coral in Chapter 15).

- **Some People Call it Swamp Potato:** Perhaps the most obvious callback in *Ballad* is taken almost directly from Collins' prequel. While relaxing out at the lake, Clerk Carmine hands Lucy Gray a plant, which she shows Coriolanus. The cinematic version has Lucy Gray saying, "It's a pretty little thing, but it's determined," which could easily describe either herself or Katniss. She then adds, "Some people call it swamp potato, but

I think katniss has a much nicer ring, don't you?" At which point, we hear Katniss' theme kick in from the beginning of *Catching Fire*. The prop used for the plant is indeed realistic (whether real or otherwise), with its distinctive white flowers and arrowhead-shaped leaves.

Of course, it was Katniss' father who informed us in the first novel about the plant for which she is named. Prior to the 74th Games, Katniss is remembering back to her childhood when she noticed a unique tuber plant growing near a pond. Her father joked that as long as she could "find herself," she would never starve (THG 52). Beyond the literal meaning of this statement, this can be further viewed as a metaphor for Katniss recognizing her own sense of self as she matures into adulthood (Paradis). In either case, Katniss' personal identity is indelibly tied to nature, the wilderness, and more specifically to the woods where she once thrived.

- **Billy Taupe's Last Words:** Just before Spruce shoots Billy Taupe in *Ballad*, he threatens Coriolanus with, "You've got a surprise coming, Capitol boy; If I'm gonna swing for this, you swing with me." This phrase is eerily similar to Katniss' threat to Snow decades later when she screams, "If we burn, you burn with us!" in *Mockingjay – Part 1*. This latter phrase is quickly adopted as a rallying cry for the rebel cause and is placed within Plutarch's *propos* against the Capitol. In both cases we have rebels threatening Snow with a similar turn of phrase, though nearly seven decades apart.

- **Rue's Four-Note Theme:** While Peacekeepers in District 12 are conducting a search for the weapon that killed Mayfair, Lucy Gray is hiding inside a building entranceway. She then whistles a quick, four-note theme to grab Coriolanus' attention. At this point they make plans to escape to the woods the next morning.

This is likely one of the more subtle Easter eggs of *Ballad*, as one must listen carefully to discern what Lucy Gray is whistling. Upon closer scrutiny, there is no mistaking this crude yet similar version of Rue's famous four-note theme from *The Hunger Games*.

- **A Familiar Earring:** While Coriolanus is attempting to pick up Lucy Gray's trail in the forest, he eventually finds one of her earrings on the ground. As Elizabeth Hardy observes, it is difficult not to compare its size, design, and metallic, circular shape with Katniss' now famous mockingjay pin that would eventually grace her own outfits (Hardy, "Hollywood"). While this may not be a planned Easter egg, the fact that we see such an up-close image of the earring is suspicious indeed. It is further instructive to recall the origin of the mockingjay pin from the original trilogy. The pin is actually gifted to Katniss by Madge Undersee in the first novel. Prior to that, the pin had essentially been a family heirloom handed down from Madge's aunt, Maysilee Donner. She had worn the pin during the 50th Games with Haymitch. The pin's history and design therefore go back decades prior to the emergence of Katniss Everdeen.

- **All the Rage in the Capitol:** In the final apartment scene with Coriolanus, we see Grandma'am (Fionnula Flanagan) wearing a turban hair style with a distinctive head wrap. This could be the very style that Effie Trinket portrays in *Mockingjay – Part 1*, when we learn that she has become a rebel captive in District 13. Effie features her own hair wrap and mentions they were all the rage when she was growing up. While Effie was certainly not alive during the 10th Games, the style could have held on for a few decades, lasting into Effie's impressionistic childhood years.

Works Cited

Allen, Kelly. "The Hunger Games: The Ballad of Songbirds & Snakes Showcases Panem in a Bygone Era." *House Beautiful*, 17 November, 2023.
https://www.housebeautiful.com/lifestyle/entertainment/a45878149/hunger-games-ballad-of-songbirds-and-snakes-filming-locations/

"Altes Stadthaus, Berlin." *Wikipedia*.
https://en.wikipedia.org/wiki/Altes_Stadthaus,_Berlin

Amorosi, A.D. "Rachel Zegler and Dave Cobb Explore the Music of 'Hunger Games: Ballad of Songbirds and Snakes,' From Why She Sang Live On-Set to How the Smiths Figured In." *Variety*, 01 December, 2023.
https://variety.com/2023/music/news/hunger-games-music-rachel-zegler-dave-cobb-soundtrack-ballad-songbirds-snakes-1235816713/

Arrow, V. *The Panem Companion: An Unofficial Guide to Suzanne Collins' Hunger Games, from Mellark Bakery to Mockingjays*. Dallas: BenBella Books, 2012.

"The Ballad Auditions and How the Cast Landed their Roles." *Still Watching?*, 01 December, 2023. https://www.youtube.com/watch?v=-uHq1t1k_2M

"Barb Azure Baird." The Hunger Games Wiki.
https://thehungergames.fandom.com/wiki/Barb_Azure_Baird#cite_note-Ballad_27-7

Butcher, Sophie. "The Hunger Games: The Ballad of Songbirds and Snakes' Lucy Gray Baird is the 'Opposite' of Katniss Everdeen, Says Director Francis Lawrence: 'She's a Performer—Exclusive Image." *Empire*, 29 August, 2023. https://www.empireonline.com/movies/news/hunger-games-ballad-of-songbirds-snakes-lucy-gray-baird-opposite-katniss-everdeen/

Bythrow, Nick. "'Tangible Feeling of Terror': Hunger Games Prequel's Arena Location Has a Dark Real-Life History." *Screen Rant*, 20 November, 2023. https://screenrant.com/hunger-games-ballad-songbirds-snakes-arena-location-history/

Campione, Katie, and D'Alessandro, Anthony. "Fly, 'Songbirds,' Fly: 'Hunger Games' Star Rachel Zegler & More on 'Emotion' of Singing

Pic's 'Timeless and Classic' Country Songs Live on Set." *Deadline*, 14 November, 2023. https://deadline.com/2023/11/hunger-games-ballad-of-songbirds-and-snakes-rachel-zegler-olivia-rodrigo-1235611855/

"Cast Interviews." *Behind the Clapperboard*, 28 October, 2023. https://www.youtube.com/watch?v=YfXbxzNQb2w

"Centennial Hall in Wroclaw." *UNESCO World Heritage Convention*. https://whc.unesco.org/en/list/1165/#:~:text=The%20Centennial%20Hall%2C%20a%20landmark,can%20seat%20some%206%2C000%20persons.

Clark, Justin. "The Hunger Games: The Ballad of Songbirds & Snakes Review: The Atrocity of Hope." *Slant*, 14 November, 2023. https://www.slantmagazine.com/film/the-hunger-games-the-ballad-of-songbirds-and-snakes-review/

Collins, Suzanne. *The Ballad of Songbirds and Snakes*. Scholastic Press, 2020.

____. *Catching Fire*. Scholastic Press, 2009.

____. *The Hunger Games*. Scholastic Press, 2008.

____. *Mockingjay*. Scholastic Press, 2010.

Conway, Cecelia. "Black Banjo Songsters in Appalachia." *Black Music Research Journal* 23, no. 1-2 (March 1 2003).

Davids, Brian. "Hunger Games Director Talks That Ending and 'Constantine 2' Optimism." *The Hollywood Reporter*, 21 November, 2023. https://www.hollywoodreporter.com/movies/movie-features/hunger-games-ballad-songbirds-snakes-ending-1235669343/

Diedrich, Lisa. "No Politics, No Park" The Duisburg-Nord Model." *Topos: European Landscape Magazine*, no. 26 (1999): 69-78.

"Director Breaks Down Scenes from 'Mockingjay', 'Ballad of Songbirds & Snakes' and More." *Vanity Fair*, 16 November, 2023. https://www.youtube.com/watch?v=vcbki4nmLfE

Dominick, Nora. "Here are 6 Side-By-Sides That Show These 'Hunger Games: The Ballad of Songbirds and Snakes' Costume Sketches Vs. the Movie." *BuzzFeed*. 26 October, 2023. https://www.buzzfeed.com/noradominick/hunger-games-songbirds-and-snakes-costumes

____. "I Genuinely Can't Watch 'The Hunger Games: The Ballad of Songbirds and Snakes' the Same Way After Reading These BTS Facts." *BuzzFeed*, 20 November, 2023.

El-Mahmoud, Sarah. "The Ballad of Songbirds and Snakes Star Rachel Zegler Reveals Why She Originally Turned Down the Role in The Hunger Games Prequel." *Cinemablend.com*, 29 January, 2023. https://www.cinemablend.com/movies/the-ballad-of-songbirds-and-snakes-star-rachel-zegler-reveals-why-she-originally-turned-down-the-role-in-the-hunger-games-prequel

"Episode 76 – Cast Interview with District 4's 'Coral' Mackenzie Lansing." *Into the Arena: Hunger Games Podcast*, 10 December, 2023. https://www.youtube.com/watch?v=DCfReycCRCw

Fazzare, Elizabeth. "The Ballad of Songbirds and Snakes: Unpacking the Dark Symbolism in the Architecture of the Hunger Games Movies." *Architectural Digest*, 21 November, 2023. https://www.msn.com/en-us/lifestyle/lifestyle-buzz/the-ballad-of-songbirds-and-snakes-unpacking-the-dark-symbolism-in-the-architecture-of-the-hunger-games-movies/ar-AA1kiRoU?domshim=1

"Featurette – Music." *Rotten Tomatoes*, 26 October, 2023. https://www.youtube.com/watch?v=dUw6R9VPFE4

"The Former Stalinallee in Berlin." *Visit Berlin*. https://www.visitberlin.de/en/stalinallee

"Fourteen-Year-Old with Down Syndrome Lands 'Hunger Games' Role." *Inside Edition*, 17 November, 2023. https://www.youtube.com/watch?v=rB6TiguQvUw

Frankel, Valerie Estelle. *Katniss the Cattail: An Unauthorized Guide to Names and Symbols in The Hunger Games*. LitCrit Press, 2012.

———. *Songbirds, Snakes & Sacrifice: Collins' Prequel References and Philosophies Explained*. LitCrit Press, 2020.

Garafano, Lauren. "19 'Hunger Games' Details, Easter Eggs, and Parallels that are in 'The Ballad of Songbirds & Snakes'." *BuzzFeed*, 21 November, 2023. https://www.buzzfeed.com/laurengarafano/ballad-of-songbirds-snakes-hunger-games-easter-eggs

Gawaran, Alyssa. "10 Best Songs on The Ballad of Songbirds and Snakes Official Soundtrack, Ranked." *Movieweb*, 23 November, 2023. https://movieweb.com/the-ballad-of-songbirds-and-snakes-best-songs-soundtrack/#district-12-stomp

Goffe, Nadira. "The New Hunger Games Movie is a Musical, Thank God." *Slate*, 17 November, 2023. https://slate.com/culture/2023/11/hunger-games-ballad-songbirds-snakes-2023-movie-music.html

Goldstein, Mathias. "Nottingham-Born Actor Tom Blyth on his Journey from the TV Workshop to HBO's The Gilded Age." *Leftlion*, 23 February, 2021.
https://leftlion.co.uk/features/2021/02/interview-with-tom-blyth-actor-nottingham-hbo-the-gilded-age/

Gomez, Dessi. "Hunger Games: The Ballad of Songbirds and Snakes' Director Explains 'Hanging Tree' Connection." *The Wrap*, 17 November, 2023.
https://www.thewrap.com/hunger-games-ballad-of-songbirds-and-snakes-hanging-tree-song-explained/

Granger, John. "Mockingjay Discussion 15: The Hanging Tree." *Hogwarts Professor*, 25 August, 2010.
https://www.hogwartsprofessor.com/mockingjay-discussion-15-the-hanging-tree

Hamilton, Lee. "The Musical 'One Genre to Rule Them All?'" *Shore Scripts*, 10 June, 2015. https://www.shorescripts.com/the-musical-one-genre-to-rule-them-all/

Hanlon, Tina. "Coal Dust and Ballads: Appalachia and District 12." In *Of Bread, Blood, and the Hunger Games: Critical Essays on the Suzanne Collins Trilogy*, 59-68. Edited by Mary F. Pharr, Leisa A. Clark, Donald E. Palumbo, and C.W. Sullivan III. Jefferson, NC: McFarland, 2012.

Hardy, Elizabeth Baird. "The Ballad of Songbirds and Snakes, First Thoughts on a Sad, Familiar Song." *Hogwarts Professor*, 22 May, 2020.
https://www.hogwartsprofessor.com/the-ballad-of-songbirds-and-snakes-first-thoughts-on-a-sad-familiar-song/

____. "Hollywood Gamemakers and Some Lovely Tunes: The Ballad of Songbirds and Snakes Comes to the Big Screen." *Hogwarts Professor*, 19 November, 2023.
https://www.hogwartsprofessor.com/hollywood-gamemakers-and-some-lovely-tunes-the-ballad-of-songbirds-and-snakes-comes-to-the-big-screen/#more-30539

Haring, Bruce. "The Hunger Games Director Francis Lawrence Says New Prequel Won't be Split, Voices Regrets on 'Mockingjay' Divide." *Deadline*.
https://deadline.com/2023/10/the-hunger-games-director-francis-lawrence-says-new-prequel-wont-split-1235573412/

Havighurst, Craig. "'Songbirds' are Enlisted for the New Hunger Games Movie." *WMOT Roots Radio*, 29 November, 2023.

https://www.wmot.org/roots-radio-news/2023-11-29/roots-songbirds-are-enlisted-for-the-new-hunger-games-movie

Hellerman, Jason. "The Musical Genre in Film and TV (Definition & Examples)." *No Film School*, 25 August, 2023. https://nofilmschool.com/musical-genre

Hemenway, Megan. "The Hunger Games Prequel Movie Improves Mockingjay Part 2's Rebel Story." *Screen Rant*, 21 November, 2023. https://screenrant.com/hunger-games-ballad-songbirds-snakes-tigris-mockingjay-improve/

Hobbes, Thomas. *Leviathan*, edited by Edward White and David Widger. 1651. Project Gutenberg, 2009.

Hood, Cooper. "Every Song in the Hunger Games: The Ballad of Songbirds & Snakes." *Screen Rant*, 17 November, 2023.

"Hobbes's Moral and Political Philosophy." *Stanford Encyclopedia of Philosophy*, revised 12 September, 2022. https://plato.stanford.edu/entries/hobbes-moral/

"How to Recognize Signs of Sociopathy." *Cleveland Clinic*, 09 September, 2021. https://health.clevelandclinic.org/sociopath-personality-disorder

Hunter, Jim. "The Hunger Games: The Ballad of Songbirds and Snakes Review: Good Acting Reinvents YA Franchise." *Tristate*, 17 November, 2023. https://www.tristatehomepage.com/community/movie-reviews/the-hunger-games-the-ballad-of-songbirds-and-snakes-review-good-acting-reinvents-ya-franchise/

"Jason Schwartzman on the 'Freedom he was Given to Shape his 'The Hunger Games' Prequel Character." *The Hollywood Reporter*. https://www.hollywoodreporter.com/video/jason-schwartzman-on-freedom-given-to-shape-his-hunger-games-prequel-character/

"Jean Jacques Rousseau." *Stanford Encyclopedia of Philosophy*, revised 21 April, 2023. https://plato.stanford.edu/entries/rousseau/

Jefferson, J'na. "Strange Fruit: Billie Holiday and Nina Simone Transform a Haunting Poem." *Udiscovermusic.com*, 11 December, 2022. https://www.udiscovermusic.com/stories/strange-fruit-feature/

"John Locke." *Stanford Encyclopedia of Philosophy*, revised 07 July, 2022. https://plato.stanford.edu/entries/locke/

Jones, Tamera. "Hunger Games Director Francis Lawrence Reveals When He First Found Out About 'The Ballad of Songbirds and Snakes'." *Collider*, 11 November, 2023.
https://collider.com/hunger-games-prequel-ballad-of-songbirds-and-snakes-francis-lawrence-comments/

"Josh Andrés Rivera." *The Hunger Games Wiki*.
https://thehungergames.fandom.com/wiki/Josh_Andr%C3%A9s_Rivera

Korrs, Ivan. "Here's What Critics are Saying About 'The Ballad of Songbirds and Snakes' Soundtrack." *Music Times*, 19 November, 2023.
https://www.musictimes.com/articles/97926/20231119/heres-what-critics-saying-ballad-songbirds-snakes-soundtrack.htm

Kostof, Spiro. *The City Shaped: Urban Patterns and Meanings Through History*. London: Thames & Hudson, 1991.

"Landscape Park Duisburg Nord." *NRW Tourism*.
https://www.nrw-tourism.com/landscape-park-duisburg-nord

Lapid, Alyssa. "Hunger Games' Costume Designer Hid Fashion Easter Eggs in the New Movie." *Bustle*, 08 November, 2023.
https://www.bustle.com/style/trish-summerville-hunger-games-easter-eggs-ballad-of-songbirds-and-snakes

LeBlanc, Jason. "James Newton Howard to Score Francis Lawrence's 'The Ballad of Songbirds and Snakes'." *Film Score*, 18 July, 2022.
https://www.filmscoremonthly.com/board/posts.cfm?threadID=148258&forumID=1&archive=0

Ledgin, Stephanie. *Homegrown Music: Discovering Bluegrass*. Westport: ABC-CLIO, 2004.

Leipholtz, Beth. "3 Challenges of Being a High-Bottom Alcoholic." *Alcohol Rehab Guide*, 26 September, 2017.
https://www.alcoholrehabguide.org/blog/challenges-high-bottom-alcoholic/

Leishman, Rachel. "The Hunger Games: The Ballad of Songbirds and Snakes has a Surprising Musical Inspiration." *The Mary Sue*, 19 November, 2023.
https://www.themarysue.com/the-hunger-games-the-ballad-of-songbirds-and-snakes-has-a-surprising-musical-inspiration/

"Local Hunger Games Actress!" Good Day Sacramento, 16 November, 2023.
https://www.youtube.com/watch?v=1SfQzMrKszw

Locke, John. *Two Treatises of Government*, edited by Thomas Hollis. 1764. A. Miller et. al., 2019.

Lopez, Kristen. "Rachel Zegler Took Inspiration from an Audrey Hepburn Classic for Her 'Hunger Games' Performance." *The Wrap*, 17 November, 2023. https://nz.finance.yahoo.com

Lynch, Joe. "Inside the Gritty, 'Dangerous' Music of 'Hunger Games: The Ballad of Songbirds & Snakes'." *Billboard*, 25 October, 2023. https://www.billboard.com/music/music-news/hunger-games-songbirds-snakes-songs-music-1235453797/

"Makeup Designer Sherri Berman on the Film's Period Looks & Character Inspiration in 'On Makeup Magazine.'" *Panem Propaganda*, 01 October, 2023. https://www.panempropaganda.com/movie-countdown/2023/10/1/the-ballad-of-songbirds-snakes-makeup-designer-sherri-berman.html

Malone, Bill. "Music." In *High Mountains Rising: Appalachia in Time and Place*, 114-134. Edited by Richard Straw and H. Tyler Blethen. Urbana: University of Illinois Press, 2004.

Martin, Kevin. "Nazi Architecture: Hitler's Grandiose Plans for Imperial Berlin." *Magellan TV*, 04 April, 2021. https://www.magellantv.com/articles/nazi-architecture-hitlers-grandiose-plans-for-imperial-berlin

"Masterplan Museumsinsel A Projection into the Future: Altes Museum." https://www.museumsinsel-berlin.de/en/buildings/altes-museum/

McClatchy, Debby. "Appalachian Traditional Music: A Short History." 27 June, 2000. https://www.mustrad.org.uk/articles/appalach.htm.

Meszoros, Mark. "Hunger Games: The Ballad of Songbirds & Snakes: The Villain's Journey." *The News-Herald*, 15 November, 2023. https://www.news-herald.com/2023/11/15/hunger-games-the-ballad-of-songbirds-snakes-the-villains-journey/

Miller, Laura. "All the Hidden Meanings of the Names in the New Hunger Games." *Slate*, 22 May, 2020. https://slate.com/culture/2020/05/hunger-games-songbirds-snakes-names-meanings-explained.html

"Monument to the Battle of the Nations." *Atlas Obscura*. https://www.atlasobscura.com/places/monument-to-the-battle-of-the-nations

Moon, Ra. "The Biggest Monument in Europe: Völkerschlachtdenkmal." *Atlas of Wonders*. https://www.atlasofwonders.com/2015/01/monument-battle-nations-leipzig.html

Moore, Nicole. "Viola Davis Had One Request for her Hunger Games Villain Look." *Looper*, 03 November, 2023. https://www.looper.com/1436040/viola-davis-hunger-games-villain-look-request/

Morona, Joey. "The Hunger Games: The Ballad of Songbirds and Snakes Review: Prequel Thrills but Fails to Justify its Existence." *Cleveland.com, Entertainment*, 15 November 2023. https://www.cleveland.com/entertainment/2023/11/the-hunger-games-the-ballad-of-songbirds-and-snakes-review-prequel-thrills-but-fails-to-justify-its-existence.html

Mower, Maxim. "Molly Tuttle Talks Orange Blossom Revue, Grammys, The Hunger Games and More." *Holler*, 30 November, 2023. https://holler.country/news/breaking/exclusive-molly-tuttle-talks-orange-blossom-revue-grammys-the-hunger-games-and-more/

"Nashville Cat Dominick Leslie's Been Playing Since he was a Baby." *Mandolin Café*, 11 August, 2020. https://www.mandolincafe.com/forum/content/690-Nashville-Cat-Dominick-Leslie-s-been-Playing-Since-he-was-a-Baby

"New Behind the Scenes Image from The Hunger Games: The Ballad of Songbirds and Snakes + Interview with Producer Nina Jacobson." *Panem Propaganda*, 06 September, 2023. https://www.panempropaganda.com/movie-countdown/2023/9/6/new-behind-the-scenes-image-from-the-hunger-games-the-ballad.html

"News Room," *Scholastic.com*, 04 October 2019. http://mediaroom.scholastic.com/press-release/scholastic-announces-title-and-cover-new-novel-worldwide-bestselling-hunger-games-seri

"Nina Jacobson Interview on The Hunger Games: The Ballad of Songbirds & Snakes." *The Upcoming*. https://www.youtube.com/watch?v=8x9z31SVBWI

O'Dell, Cary. "Strange Fruit—Billie Holiday (1939)." *Library of Congress*, 2002. https://www.loc.gov/static/programs/national-recording-preservation-board/documents/StrangeFruit.pdf

Paradis, Thomas. *A Place Called District 12: Appalachian Geography and Music in the Hunger Games*. McFarland & Co., Inc. 2022.

Piña, Christy. "Hunger Games Prequel Director Improvised Lucy Gray Baird-Katniss Everdeen Curtsy Callback to Original Film." *The Hollywood Reporter*, 29 October, 2023. https://www.hollywoodreporter.com/movies/movie-news/hunger-games-director-lucy-gray-baird-katniss-everdeen-callback-curtsy-1235631324/

Poe, Jim. "A Look at Appalachian Culture and History in 'The Hunger Games.'" *Times West Virginian*, 15 November, 2015. https://www.timeswv.com/news/a-look-at-appalachian-culture-and-history-in-the-hunger-games/article_2a9f14a6-8b7c-11e5-ad77-1fe4f69156e0.html

Puckett-Pope, Lauren. "Inside the 'Big Message' Behind the Costumes of The Hunger Games: The Ballad of Songbirds and Snakes." *Elle*, 08 November, 2023. https://www.elle.com/culture/movies-tv/a45767540/the-hunger-games-ballad-songbirds-snakes-fashion-costumes/

"Rachel Zegler 'Pure as the Driven Snow.'" *RachelZeglerMedia*, 17 November, 2023. https://www.youtube.com/watch?v=sS8B74dw0Dg

Rasker, Rachel. "The Hunger Games Prequel's Easter Eggs and Influences from Nazi Germany." *ABC News*, 27 November, 2023. https://www.abc.net.au/news/2023-11-28/hunger-games-ballad-of-songbirds-snakes-production-designer/103154170

Rousseau, Jean-Jacques. *The Social Contract and Other Later Political Writings*, edited and translated by Victor Gourevitch, Cambridge University Press, 1997.

Roxborough, Scott. "New 'Hunger Games' Transforms German Locations into Panem." *DW*, 16 November, 2023. https://www.dw.com/en/new-hunger-games-transforms-german-locations-into-panem/a-67393497

"Scene Breakdown with Director Francis Lawrence." *Fandango*, 06 November, 2023. https://www.youtube.com/watch?v=j7k4_zaZE00

"Scholastic Releases New Interview with Suzanne Collins, Author of the Worldwide Bestselling Hunger Games Series." *PR Newswire*, 19 May, 2020.

http://mediaroom.scholastic.com/press-release/scholastic-releases-new-interview-suzanne-collins-author-worldwide-bestselling-hunger-

"Sejanus Plinth." *The Hunger Games Wiki.*
https://thehungergames.fandom.com/wiki/Sejanus_Plinth

Shaw, Angel. "Ten Reasons Ballad of Songbirds & Snakes' Box Office is Disappointing After $98 Million Opening." *Screen Rant*, 20 November, 2023.
https://screenrant.com/hunger-games-ballad-songbirds-snakes-box-office-opening-bomb/

Smith, Mayne. "An Introduction to Bluegrass." *Journal of American Folklore* 78, no. 309 (July-September 1965): 245-256.

"Sofia Sanchez, 'Hunger Games' star with Down Syndrome, Says Being in the Movie was 'Awesome.'" *Yahoo Entertainment*, 21 November, 2023.
https://www.youtube.com/watch?v=0uvjjodYrZI

"Soundtrack Review – 'The Hunger Games: The Ballad of Songbirds and Snakes.'" *Saving Country Music*, 17 November, 2023.
https://www.savingcountrymusic.com/soundtrack-review-the-hunger-games-the-ballad-of-songbirds-and-snakes/

Stedman, Alex. "The Ballad Director on Why He Never Would've Split It Into Two Parts." *IGN*, 07 November 2023.
https://www.ign.com/articles/the-ballad-of-songbirds-snakes-director-on-why-he-never-wouldve-split-it-into-two-parts

"Strausberger Platz: Living Between an Eventful Past and Future." *Adelto.*
https://www.adelto.co.uk/strausberger-platz-living-between-an-eventful-past-and-future/

Sweet, Erin. "Resilience in Dystopia: Women of the Hunger Games Series Defending Appalachia." *Urban Appalachian Community Coalition*, 05 December, 2023.
https://uacvoice.org/2023/11/resilience-in-dystopia-women-of-the-hunger-games-series-defending-appalachia/

Tangcay, Jazz. "'Hunger Games: The Ballad of Songbirds and Snakes': How Lucy Gray's Rainbow Dress Connects to Katniss." *Variety*. 18 November, 2023.
https://variety.com/2023/artisans/news/hunger-games-ballad-of-songbirds-and-snakes-how-lucy-grays-rainbow-dress-connects-to-katniss-everdeen-1235782433/

"Thomas Hobbes." *Stanford Encyclopedia of Philosophy*, revised 12 February, 2021.
https://plato.stanford.edu/entries/hobbes/

"Tieranatomisches Theater (1)." *Atlas Obscura*.
https://www.atlasobscura.com/places/tieranatomisches-theater

"Tieranatomisches Theater (2)." *Museumsportal Berlin*.
https://www.museumsportal-berlin.de/en/museums/tieranatomisches-theater/

Tonkin, Boyd. "Wroclaw: How the Former German City Became a Testing-ground for Europe's Aspirations After Winning Capital of Culture." *Independent*, 17 January, 2016.
https://www.independent.co.uk/news/world/europe/wroclaw-how-the-former-german-city-became-a-testingground-for-europe-s-aspirations-after-winning-capital-of-culture-a6818016.html

Ulatowski, Rachel. "Ballad of Songbirds and Snakes' Inclusion Makes One Aspect of the Film Better Than the Book." *The Mary Sue*, 21 November, 2023.
https://www.themarysue.com/ballad-of-songbirds-and-snakes-diversity-makes-one-aspect-of-the-film-better-than-the-book/

"Ullsteinhaus." *Berlin Companion*.
https://indmajor.github.io/berlincompanion/2019/08/16/ullsteinhaus.html

Valby, Karen. "Team 'Hunger Games' Talks: Author Suzanne Collins and Director Gary Ross on Their Allegiance to Each Other, and Their Actors—EXCLUSIVE." *Entertainment Weekly*, 07 April, 2011.
https://ew.com/article/2011/04/07/hunger-games-suzanne-collins-gary-ross-exclusive/

VanHoose, Benjamin. "Behind Viola Davis' Whimsical Yet Devious Hunger Games Look Inspired by Willy Wonka." *People*, 25 October, 2023.
https://people.com/viola-davis-hunger-games-ballad-songbirds-snakes-costume-look-exclusive-8379499

"Viola Davis Talks About Hunger Is." *The Ellen Show*, 09 April, 2014.
https://www.youtube.com/watch?v=SBrHcudhWtg

Wagner, Emma. "Will There Be More Hunger Games Books & Movies After Songbirds & Snakes?" *Screen Rant*, 17 November, 2023.
https://screenrant.com/will-there-be-more-hunger-games-books-movies/

Wainwright, Oliver. "David Chipperfield's Berlin Temple: 'Like Ascending to the Realm of the Gods.'" *The Guardian*, 08 July, 2019. https://www.theguardian.com/artanddesign/2019/jul/08/david-chipperfield-james-simon-gallery-berlin-museum-island

Walbank, Frank. "Plutarch: Greek Biographer." *Britannica*, updated 08 March, 2024. https://www.britannica.com/biography/Plutarch

Walsh, Savannah. "Inside the Dystopian Appalachia Music of the Hunger Games Prequel." *Vanity Fair*, 17 November, 2023. https://www.vanityfair.com/hollywood/2023/11/inside-the-dystopian-appalachia-music-of-the-hunger-games-prequel

Wang, Jessica. "...Director on the Sinister Viola Davis Meme That Inspired her Casting." *Entertainment Weekly*, 25 September, 2023. https://ew.com/movies/ballad-of-songbirds-and-snakes-viola-davis-hunger-games-villain-preview/

————. "Game On: How The Ballad of Songbirds and Snakes Brings Young Coriolanus Snow to Life in the Hunger Games Prequel." *Entertainment Weekly*, 25 September, 2023. https://ew.com/movies/hunger-games-prequel-ballad-songbirds-and-snakes-director-interview-cover-story/

————. "...Mysterious Ending, Explained." *Entertainment Weekly*, 17 November, 2023. https://ew.com/hunger-games-ballad-of-songbirds-and-snakes-ending-explained-8401917

————. "Olivia Rodrigo Joins the Hunger Games with New Ballad of Songbirds and Snakes song." *Entertainment Weekly*, 01 November, 2023. https://ew.com/movies/olivia-rodrigo-hunger-games-ballad-of-songbirds-and-snakes-song/

————. "Rachel Zegler's Big Arena Song in The Hunger Games Prequel Made the Crew Tear Up." *Entertainment Weekly*, 19 November, 2023.

"What Fans Should Expect." *Fandango*, 16 November 2023. https://www.youtube.com/watch?v=w3NRJDBJImU

Williams, Spencer. "Costume Designer Trish Summerville Returns to Panem for The Hunger Games: The Ballad of Songbirds and Snakes." *The Art of Costume*. https://theartofcostume.com/2023/10/25/costume-designer-trish-summerville-returns-to-panem-for-the-hunger-games-the-ballad-of-songbirds-and-snakes/

Wilmering, Antoine. "Keeping it Modern in Poland: The Conservation of Max Berg's Centennial Hall." *Getty*, 18 April, 2016. https://blogs.getty.edu/iris/keeping-it-modern-in-poland-the-conservation-of-max-bergs-centennial-hall/

Wordsworth, William. "Lucy Gray." *The Reader*, 1799. https://www.poetryfoundation.org/poems/45557/the-tables-turned

Zelmer, Emily. "On Location: 'The Hunger Games: The Ballad of Songbirds and Snakes' Brings the Saga to Germany and Poland." *CN Traveler*, 17 November, 2023. https://www.cntraveler.com/story/on-location-hunger-games-ballad-of-songbirds-and-snakes

ABOUT THE AUTHOR

At Henry River Mill Village, North Carolina, filming location for the Seam and Peeta's bakery in *The Hunger Games*. (Photo: Ed Tatsch)

Thomas (Tom) Paradis is professor of geography and community planning at Butler University in Indianapolis, Indiana, USA, where he teaches a full slate of courses on urban, cultural, and historical geography, urban design and planning, architectural history, and world regional geography. He has also taught and led study abroad programs in Siena, Viterbo, and Rome, Italy. A favorite annual course is his first-year seminar (FYS) titled *Unpacking the Hunger Games*, in which students enjoy deeper dives into the World of Panem. His previous book is *A Place Called District 12: Appalachian Geography and Music in the Hunger Games* (McFarland, 2022).

www.ingramcontent.com/pod-product-compliance
Lightning Source LLC
Chambersburg PA
CBHW030545080526
44585CB00012B/270